Trading Up

The New American Luxury

Michael J. Silverstein and **Neil Fiske**
with **John Butman**

PORTFOLIO

PORTFOLIO

Published by the Penguin Group
Penguin Group (USA) Inc., 375 Hudson Street, New York, New York 10014, U.S.A.
Penguin Books Ltd, 80 Strand, London WC2R 0RL, England
Penguin Books Australia Ltd, 250 Camberwell Road, Camberwell, Victoria 3124, Australia
Penguin Books Canada Ltd, 10 Alcorn Avenue, Toronto, Ontario, Canada M4V 3B2
Penguin Books India (P) Ltd, 11 Community Centre, Panchsheel Park,
New Delhi - 110 017, India
Penguin Books (N.Z.) Ltd, Cnr Rosedale and Airborne Roads, Albany, Auckland,
New Zealand
Penguin Books (South Africa) (Pty) Ltd, 24 Sturdee Avenue,
Rosebank, Johannesburg 2196, South Africa

Penguin Books Ltd, Registered Offices:
80 Strand, London WC2R 0RL, England

First published in 2003 by Portfolio,
a member of Penguin Group (USA) Inc.

10 9 8 7 6 5 4 3 2 1

Grateful acknowledgment is made for permission to reprint excerpts from the following
copyrighted works:
American Vintage: The Rise of American Wine by Paul Lukacs. Copyright © 2000 by Paul
Lukacs. Reprinted by permission of Houghton Mifflin Company. All rights reserved.
Harvests of Joys: My Passion for Excellence by Robert Mondavi with Paul Chutkow. Copy-
right © 1998 by Robert Mondavi. Reprinted by permission of Harcourt, Inc.
"Cadillac Ranch" by Bruce Springsteen. Copyright © 1980 Bruce Springsteen. Reprinted
by permission.

PUBLISHER'S NOTE
This publication is designed to provide accurate and authoritative information in regard to
the subject matter covered. It is sold with the understanding that the publisher is not engaged
in rendering legal, accounting or other professional services. If you require legal advice or
other expert assistance, you should seek the services of a competent professional.

LIBRARY OF CONGRESS CATALOGING IN PUBLICATION DATA
Silverstein, Michael.
    Trading up : the new American luxury / Michael Silverstein and Neil Fiske ; with John
Butman.
        p.   cm.
    Includes index.
    ISBN 1-59184-013-9 (alk. paper)
        1. Luxury.   2. Cost and standard of living—United States.   3. Quality of
products—United States.   I. Fiske, Neil.   II. Butman, John.   III. Title.
HB841.S55   2003
339.4'7'0973—dc21   2003048675

This book is printed on acid-free paper. ∞

Printed in the United States of America
Set in Janson Text
Designed by Joseph Rutt

I am deeply grateful to my family, who gave me encouragement, amazing support, and time to write. I dedicate this book to my beautiful wife, Gerry, for her kindness and unconditional love, draft reviews, and much more, and to my fantastic children, Charlie and Heather, for their love, taste, and inspiration.
—Michael

To my family.
—Neil

As we were putting the finishing touches on this book, America declared war on Iraq and consumer confidence slipped to its lowest point in ten years. Many of our partners at The Boston Consulting Group (BCG), while supportive of our research, worried that our thinking about luxury and how middle-market consumers were redefining it would be perceived as out of step with the times. A few of them probably wondered whether our thinking was up to the standard of such well-known BCG ideas as the experience curve, the growth share matrix, and time-based competition. Were we writing about a fundamental aspect of how the world of business works or were we reporting on a fad?

Part of the problem was the word itself: luxury. To some, it sounded trivial. These aren't essentials, the guns and butter that drive an economy. People don't need luxury, after all. They need, well, necessities. So, we stopped using the word to introduce our thinking and began describing what consumers were doing: trading up. We talked about how twenty-five million households in the United States, with billions of dollars of discretionary spending power, were magnifying the impact of those dollars by focusing their purchases on a new level of goods and services that cost more than conventional products—sometimes a lot more—but seemed to deliver a lot more value, particularly emotional value, to them.

⁓ That story interested our partners, particularly in an economy where the loss of pricing power and the elusiveness of growth were constantly in the business headlines. But they still were not convinced that the emotional benefits—the sense of adventure, security, self-expression, and connectedness that these products and services brought—were real and durable. Then we got the first-quarter results from some of the companies featured in the book, and they corroborated what we believed: there was a new and important strategy being invented, and it was restructuring and polarizing markets. This news of strong performance, even in very bad times, could not be ignored.

Our partners were also interested in the way the new players were competing. To use a central BCG theme, they were "breaking compromises"—breaking many of the traditional rules of marketing, pricing, promotion, and product development, rules that should have been broken before now.

The real star of this book is the American middle-market consumer. This is the consumer that demographers love because he or she is so predictable and easy to identify and that companies can count on because he or she is so easy to satisfy. But that consumer is rapidly disappearing. More and more, the middle-market consumer is a person who selectively trades up to new and better products and services, trades down in others to pay for his or her premium purchases, and, in the process, drives innovation and growth in previously stale—or in BCG parlance, "stalemated"—markets.

It is a marvelous story unless you're a snob and deplore the fact that your no-taste brother-in-law has discovered good wine. (Not at your price point, of course, but perhaps a better value!) Or unless you're an elitist who believes that only rich people should go on cruises. Or unless you're a purist who thinks that dog food should just be dog food. But even such doubters have to recognize the wisdom of one woman who told us, "One piece of good chocolate is worth twenty-two Hershey's bars."

Even so, social critics argue that trading up is a negative force, and many consumers wonder whether they're right. While acknowledging their concerns, we believe that the trend is not fundamentally driven by credit card debt, pathological spending, or mindless emulation. New Luxury consumers and producers love their products, but they know the products' limitations.

In fact, the redefinition of luxury is a particularly American story because it is about people's resisting the stratification and segmentation that society would impose on them. Because the movement to New Luxury markets is happening first and fast in the United States, driven by the enormous spending power of households earning more than $50,000 per year, it will give the United States a competitive advantage vis-à-vis other countries. But not for long.

This is a global story, too. *The New York Times* reported on the rising divorce rate in Japan, especially among older women. It seems that many of these women are taking unusual steps, such as dating, to reconnect with society. They are willing to spend money on themselves to rediscover and redevelop their lives. In a very traditional society, these women are embracing novel concepts such as individualism, materialism, and personal happiness. They are redefining age-old notions of the collective good, harmony, and, above all, *gaman,* or self-denial. We have seen similar patterns of behavior in societies around the world. New Luxury is global; it's here to stay, and so are the powerful financial and societal forces that drive it.

In the last chapter of the book, we take some swipes at executives in marketing positions at large American companies. We have many friends among them, and our goal is not to criticize them but to embolden them to chart a different course and abandon incremental tactics that rarely lead to competitive advantage. We ask them to dream again with their customers and understand the emotions that drive their behavior. Business leaders need to move now. Not just executives in consumer and retail, but also in financial services, health care, education, travel, and other industries, or they will likely lose significant market value to new players willing to make the right investments to attract an increasingly powerful and discerning American consumer.

May our world be at peace and in good economic health when our book is published. Whatever the situation, we will continue to need the new luxuries of life we describe.

Neil Fiske
Michael J. Silverstein
March 31, 2003

First, let me say right up front, I'm a believer in this book. In one way or another, I've been practicing the principles Michael and Neil describe since I opened my first Limited store in Columbus, Ohio, in 1963. I know these ideas work. And I believe they are the "sweet spot" in virtually every significant brand success today, and well into the foreseeable future.

Before I get into why I'm so enthusiastic about these ideas, a little background on my relationship with Michael, Neil, and The Boston Consulting Group.

Several years ago, I could see that the business model we had used so successfully for over twenty years—one that revolved around fast fashion, significant promotions, and dominant real estate positions—would not sustain us into the future.

The future was in brands.

At that point, I had never really talked to any business consultant or group. A classic entrepreneur, I relied on my instincts and the things that had made us successful.

Having determined that fundamental change was a must, I scheduled meetings with a few of the major business consultancies. I was looking for some outside objectivity. BCG sent Michael Silverstein, and I liked him immediately. Michael is wise, pragmatic, funny, and practical. He gets right to the heart of the issue, and he has sound business judgment. Michael brought in Neil, and they—along with a number of other bright, energetic BCG people—became solid contributing strategic partners.

They still are.

Our business has made the shift to brands, and *Fortune* recently named us "the world's most admired specialty retailer." Our business model works, and I'm very pleased with the progress that continues to be made.

So, back to the beginning. Michael and Neil are right: the customer is more sophisticated than ever. But I've always given our customer credit for having the same taste that I have. Nothing is more annoying to me than sitting in a merchant meeting and hearing some buyer say, "I like it, but the customer won't." Bull. I've been shopping the world for over forty years, and I've never overreached our customer. They stay with you if you pay them the compliment of acknowledging their good taste. Of course price points are an issue. That goes without saying. But they will reach, in virtually any category, if you create demand.

Clearly, Victoria's Secret is an example—the world's best-known, bestselling, most-profitable lingerie brand. But analysts thought we were crazy when we bought the business. Like most people, all they could see was that American women shopped for underwear in department stores—and, therefore, they always would.

That was not my experience. I had seen women in Paris, London, Vienna, and Milan buying lingerie in marvelous little boutiques. They saw it as fashion. I was convinced that American women would, too. And I was determined to design and market a specialty lingerie boutique that would be the best in the world. Over the past twenty years, I believe we've managed to do just that. And, as the business has grown, we've continued to increase margins by constantly presenting fresh lingerie and fashion and beauty offerings. By creating demand.

I'm happy that Michael and Neil chose to share the Victoria's Secret story in their book. And I find it comforting to see so many stories here that echo my philosophy. I found myself wondering whether Howard Schultz of Starbucks was sitting in the same Italian coffee shop I was, thinking to himself, "This is great. They'd love this in America." He applied it to coffee. I, to lingerie and fashion.

But we were both right. And, clearly, we've managed to "trade up the customer." Today it's more prevalent than ever. And "trading up" is happening across virtually every product category. The evidence is everywhere.

To their credit, Michael and Neil have managed to succinctly crystallize it in this important book.

Leslie H. Wexner
Chairman and CEO
Limited Brands

Contents

Part One

Trading Up to New Luxury

One

Trading Up to New Luxury: An Overview

America's middle-market consumers are trading up.

They are willing, even eager, to pay a premium price for remarkable kinds of goods that we call New Luxury—products and services that possess higher levels of quality, taste, and aspiration than other goods in the category but are not so expensive as to be out of reach. So many middle-market consumers want to trade up, and so many can now afford to, that New Luxury goods have flouted the conventional wisdom that says, "The higher the price, the lower the volume." They sell at much higher prices than conventional goods *and* in much higher volumes than traditional luxury goods and, as a result, have soared into previously uncharted territory high above the familiar price-volume demand curve. In category after category of consumer goods and services, New Luxury winners have emerged, traditional leaders have been dethroned, and the entire category has been transformed. The phenomenon forces us to think in new ways about the relationship between consumer needs and consumer goods, and it offers a huge opportunity for business leaders to pursue their own aspirations and realize growth and profit as well. America is trading up, and it's good for both business and society.

The trading-up phenomenon is happening in scores of categories of goods and services, at prices ranging from just a few dollars to tens of thousands. It involves consumers who earn $50,000 a year and those who earn $200,000. Single moms do it, retired couples do it—working singles, families with kids, and even their pets do it. We have interviewed hundreds of middle-market consumers, observed hundreds more in their homes and workplaces, and conducted a survey of more than 2,300 people earning $50,000 and above. Ninety-six percent of them say they will pay a premium for at least one type of product. With forty-seven million households in the United States with incomes of $50,000 or more, and an average household size of 2.6 people, that's nearly 122 million Americans with the means and the desire to trade up.

Who are these consumers and what are they buying? All kinds of people trade up every day to many types of goods and for many reasons—some of them unexpected and counterintuitive. Perhaps the most startling traders up we talked with were a group of consumers who were ecstatic about a product category that most people would like to forget—a washer-dryer combination from Whirlpool® called Duet®. The pair sells for more than $2,000, compared to about $600 for a conventional washer-dryer combination. Believe it or not, consumers made the following comments about these European-styled front-loading machines: "I love them." "They are part of my family." "They are like our little mechanical buddies—they have personality." We are not making this up, and these people are not paid spokespeople or company employees. These are both women and men, with a range of demographic characteristics, who told us, again and again, that Duet makes them feel happy, like a better person, less stressed, prouder of their children, loved and appreciated, and accomplished. In our fifty combined years of listening to consumers, we have never heard more heartfelt expressions of emotion about a product that even industry insiders think of as mundane and unworthy of much attention. Five years ago, the Whirlpool brand managers, in their wildest dreams, had not imagined there could be that much unit volume for a washer-dryer at that price. Even today they are astonished by their own success—and are struggling to build enough machines to keep up with consumer demand.

Another trader up who stands out is Jake, a thirty-four-year-old construction worker earning about $50,000 a year, whose great passion is golf. It took Jake a year to save enough money to buy a complete set of Callaway golf clubs—$3,000 worth of premium titanium-faced drivers, putters, and wedges—although he could have bought a decent set from a conventional producer for under $1,000. During the eight-month golf season in Chicago, Jake works the 6 A.M. shift so he can be on the course by 2 P.M.; he plays eighteen holes nearly every weekday after work and—again, believe it or not—twice on Saturday and twice more on Sunday. He is a three-index golfer, which means he is in the top 1 percent of all recreational golfers in terms of skill. We played a round of golf with him at a public course, during which he described in detail the technical differences and performance benefits of his Great Big Bertha clubs. "But the real reason I bought them," he told us at last, "is that they make me feel rich. You can run the biggest company in the world and be one of the richest guys in the world, but you can't buy any clubs better than these." Then, looking at us with a hint of a smile, Jake said, "When I kick your butt on the course, I feel good. I feel equal. I may make a lot less money than you do, but I think I have a better life." After the round (during which he did, in fact, kick our butt), Jake carefully placed his clubs in his pickup truck and said, "Thank you, Mr. Callaway, for another fine day." In 1989, Callaway Golf was not a top-ten golf equipment supplier. Within three years of the introduction of the Big Bertha driver in 1990, Callaway soared to number one in the world.

Not all traders up are driven by feelings of happiness and accomplishment; many trade up to manage feelings of stress and difficulty. Frances, a divorced art director earning more than $100,000 a year, had been dating a guy for three years. On the eve of her fiftieth birthday, he told her he was leaving her for a thirty-year-old woman and they were going to start a family. "It sounds like a bad novel," Frances told us. "I was unhappy. During that time, I bought a lot of jewelry, not only because it was beautiful and I loved it, but because I knew there wasn't anybody who was going to buy it for me." She realized what she was doing, and she didn't jeopardize her financial well-being to do it. "At that particular time," she said, "I just felt like I needed to give myself a happy pill." With more women working in the United States, divorce rates on the rise, people marrying later, and more singles choosing to stay that way, there are a lot of consumers—men and women—looking for an emotional lift in the form of a New Luxury purchase.

Trading up spans so many categories and appeals to such a broad range of consumers, that it has come to represent a major and growing segment of the economy. In twenty-three categories of consumer products and services worth $1.8 trillion in annual sales, New Luxury already accounts for 19 percent of the total, or about $350 billion per year—and it's growing 10 to 15 percent annually. And the demand is highly elastic because it can be created in categories that have never had a premium offering before and because even a category that has been transformed by a New Luxury product can be traded up again.

The Characteristics of New Luxury

From our analysis of the most successful New Luxury goods in more than thirty categories, we have identified three major types.

"Accessible superpremium" products are priced at or near the top of their category, and at a considerable premium to conventional offerings. They are still affordable to the middle-market consumer, however, because they are relatively low-ticket items. For example, Belvedere vodka sells for about $28 a bottle, an 88 percent premium over Absolut at $16. Nutro pet food sells at $.71 per pound, a 58 percent premium to Alpo at $.45 per pound. Almost anyone can afford a bottle of Belvedere or a bag of Nutro if those categories are emotionally important to him or her.

"Old Luxury brand extensions" are lower-priced versions of products created by companies whose brands have traditionally been affordable only for the rich—households earning $200,000 and above. Mercedes-Benz, for example, has dramatically changed its product mix in the past ten years, with continual reductions in the price of the entry-level C-class coupe—now about $26,000—and a steady increase in revenue from this model. Mercedes-Benz has also worked to keep the brand aspirational by extending it up-market as well. The Maybach sells for over $300,000—more than ten times the price of the entry-level C-class coupe. Such Old Luxury brands have mastered a neat trick: becoming simultaneously more accessible and more aspirational.

"Masstige" goods—a neologism for "mass prestige"—are neither at the top of their category in price nor related to other iterations of the brand. They occupy a sweet spot in the market "between mass and class," commanding a premium over conventional products, but priced well below superpremium or Old Luxury goods. Bath & Body Works body lotion, for example, sells at $9.00 for an eight-ounce bottle ($1.13 per ounce), a premium of about 275 percent over Vaseline Intensive Care, which sells at $3.29 for 11 ounces, or $.30 an ounce. But it is far from the highest-priced product in the category—Kiehl's Creme de Corps, one of many superpremium skin creams, retails at $24 for the eight-ounce bottle, a 167 percent premium over the Bath & Body Works product, and there are many other brands that sell for far more.

Despite the wide price range of New Luxury goods and the variety of categories in which they appear, they have particular characteristics that are common across all categories and prices—and they are different from those of superpremium or Old Luxury goods, and also from those of conventional, midprice, middle-market products. Most important, New Luxury goods are always based on emotions, and consumers have a much stronger emotional engagement with them than with other goods. Even relatively low-ticket items, such as premium vodkas that sell for around $30 a bottle, have a well-defined emotional appeal for their consumers. The engagement tends to get more intense and long lasting with big-ticket items, such as home appliances and automobiles. BMW drivers, for example, are particularly engaged with their cars. Dr. Michael Ganal, a BMW board member, told us that BMW owners wash their cars more frequently than owners of other cars do. They park them on the street and then turn back to gaze lovingly at them as they walk away. They say that the first sight of their BMW in the airport parking lot is like a warm welcome home. By contrast, very expensive Old Luxury goods—such as Chanel handbags and Rolls-Royce cars—are based primarily on status, class, and exclusivity rather than on genuine, personal emotional engagement. And the appeal of traditional middle-market goods is based more on price, functionality, and convenience than on emotional connection: it's a rare Taurus driver who can be found gazing fondly at his parked car.

Emotional engagement is essential, but not sufficient, to qualify a product as New Luxury; it must connect with the consumer on all three levels of a "ladder of benefits." First, it must have technical differences in design, technology, or both. Subsumed within this technical level is an assumption of quality—that the product will be free from defects and perform as promised. Second, those technical differences must contribute to superior functional performance. It's not enough to incorporate "improvements" that don't actually improve anything but are intended only to make the product look different or appear to be changed. (American carmakers played that game for years.) Finally, the technical and functional benefits must combine—along with other factors, such as brand values and company ethos—to engage the consumer emotionally. Most consumers make one dominant emotional connection with a product, but there are usually others involved as well.

When a New Luxury brand solidly delivers the ladder of benefits, it can catch fire. It will take hold in the minds of consumers, quickly change the rules of its category, grow to market dominance—as Starbucks, Kendall-Jackson, and Victoria's Secret have—and force a redrawing of the demand curve. As that happens, the category tends to polarize. Consumers shop more selectively. They trade up to the premium New Luxury product if the category is important to them. If it isn't, they trade down to the low-cost or private-label brand, or even go without. They scrimp and save across a broad swath of spending in order to afford their New Luxury purchases—polarizing the household budget. Almost every American engages in this practice of "rocketing"—spending a disproportionate amount of his income in a category of great meaning. The combination of trading up and trading down leads to a "disharmony of consumption," meaning that a consumer's buying habits do not always conform to her income level. She may shop at Costco but drive a Mercedes, for example, or buy private-label dishwashing liquid but drink premium Sam Adams beer.

As consumers buy more selectively, trading up and trading

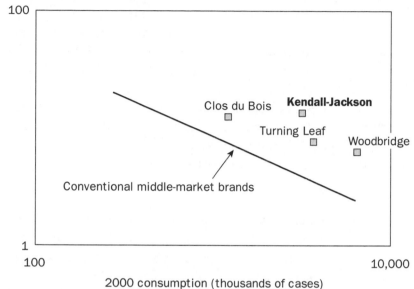

Kendall-Jackson wines are off the price-volume demand curve, selling at higher prices and in higher volumes than conventional wines and than competitive premium labels.

down, they increasingly ignore the conventional, midprice product that fails to deliver the ladder of benefits. Why bother with a product that offers neither a price advantage nor a functional or emotional benefit? Companies that offer such products are in grave danger of "death in the middle"—they will be unable to match the price of low-cost products or the emotional engagement of New Luxury goods. They will lose sales, profitability, market share, and consumer interest. To survive, they must lower prices, revitalize and reposition their products, or exit the market.

The Forces Behind New Luxury

What has caused the rise of New Luxury, and what forces are fueling its growth? We believe that the trading-up phenomenon has come about as the result of a confluence of social forces and business factors. Not since the spread of suburbia and the rise of "convenience" goods in the post–World War II era have we seen this kind of alignment of consumer wants and needs with the capabilities and drives of industry. At that time, consumers' desire for manufactured goods soared in an arc parallel to that of industry's ability to produce them. After the emotional and psychic hardships of the war, Americans wanted cars, refrigerators, and household goods in unprecedented quantities. And thanks to newfound capabilities developed and sharpened in the hurry-up production of war materiel, including aircraft, weapons, uniforms, and packaged goods, American industry was ready and eager to meet the demand. Americans wanted to put the pain of war behind them and stretch their new muscles of world dominance. Similarly, today the American consumer is in a state of heightened emotionalism, and, similarly, American businesses have at their command a new set of skills and capabilities. And, like that earlier consumer-goods boom, New Luxury is no fad: it is driven by fundamental, long-term forces on both the demand and supply sides, forces that will keep it thriving for years to come.

On the demand side, trading up is being driven by a combination of demographic and cultural shifts that have been building for decades.

Most important, American households simply have more discretionary wealth available to be spent on premium goods than ever before. Real household income has risen for all Americans over the past thirty years, and it has risen fastest for the highest earners. Income for the top fifth or quintile—households earning over $82,000—has risen nearly 70 percent in real terms. As a result, those twenty-one million affluent households control nearly 60 percent of the nation's discretionary purchasing power. Home ownership has also contributed to consumers' increased wealth. Homeowners, on average, have $50,000 worth of equity in their homes, and the entire pool of U.S. home equity is $7 trillion. Another less obvious contributor to consumer wealth is the savings that have been passed on to them by large discount retailers. Over the years, mass retailers have reduced costs and compressed margins so much that they have reduced the cost of living for middle-market consumers. We estimate that in 2001, approximately $100 billion was freed up in this way and became available for New Luxury spending.

Just as important as the increased wealth of Americans is the newly dominant role played by women, both as consumers and as influencers of consumption. The percentage of women in the workforce has risen steadily and dramatically over the past four decades, and the percentage of married couples with a wife in the paid labor force has nearly doubled. Not only are more women working, they are earning higher salaries than ever before; nearly a quarter of married women make more money than their husbands do. Women feel they have the right to spend on themselves. Over and over again, they told us, "I earned it. I can spend it however I want, including on myself."

Partly as a result of these demographic shifts, the traditional American family is becoming less dominant—only 24 percent of American households contain a married couple with kids living at home. Both men and women are getting married much later in life and they are having fewer children together. The result is that there are more singles with more money to spend on themselves. And because families are smaller and have higher incomes, there is more per capita wealth. Although people are getting married later, they are no more successful in making their marriages work. Half of all first marriages end in divorce; a third of all marriages fail in the first ten years. When couples break up, their consumption patterns change dramatically—the new singles spend more of their money on themselves, both to rebuild their personal brand (how they present themselves to the world) and as a salve for their emotional distress. Although women tend to have less wealth after a divorce than when they were married, divorced women are pronounced rocketers—they tell us they spend disproportionate amounts of their money on a wide range of goods that they believe will make them more attractive and help to ease the pain of the breakup.

The profile of the American consumer is also changing. The middle-market consumer of today is better educated, more sophisticated, better traveled, more adventurous, and more discerning than ever before. Today, more than half of all Americans over the age of twenty-five have completed some college. Educated consumers are eager to know about the products they use and the context of their categories. In 1970, three million Americans visited Europe; eleven million visited in 2000. And their travels have exposed them to the styles and tastes of other countries, particularly those of Europe. Well-traveled consumers seek out the tastes and styles they discovered in foreign places in goods they can buy and enjoy at home.

Finally, middle-market consumers are more aware of their emotional states and are more willing to acknowledge their needs, talk about them, and try to respond to them. We all receive countless messages every day—especially from media influencers and celebrity endorsers—urging us to reach for our dreams, fulfill our emotional needs, go for the gusto, self-actualize, take care of ourselves, and feel good about who we are. What's more, these messages are often intertwined with, or linked to, New Luxury goods. Oprah Winfrey endorses products, Martha Stewart sells them, Sarah Jessica Parker and her friends on *Sex and the City* display them.

These factors have transformed the profile of the "average" middle-market American consumer from an unassuming and unsophisticated person of modest means and limited influence into a sophisticated and discerning consumer with high aspirations and substantial buying power and clout.

The supply-side forces have been just as important in producing the New Luxury business endeavor. Perhaps most important is the increased acceptance and role of the "outsider"—the entrepreneur or innovator who gathers ideas and inspiration from sources outside the category, rejects the conventional wisdom of the leaders, and works outside the system. (At least initially: often the "outsider's way" eventually becomes the established system.) Like the consumers of their goods, these innovators are usually more knowledgeable, more sophisticated and emotionally driven, and less willing to settle for creating conventional goods than established managers in the category. Pleasant Rowland, for example, created the American Girl doll because she wanted to buy a gift for her niece but was completely dissatisfied with Cabbage Patch Kids and the other dolls she found on the market. She built her company into a $300 million business, selling dolls with historical characters and finely detailed and accurate accessories at $84 each.

Changes in retailing have also contributed to the trading-up phenomenon, by increasing the availability of New Luxury goods in retail outlets across America. The proliferation of malls throughout the country has made it possible for premium specialty retailers, such as Williams-Sonoma and Victoria's Secret, to expand quickly. Mass merchandisers have also played an important role in the spread of New Luxury goods, stocking more and more premium items on their shelves. Costco, for example, now stocks a larger selection and sells a larger volume of premium wine than any other retailer. Costco stores sell more first-growth wines from the Bordeaux region in France than any other retailer, including wine specialty chains. As retailing has polarized, traditional department stores have found themselves stuck in the middle. They offer similar assortments of goods, display them in similar ways, and provide little emotional engagement or uplift for the shopper. As a result, traditional department stores are in a state of decline.

New Luxury creators have also benefited from the globalization of business and trade. The easing of international trade barriers, the improving capabilities of global supply-chain-services providers, and the reduced costs of international shipping have enabled companies of almost every size to take advantage of foreign labor markets and put together and manage complex global networks for sourcing, manufacturing, assembling, and distributing their goods.

These supply-side factors have made it easier for New Luxury companies to attract investment for the creation of their goods, to develop their products faster and produce them at lower cost, and to quickly increase production volume when consumer demand increases.

Seeing the Pattern

There is a fascinating exercise (developed by Dr. Otfried Spreen, who is not a New Luxury creator, but rather a developmental psychologist at the University of Victoria in British Columbia) that is used to study the dynamics of human perception, learning, and creativity. Participants in this exercise are shown a piece of white paper that has a number of black shapes printed on it. The shapes seem to be randomly organized and disconnected. The participants are asked to study the paper and then describe the complete image that the pieces suggest. Some make a guess; others are stumped. Next, the psychologist shows the participants a second piece of paper that has more black shapes—more elements of the larger graphic—and the pattern instantly becomes clear: the image is of a cowboy sitting on his horse. With the new pattern as a frame of reference, the psychologist then shows the participants the original picture. The new frame of reference completely changes the participants' perception of the original page and unlocks the pattern that was there all along. "It's a cowboy on his horse," they now say of the first graphic, with force and conviction. Psychologists conclude from this exercise that our perception of reality is based on past patterns—our frame of reference—even if that frame of reference doesn't apply to or fully explain reality itself. Breakthroughs in creativity and innovation come from finding a new frame of reference, a new pattern to explain a changing reality.

In coming to an understanding of the trading-up phenomenon and New Luxury, we have gone through a process not dissimilar to the one involved in the cowboy test—except that we had no second sheet of paper available that revealed the whole pattern. We had to create that second sheet of paper for ourselves, and it is, in effect, this book. We began studying the trading-up phenomenon nearly ten years ago, a result of consulting work with companies in a number of consumer goods categories. Early on, we identified many of the large shapes contained in the pattern—such as the redrawing of the demand curve and the transformation of certain categories—but we did not immediately guess how they might all come together. We suspected, however, that they would reveal a new and unexpected picture of the world of consumer goods. We discovered that other people who were looking at the same set of blocks had a similar suspicion and were beginning to put names to the emerging pattern. People in the fashion industry said the big picture was of "the collapsing fashion cycle." Retailers guessed it showed the "demise of the department store." Producers talked of the "globalization of the supply chain." Some observers said it depicted "the democratization of taste" or a "new consumerism." Callaway Golf talked of its mission as the "democratization of golf."

We thought the pattern was even bigger, more fundamental, and more important than these various interpretations suggested. About two years ago, we decided to do a deep dive into the subject—which we tentatively called the "democratization of luxury"—primarily to learn more about it so we could offer our knowledge to companies and help them succeed. Our research revealed such fascinating material that we thought we had, as a useful adjunct to our consulting work, a subject for a book. The publishing world agreed, so we intensified our efforts and dove even deeper into the subject, with the help of a team of colleagues and expert partners from The Boston Consulting Group. We analyzed more than thirty categories of consumer goods and services and did extensive research into consumer and economic data. We visited and talked with many New Luxury leaders, interviewed dozens of consumers around the country, and, with Harris-Interactive, we conducted a survey of 2,300 consumers about their buying habits and attitudes toward New Luxury consumption. We did field research and observation on the streets and in retail outlets. We did a literature review of more than eight hundred books, articles, and other related materials, and created a database to manage those sources. Most satisfying, we had extensive discussions among the members of our trading-up team about which shapes were the most important and how they all fitted together.

Our conclusion, as described above and further explored in this book, is that the big blocks are all fundamental forces that fit into a powerful, long-lasting, and resilient social and business pattern that we decided to call "trading up." It is a pattern that we wanted to share with businesspeople (as well as consumers) because we believe it can provide a new lens through which we can view the world and a new path toward innovation, profitability, and growth.

The phenomenon affects, or will soon affect, a wide range of businesspeople in almost every consumer-goods category, including consumables, durables, and services. New Luxury is a business strategy and, as such, must be developed and executed by CEOs and divisional leaders of large companies, as well as entrepreneurs and innovators in smaller companies. New Luxury is product centered, and so it affects product developers as well as supply chain managers. It also requires a keen understanding of consumer motivations and buying behavior, and so it has significance for market researchers and marketers.

Trading up poses an imminent threat or presents an immediate opportunity, depending on one's circumstances and point of view. The threat is mostly felt (or should be) by companies offering conventional midprice products to the middle market, because when a New Luxury competitor enters the category, the polarization can happen so fast that it becomes difficult to escape death in the middle. The opportunity is most potent for an entrepreneur or a business with the vision and resources to enter a category that has stagnated and can be traded up. New Luxury creators can move very rapidly from idea to prototype, sometimes in as little as a year. They can create initial product runs, in low volumes, with minimal capital investment. They can often build out their business within five years. When they're ready to sell, there are eager buyers.

We have learned that New Luxury goods cannot be created, by either entrepreneurs or established companies, with the methods traditionally used to develop products and bring them to market. Across categories and in very different kinds of organizations, New Luxury leaders follow eight practices that we'll talk about throughout this book:

1. They *never underestimate their customers*. They believe the consumer has the desire, interest, intelligence, and capability to trade up—even when the entrepreneur has no data to prove his contention or a business model to follow.

2. They *shatter the price-volume demand curve*. They don't settle for incremental improvements or price increases. They prefer the major leap and the big premium. They go for higher prices and higher volume, earning disproportionate profits as a result.

3. They *create a ladder of genuine benefits.* They don't try to fool their customers with meaningless innovations, nor do they try to get by on brand image alone. They make technical improvements that produce functional benefits that result in emotional engagement for the consumer. They don't try to pretend that better cosmetics are true innovations.

4. They *escalate innovation, elevate quality, and deliver a flawless experience*. The market for New Luxury is rich in opportunity, but it is also very unstable. This is because technical and functional advantages are increasingly short-lived as new competitors enter the market and because of the acceleration of the cascade of innovations from high-end products to lower-priced ones. What is luxurious and different today becomes the standard brand of tomorrow. Nearly 80 percent of all cars have such standard features as antilock brakes and power locks that were exclusively luxury features a few years ago. A well-established brand can't maintain an emotional position for long if the technical and functional benefits become undifferentiated.

5. They *extend the price range and positioning of the brand*. Many New Luxury brands extend the brand upmarket to create aspirational appeal and down-market to make it more accessible and more competitive and to build demand. A traditional competitor's highest price may be three to four times its lowest; New Luxury players often have a fivefold to tenfold difference between their highest and lowest price points. They are careful, however, to create, define, and maintain a distinct character and meaning for each product at every level, as well as to articulate the brand essence all the products share.

6. They *customize their value chains to deliver on the benefit ladder*. They put the emphasis on control of the value chain rather than on ownership of it, and they become masters at orchestrating it. Jim Koch, founder of The Boston Beer Company, specified the process for making Samuel Adams Boston Lager (which combined aspects of nineteenth-century brewing with twentieth-century quality-control methods), selected the ingredients, and managed distribution; but he did not choose to grow his own hops or to build extensive production facilities.

7. They *use influence marketing and seed their success through brand apostles*. In New Luxury goods, a small percentage of category consumers contribute the dominant share of value. In categories with frequent repeat purchases, such as lingerie and spirits, the

top 10 percent of customers typically generate up to half of category sales and profits. New Luxury leaders do not rely solely
on traditional consumer-research methods, such as polling and
focus groups, to understand who those core customers are; they
work harder to define their core audience and spend more time
interacting with customers, often one-on-one. Reaching them
requires a different kind of launch, which involves carefully managed initial sales to specific groups in specific venues, frequent
feedback from early purchasers, and word-of-mouth recommendations.

8. They *continually attack the category like an outsider.* They think
    like outsiders, act like mavericks, talk like iconoclasts, and strive
    never to think of themselves as insiders, even after they have be-
    come the leaders in their categories.

A Preview of the Chapters

This book is organized in four parts. Part One describes the
trading-up phenomenon and the forces that drive it. Part Two tells
stories of consumers and goods in specific categories. Part Three
provides tools and encouragement for seizing the New Luxury
opportunity. Part Four provides context and background information.

Part One: Trading Up to New Luxury

Chapter 2: The Spenders and Their Needs. Deep analysis reveals that
key demand-side factors have given rise to the trading-up phenomenon. They include the rise in real incomes and home equity, the
cash windfall delivered by mass retailers, the changing role of
women and the family structure, the rise in divorce rates, the increasing worldliness and sophistication of the American consumer,
and the increased focus on emotions and the growing cultural permission to spend. This chapter also defines the four emotional
spaces that drive consumer purchases: Taking Care of Me, Questing, Connecting, and Individual Style.

Chapter 3: The Creators and Their Goods. An exploration of the supply-side factors shows how they have contributed to the rise of New Luxury, including the role of the outsider entrepreneur, shifts in dynamics of retailing, and the increased access to flexible supply-chain networks and global resources. It also further details the eight key practices of New Luxury leaders.

Chapter 4: Where Goods and Emotions Intersect. This is an overview of the most important categories of New Luxury goods and the primary and secondary emotional drivers in each one. This chapter is based largely on our survey of 2,300 American consumers, the results of which are summarized.

Part Two: The Leaders

Chapter 5: The World Is a Sexy Place. The story tells how Leslie Wexner built Victoria's Secret into a masstige brand and the leader in its category, by understanding the emotional drivers of young women. In our talks with Wexner, he described how he built a $10 billion retail empire with an initial investment of $5,000, and how he continues to imagine, "pattern," invest, and build new enterprises.

Chapter 6: Eating As an Emotional Experience. Panera Bread, The Cheesecake Factory, and Trader Joe's have helped to redefine how, where, and when Americans eat by understanding that food is as much about connecting with others and questing for new tastes and experiences as it is about survival. Ronald Shaich, CEO of Panera Bread, tells us how he built his business around the emotional connection with bread.

Chapter 7: Only the Best for Members of the Family. Although there are fewer traditional families, and families are smaller, American consumers still highly value and want to maintain and strengthen their connections with family members—even if they are pet animals. We tell the story of the "girl business" in historical dolls and explore the new status of dogs and cats (and gerbils and snakes) as family members who deserve only the best.

Chapter 8: Inside the New American Home. The home is a primary category of trading-up activity—the most valuable financial and emotional asset for most consumers. This is the story of how Sub-Zero, Viking, and (amazingly) Whirlpool have transformed the average middle-market home from a modest nest to a showplace of Individual Style.

Chapter 9: Awakening the American Palate to Wine. Jess Jackson and other winemakers acted on their belief that the American consumer would appreciate better wines. Jackson takes us on a helicopter tour of his vineyards and treats us to lunch and a nice bottle of wine on a hilltop near his estate.

Chapter 10: The Old World in New Luxury Bottles. Both Belvedere vodka and The Boston Beer Company's Samuel Adams Boston Lager are adaptations of old-world beverages, created with processes based on traditional craft but updated with new technologies. The result is a drink with an artisanal character that can be produced in large volumes with consistency. Edward Phillips, CEO of Millennium Import LLC, talks about the traditional Polish provenance of Belvedere and how he discovered its power.

Chapter 11: Demonstrably Superior and Pleasingly Different. Ely Callaway is the quintessential New Luxury entrepreneur. He helped transform the wine industry with his Callaway Vineyard & Winery, and he revolutionized the world of golf with the introduction of his Big Bertha driver. We visit the Carlsbad, California, headquarters of Callaway Golf not long after Ely's death and find that the outsider thinking continues.

Chapter 12: A Cautionary Tale of an Old Luxury Brand. The story of the decline of Cadillac shows what can happen when an Old Luxury icon tries to maintain share by relying on brand image to make an emotional connection with consumers while failing to deliver on the other rungs of the benefit ladder. When new competitors do—especially Lexus, Mercedes-Benz, and BMW—it's often too late for the emotionally empty brand. In sharp contrast, the senior BMW executives in the United States describe how BMW has become the most profitable automaker in the world.

Part Three: Excelsior

Chapter 13: The Opportunity. In this chapter, we offer our thoughts on the potential of the market and the categories of greatest opportunity.

Chapter 14: A Work Plan. This discussion provides specific steps to take in the three phases of launching and managing a New Luxury business: Visioning, Translating, and Executing. We talk about how entrepreneurs, and entrepreneurial managers, can find opportunity, create a vision, develop a product, and take it to market.

Chapter 15: A Call to Action. We have words of encouragement and, we hope, insight for leaders and innovators.

Part Four: The Back Story

Luxury: A Philosophical and Historical Context. We summarize the important ideas that have shaped our thinking about luxury and necessity.

About Our Sources. This discussion describes the major sources from which we have drawn data and information.

Acknowledgments. To many people who helped us create this book, we extend our thanks and gratitude.

Trading Up Brings Benefits to Business and Society

Americans have not finished trading up. There remains vast potential to reshape categories, create new winners, dethrone market leaders, simultaneously destroy and create immense value, and unleash growth and rebirth in mature industries.

Overall, New Luxury is good news for America because it brings benefits to both its creators and its consumers. It is an opportunity and a call to action for businesses because New Luxury goods do what has long been considered impossible—they generate much higher profit margins than conventional middle-market products at much higher unit volumes than superpremium goods. What's more, they enable the entrepreneur and innovator to participate in a business that is personally meaningful and emotionally engaging and that connects them to consumers whose values they share.

For the consumer, New Luxury brings even more than goods with a valuable ladder of benefits: it brings them unprecedented power and influence. America has always moved forward on the two great tracks of production and consumption. Production has long been given the lion's share of the attention and credit for America's progress, which has been defined as breakthroughs in technology, productivity, quality, and service. The consumer was important, but primarily as a relatively passive partner whose duty was to consume in ever greater quantities in order to keep the engine of production rolling. But New Luxury consumers are so knowledgeable, selective, affluent, and discerning that businesses must listen and respond to them as never before. And although the primary traders up are relatively affluent—earning $50,000 and above a year—the effects of New Luxury goods spread benefits to people at all income levels. By polarizing the market, a New Luxury entry does not drive out low-cost goods; rather, it helps to ensure that they are available. And the pressure from the most affluent consumers stimulates and accelerates innovation at the high end, which cascades downward to lower-priced products more rapidly than ever before—making innovation more affordable and available to a broader set of consumers.

New Luxury, therefore, can benefit us all. For consumers, it offers a new kind of emotional engagement and business influence. For imaginative leaders, it offers a new way to think about growth, profitability, and the art of fulfilling dreams.

Two

The Spenders and Their Needs

Who are the New Luxury consumers?

They are a surprisingly diverse group of people—both male and female, all ages, single and married, and in every kind of profession. In conducting interviews with them, what's most striking is that there is no "typical" New Luxury spender—as defined by demographics, at least—any more than there is a typical American.

But they have certain behaviors in common. As our survey shows, almost everyone (96.2 percent) will "pay more" for at least one type of product that is of importance to them, and almost 70 percent identified as many as ten categories in which they will rocket—that is, spend a disproportionate amount of their income, as compared to their spending on other categories. However, only half (48.4 percent) of the consumers we surveyed are prepared to spend "as much as they can" for goods in a specific category, and only half of those will rocket in as many as three categories.

These results confirm our anecdotal findings: New Luxury consumers are defined by their highly selective buying behavior. They carefully and deliberately trade up to premium goods in specific categories while paying less or "trading down" in many, or most, others. (Some categories, too, are simply of no interest or relevance to them.) The criteria for their selective purchases are both rational—involving technical and functional considerations—and emotional.

Trading up is an important phenomenon because millions of consumers are involved in selective buying in a very wide range of categories. Although trading up involves people of all descriptions, some consumer profiles are more likely to be New Luxury spenders than others: many are single working people in their twenties. Kathy, for example, is twenty-two, lives alone in an apartment in Chicago, and works as a business professional, a job that pays $60,000 a year. "Right now," she told us, "I do not have anything to pay for except rent and utilities and my telephone. I have a lot of disposable income." She buys Coach handbags, premium wines, and Panera Bread lunches, and she "has a thing for grocery shopping," which takes her to specialty and gourmet food shops. But when it comes to shampoo, she "just gets drugstore stuff." Nor does she trade up on clothing, because "fashion comes and goes, and I can easily cut back in that area."

Empty nesters are important traders up—married couples, widows, or widowers, with good incomes, whose children no longer live at home. Charles and Judith are in their mid-fifties, with a household income of more than $200,000 and four kids, none of whom live with them, from two previous marriages. Like many empty nesters, Charles and Judith spend on travel, their home, and cars. He owns a BMW 3-Series and a Jaguar. She bought a Thermador six-burner range and other premium appliances when they did over the kitchen. But they don't like to overspend, and they don't believe in status buying; Charles scoffs at the idea of buying a fancy watch. "We do not make big money decisions without a lot of careful reflection," Charles told us. "We are willing to spend a lot of money for certain things if we think they have value and we want them and can afford them."

Divorced women are among the most pronounced traders up. In our survey, divorced women said they would trade up in as many as thirty categories, far more than any other consumer profile. Valerie, fifty-one, has been divorced for twenty-five years. She raised two kids while earning about $60,000 as a coal miner. (That's right, even coal miners like to trade up.) "Money does not stop me if I really like something," she says. "I will work overtime to get what I really want. I want what I think is the best for me." Women who have separated from their husbands, even temporarily, or have broken up with their boyfriends are also prone to disproportionate spending in key categories. Emily, thirty-one, and her husband, Paul, thirty-two, are both lawyers in the public sector, with a household income of over $100,000. They had a fight, and he moved to his own apartment; during that time, she bought a new wardrobe. "I've never in my life been a therapeutic shopper," she told us. But she did it "so that every time he saw me, I was looking good. It was revenge shopping."

Dual-income couples with no kids, or DINKs, and dual-income couples with kids, DIWKs, are also New Luxury buyers. Because they earn two incomes, they have enough disposable wealth to spend on premium goods, and because they are pressed for time, they feel the need to buy things that make their lives easier and less stressful. Paula, fifty-eight, remembers what it was like to raise three children. "I was working forty hours a week and taking classes. I had to use every minute. It was like I was on a treadmill that never stopped." Nadyenka, twenty-four, and her husband, Jake, thirty-three, both work, and they have a household income of over $120,000; they have no children. She says, "I am working a lot, so on the weekends I want to treat myself to something special. If I do not balance my hard work with something for myself, it would be too much."

Coal miners and businesspeople, single and married, parents and couples with no kids, ages from twenty-two to sixty-two, incomes of $45,000 to $200,000 per year—traders up cannot be defined, or targeted, by traditional demographics alone. But, in addition to their selective buying behavior, they do share many important characteristics.

Rising Incomes and Available Wealth

American households have more wealth available to spend on premium goods than ever before. Most of that wealth comes from increased incomes—from 1970 to 2000, real household income rose by more than 50 percent. There are about 112 million households in America today; almost 27 million of them have annual income

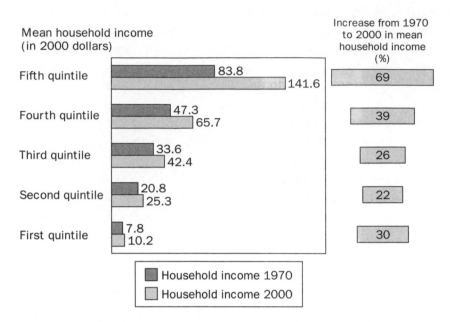

Mean household income
(in 2000 dollars)

Increase from 1970
to 2000 in mean
household income
(%)

Fifth quintile	83.8 / 141.6	69
Fourth quintile	47.3 / 65.7	39
Third quintile	33.6 / 42.4	26
Second quintile	20.8 / 25.3	22
First quintile	7.8 / 10.2	30

■ Household income 1970
□ Household income 2000

The income of the highest-earning households has grown the fastest in the past thirty years, and the gap in household income between top earners and middle earners has widened.

of $75,000 or more, and 15 million of those take in more than $100,000.

The wealth is becoming more and more concentrated at the top of the income scale. When the population is divided into five equal segments, or quintiles, the top quintile—the top 20 percent, including those earning more than $82,000 per year—accounts for nearly 50 percent of the aggregate income. And income for that segment has risen at a much faster rate than any other, rising nearly 70 percent in real terms from 1970 to 2000. The top two quintiles—the upper 40 percent—account for almost 73 percent of the aggregate. Those upper two quintiles of income constitute the most important market for New Luxury goods.

In addition to rising income, Americans have also financially benefited from a sharp increase in the aggregate value of all their financial holdings, including stock, over the past ten years. Even with the loss of value in the stock market from 2001 to 2003, Americans still have a great deal of accumulated wealth. The top quintile controls some 63 percent of that aggregate net worth; the top two control almost 80 percent of it.

_____

Increased Home Values and Equity

More Americans own homes than ever before—there were some seventy-three million owned homes in the United States in 2002, up from about forty-one million in 1970—thanks to low interest rates, smaller required down payments, a variety of financing options, and government assistance programs. Many homeowners have come to think of their houses as their safest long-term investment, and much New Luxury spending and activity revolves around the home.

American homes have grown dramatically bigger over the years. In 1950, the typical new home was about 1,000 square feet in area, with two bedrooms, one bathroom, and no garage, air-conditioning, or fireplace. In 2000, the average new home was about 2,265 square feet, with three bedrooms, 2.5 bathrooms, a two-car garage, central air-conditioning, and at least one fireplace.

Homes have gotten bigger, but they sit on smaller lots of land. The average lot size in 1985 was 17,610 square feet (about .4 acre); in 2000 it had shrunk to 12,910 square feet (about .28 acre). This means that a greater percentage of the homeowner's total domain is inside the house, making interior accoutrements all the more important.

Sales of new and existing homes have been on the rise, as have their values—and the hottest action is in high-value homes, those selling for over $250,000. The result is that we have a giant pool of home equity, some $7 trillion. The average homeowner has unrealized gains in the value of his house of about $50,000. Homeowners have not been reluctant to tap into that wealth; nearly half of them have taken a home equity loan, line of credit, or second mortgage. Twenty-two percent of those who have refinanced take out some cash as part of the transaction. Home equity has provided the fuel for much New Luxury spending, much of it for the home.

Because houses are bigger and more valuable than ever, it is no wonder that a lot of money taken out gets poured right back into

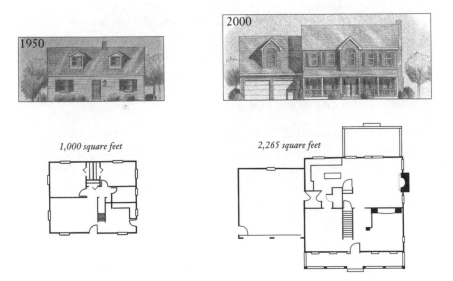

1,000 square feet   2,265 square feet

New American homes have grown dramatically bigger, doubling in size since 1950, and they have more amenities than ever before. However, they sit on smaller lots. Illustrations reprinted with permission of the National Association of Home Builders.

them in the form of improvements and new fixtures and appliances. Besides, the home is the most emotionally rich possession to most consumers, and money spent there is rarely considered to be wasted. In 2001, Americans spent some $160 billion on goods and services for their homes, up from $67 billion in 1970. (Home Depot grew from $1.6 billion in sales in 1985 to $54 billion in sales in 2001—equal to more than a third of our national spending on home improvement.)

Much of the money ends up in the kitchen. Sixty-five percent of all home-improvement projects undertaken in 2000 involved kitchen improvements such as granite countertops, flooring, lighting fixtures, commercial-grade appliances, dual dishwashers, and undercabinet refrigerators. Bathrooms run a close second: 51 percent of all projects involved upgrades to the family bath, including multiple-head or steam showers, vanities, and in-floor heating systems. These rooms, along with the bedroom, are the most emotionally meaningful areas of a home. The kitchen is the central place for connection among family members; the bathroom is an important place for individual rejuvenation and restoration.

There has also been a rise in second-home ownership. There were 1.7 million second homes in 1980; today there are over 4 million. Second homes often have at least as much emotional meaning as primary residences. As people change jobs and locations, and as families trade up to bigger and better primary homes when income and interest rates allow, they may maintain a longer and deeper relationship with the vacation house. It makes sense to buy special things for such a special place. That's why even smaller second homes by the lake or in the mountains boast granite countertops and marble baths, Pottery Barn furniture, cotton bathrobes from Restoration Hardware for the guests, and dinnerware from Crate and Barrel. The second home is a place for regeneration, and every night spent there is precious; the better the goods, the better the memories.

Reduced Cost of Living and More Discretionary Income

Another contributor to consumers' wealth is the savings that have been passed on to them by large discount retailers. Over the years, mass retailers such as Wal-Mart, Costco, Home Depot, Lowe's, Kohl's, Circuit City, and others have reduced costs and compressed margins so that consumers have been able to enjoy "everyday low prices" on a wide variety of goods and, as a result, lower their cost of living. We estimate that in 2001 at least $100 billion was freed up in this way and became available for New Luxury spending, and the trend will likely continue in years to come.

The rise in real income, combined with the increase in aggregate value of assets including the home and the reduction in the cost of living, have led to a rise in discretionary income—money left over after the necessities have been purchased—for everyone. There is no precise definition of discretionary income, however, and no standard way to measure it, because there is no absolute dividing line between what is "necessary" and what is "not necessary," or "luxury."

Most Americans, even the lowest-income earners, can afford the necessities of physical survival—food, clothing, and shelter—and have money available for other needs and wants. We estimate that, in the last thirty years, at least $3 trillion has been created and become available for spending.

Many of these needs and wants are refinements of the survival necessities. For example, it is possible to slake one's thirst with a glass of tap water or with a glass of Kendall-Jackson Late Harvest Chardonnay at $12.95 for the bottle. You can keep warm in a knit sweater from Sears for $19.99 or a cashmere turtleneck from Bloomingdale's at $99. These are matters of personal preference and style. Other needs and wants are not related to survival, but they take on great importance to the consumer—goods that bring social, intellectual, emotional, and spiritual benefit. These needs can range from a shot of Botox to a Viking stove. And society plays a role in defining what is considered a necessity and what is a luxury. In twenty-first-century America, a toilet can easily be defined as a necessity, although it would not have been one in the nineteenth century. For the consumer in the bottom quintile, that might be an American Standard toilet that costs $56; the New Luxury consumer might choose the Kohler Fables & Flowers design at $1,134.

The relative nature of needs and wants and the relative elasticity of discretionary income are at the very heart of the trading-up phenomenon, because they mean that every consumer has a different idea of what is necessary for him to survive in his own world and what he is willing to spend to do so. As one consumer put it, "Necessity is one of those relative terms that depends on who you are or where you are in your life. When things become important to you, they become necessities."

Women As New Luxury Earners and Spenders

Women are the dominant New Luxury consumers, but they are very different from the "housewife-consumers" of the 1950s.

Today, most American women participate in the workforce. Sixty percent of all women aged sixteen to sixty-four work, either full-time or part time; 76 percent of women aged twenty-five to fifty-four—the peak earning years—work. Not only are more women working, they are earning higher salaries than ever before. Real median income (in 2001 dollars) for women employed full time rose from $21,477 in 1970 to $30,240 in 2001, an increase of 41 percent.

Women are also working more hours than they used to. Twenty percent of working women put in forty hours a week or more, up from 13 percent in 1976. Twice as many women work forty-nine hours or more per week than did in 1970. And 7 percent of working women are on the job between forty-nine and fifty-nine hours a week. Although nearly a quarter of working women are part-time employees, the average number of hours they worked per week has also increased—from 16.2 in 1969 to 26.6 in 1998. This increase in working hours is significant because it adds to the strain of working women with families—there are "never enough hours in the day" to get everything done.

Many more women are single. Women are less likely to get married, and those who do marry do so later in their lives. The percentage of unmarried women aged twenty-five to twenty-nine has more than tripled in just the last thirty years, from just 11 percent in 1970 to 39 percent in 2000. That cohort of young, single, working women is highly influential in the New Luxury market, as consumers and as tastemakers.

The result of these societal shifts is that large numbers of single working women are earning lots of money—in excess of $374 billion. They have few financial obligations apart from their own living expenses and, in some cases, student loans. They have no families to buy goods for, and they are generally too young to be concerned about saving for retirement or for the education of their as-yet unborn children. The ones who cohabit—and the number of cohabiting couples has grown from 439,000 in 1960 to 4,736,000 in 2000—are in most cases living with another wage earner. So they feel free to spend and to consume as they wish, and they are prime candidates for certain categories of New Luxury goods, including fashion, food and beverage, cars, furniture, pet food, and travel.

(It's interesting to note that the influence of young single women on the economy is not a phenomenon unique to our society.

In Japan, there are about five million young, single, working women who live at home with their parents. They spend up to 10 percent of their annual salary on fashion items, and they are the largest-spending segment of Japanese society. As a result, they are powerful tastemakers: they have helped make Louis Vuitton the most successful luxury brand in Japan, so successful that LVMH, which owns Louis Vuitton, fears that consumers worldwide may come to think the company is Japanese rather than French.)

There is a final reason that women are so important in the trading-up phenomenon. Most observers agree that women have always had a particular ability to judge the value of goods, especially the goods that make up the bulk of the retail market, and a keen understanding of the complex emotional meanings and social messages contained in them. In our interviews, we found that female consumers are highly attuned to the subtle messages contained in brands, colors, and the minutest details of design, manufacture, and packaging—and from a very young age.

Their tremendous sensitivity to and understanding of products, coupled with their greater purchasing power and influence, means that women are the quintessential New Luxury consumers. They have the means, the motives, and the opportunities to purchase goods—especially goods that meet important emotional needs.

A Changing Family Structure

Just as there is no typical New Luxury consumer, there is no typical American family. The traditional image of the family composed of mom, dad, and kids all living at home together describes just 24 percent of American households. Even those households look different than you might assume, because the parents are older, there are fewer kids, and in most of them, both parents work.

Men as well as women are getting married much later in life than in the past. In 1970, the median age of people at first marriage was 20.8 years; by 2000, that figure had risen to 25.1 years. Partly as a result of later marriages, women are having their first child later in life as well. Over the last three decades, the median age of a mother at her first birth has risen from 22.5 to 26.5 years; during the same

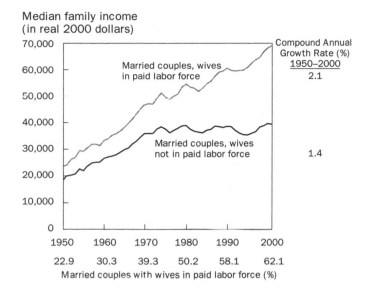

Median family income
(in real 2000 dollars)

The growth in incomes of married couples has largely been driven by the participation of wives in the labor force.

period, the percentage of women having their first child after age thirty rose from 18 percent to 38 percent. Delayed childbirth has caused an increase in the number of DINK households, and these couples are major contributors to the New Luxury market because they have money to spend and few obligations beyond their own needs and wants.

Not only are women having children later in life, they are also having fewer kids in total. From 1970 to 2000, the birthrate dropped from 87.9 for every 1,000 women of childbearing age, to 67.5 per 1,000. The reduction in the birthrate has contributed to a fall in the average household size—from a median of 3.11 people per household in 1970 to 2.60 in 2000—as well as a decline in the number of households with children under the age of eighteen. The result is that real per capita income has risen substantially. The share of income for each household member was $12,400 in 1970 and rose to almost $22,000 in 2000, a rise of more than 75 percent. That means there is more money to go around in the average family to fuel important purchases.

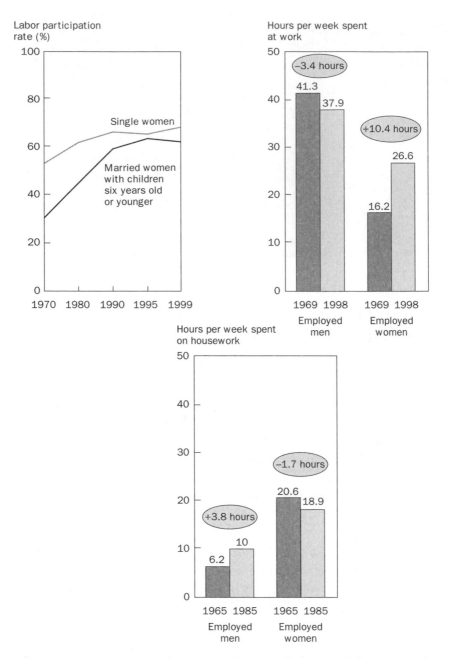

American women are working more than ever before, and they are working longer hours and still doing most of the housework; they are emotionally stressed and hard-pressed for time to get everything done.

Even when women do have their children, they are likely to keep working. In 1960, working women who were married and had kids six years old or younger were a minority, constituting just over 18 percent of the workforce. In 2000, that percentage had risen forty-four points to almost 63 percent. The percentage of married working women with kids aged six to seventeen has also jumped— from 39 percent in 1960 to 77 percent in 2000.

And yet working women continue to shoulder most of the child care responsibilities and do the vast majority of housework, including laundry, cooking, shopping for groceries, and caring for sick family members. Married working women with kids are, in effect, working two shifts. They feel overburdened and freely admit that they need help in managing their duties and that they need moments of relief and restoration whenever they can grab them. Because they have the money to spend, they will pay a premium for New Luxury goods that can lighten their workload and soothe their souls. As Nicole, a twenty-eight-year-old lawyer, comments, "Women are more willing to spend on themselves today. We think that our mothers didn't get to spend on themselves because they weren't earners, but we can because we do earn. The financial independence of women leads to the 'I can buy it if I want' attitude."

A Longer Dating Period and High Rates of Divorce

Because people are getting married later in their lives, young people spend more time and money on dating, branding themselves, and experiencing the world. Many of them choose not to marry at all, and as their incomes rise, they have increasingly large amounts of discretionary cash to spend on goods that please them. Many of those who do marry enter their first marriage with significant amounts of discretionary income and savings, which they can apply to purchases for the home and family.

Although people are entering marriage later (and presumably with more careful consideration), divorce rates remain high. From 1973 to 1995, the probability of a marriage's ending in divorce during the first ten years rose from 20 percent to 33 percent. More than 50 percent of all first marriages end in divorce, as do 58 percent of second marriages.

Though women tend to have less wealth after a divorce than when they were married, our survey shows that divorced women are pronounced rocketers. Divorced people, both male and female, dine out more often, buy cars and clothes, renovate or decorate their homes, take adventure vacations, and purchase apparel and accessories as a way to smooth the transition to a new style of life. They are an important market, with a distinct set of values and interests and a special relationship with brands.

Education, Sophistication, and Worldliness

The trading-up phenomenon would not have emerged as dramatically as it has—even with increased wealth and the influence of women—if the American consumer had not changed. Today's consumers have a higher level of education and worldliness, and they are therefore generally more discerning buyers and sophisticated consumers.

More Americans are college educated than ever before. Even so, the percentage is lower than one might think—just over 50 percent of the population aged twenty-five and older has completed at least some college. Traditionally, more men than women earned college degrees, but the ratio began to change in the 1990s. By 2000, 13 percent of women aged twenty to twenty-four had earned degrees, while only 8.6 percent of men aged twenty to twenty-four had. However, for both men and women, a higher level of education generally equates to a higher level of income. So 58.1 percent of people in the top quintile have earned a college degree, in comparison to the 27 percent average for all Americans.

The impact of a college degree is not only on consumers' ability to earn money; it also tends to increase their appreciation of learning in general and throughout the course of their lives. Consumers talk about learning as a key attraction of certain types of goods; they like to know the story of the brand and understand something about the category.

New Luxury consumers also like to learn about specific products and the companies that make them. That's why so many New Luxury brands have a narrative associated with them. Every American Girl doll is created with a complete life story from a specific era of history, told in beautifully produced full-color books. American Flatbread frozen pizza tells how its founder got the idea for his pizza and puts the story right on the back of the box.

Americans have become big travelers. The introduction of the Boeing 707 intercontinental jet in 1958 made the world more accessible to more Americans than ever before, but the cost of a ticket was still high—about $2,500 (2002 dollars) for a New York–Paris round-trip in economy class—and out of reach of the middle-market consumer. Following the deregulation of the airlines in 1978, however, ticket prices began to fall. By 1988, the New York–Paris round-trip had dropped to $687 (2002 dollars), and in 2002 the same ticket could be purchased for $332. As ticket prices have fallen, the number of travelers to Europe has risen sharply. In 1970, three million Americans visited Europe; eleven million visited in 2000. Travel to Asia also has become increasingly popular. The number of travelers there increased 93 percent from 1990 to 2000. Japan is the most popular Asian destination, but the number of travelers to China is the fastest growing.

"Travel is broadening," as the cliché goes, and it has certainly contributed to Americans' awareness of European styles and goods in a number of categories, including cars, appliances, leather goods, bath and body care, fashion and accessories, food, water, wine, and coffee. This has led to U.S. products that pick up on European styles without copying them—for example, Howard Schultz, founder of Starbucks, talks about bringing the sensibility of an Italian coffeehouse to the United States. It has also led to an increase in imports of European goods, including low-end products such as bottled waters and high-ticket items such as luggage and automobiles.

In recent years, American travelers have ceased to be content with traditional European sightseeing. Travel is increasingly seen as an educational experience rather than as just a vacation. People want unusual and special adventures and are willing to pay for them. Food lovers take a cooking tour in Paris. Adventurers visit with Samburu villagers in Kenya. For many overworked and stressed Americans, travel provides experience of cultures that seem to have a slower pace of life, greater emphasis on enjoyment, more time spent with friends and family, and greater personal fulfillment.

These travelers return with an appreciation for new tastes and looks, exotic goods and ideas, and they want to incorporate them into their lives at home. The appeal of many New Luxury goods is that they have an element of the exotic to them, or they remind the consumer of some experience or emotion she experienced during her travels. Betsy, a twenty-two-year-old professional, shops in specialty grocery stores because "they give you a better feeling, as if you're buying your food from a place that values customers like you. It's more like an Italian market."

This penchant for overseas travel—and to increasingly exotic locations—will continue to whet the American appetite for imported goods and increase the demand for products and services that remind us of our adventures abroad.

Greater Emotional Awareness and Permission to Spend

Even the increase in wealth, the influence of women, and greater sophistication might not have produced the emotionally driven New Luxury consumer because one very powerful inhibiting factor still stood in the way: guilt. Americans have always valued hard work and looked askance at overconsumption. But in the 1960s there began a barrage of messages from popular influencers that said it was important for Americans to reach for their dreams, fulfill their emotional needs, be all they can be, grab for the gusto, self-actualize, and, not only do all that, but also take care of themselves, look after number one, reward themselves, and build their self-esteem.

Products and services were always intertwined with these messages, so it gradually became clear to consumers that they were being given permission to consume a little more aggressively than they had in the past—*if consumption was in the service of a higher good, such as self-improvement or building relationships.* Not only did the influencers give American consumers permission to "go for it," they actively encouraged them to do so. And, in a final act of helpfulness, the influencers presented their audiences with lifestyles to emulate and endorsed products for them to buy.

Oprah Winfrey is a world-class encourager, especially, of course, of women. She manages an influential empire that centers around her television program, *Oprah*, watched by some twenty-two million viewers in the United States. Her magazine, *O*, was launched in 2000 and became the most successful start-up in the industry. Within a year, the circulation of *O* had zoomed past the leading lifestyle magazine for women, *Martha Stewart Living*. The 2.6 million paid subscribers to *O* have an average income of $63,000 and are avid buyers of such New Luxury brands as Coach, Lexus, and Donna Karan. Oprah's message, which she also delivers in live "guru appearances," is simple: "Live Your Best Life. If you're open to the possibilities, your life gets grander, bigger, bolder!"

Oprah's mission is an ambitious one: "To use television to transform people's lives, to make viewers see themselves differently, and to bring happiness and a sense of fulfillment into every home." She has established the credibility and authority to realize this lofty goal through her own very personal—yet very public—triumphs and travails. Her audience knows the details of her humble beginnings in rural Mississippi, childhood sexual abuse, and lifelong struggle with weight and low self-esteem. Her emotional and spiritual journey for validation, self-knowledge, and self-acceptance has been equally public, and Oprah has invited her television and magazine audiences along. She seeks wisdom and inspiration to supplement her life experience by consulting experts and gurus; challenging celebrities to share "What I Know for Sure"; and encouraging everyday heroes to recount the "Aha! Moment" that enabled them to achieve their successes.

Oprah's mantra—"Live Your Best Life"—connects with many American women's aspirations. This is the essence of Oprah, and it informs all aspects of her "brand": the advice she doles out on health, relationships, and sex; the products she selects for her "O list"; the content of her national speaking tours and workshops; the subjects of books she talks about. But as aspirational as her life and her message may be, Oprah is also accessible. She is down-to-earth and she speaks frankly and openly about her life. Janna, a forty-five-year-old single woman from California, and her mother were two of 8,500 people who paid $185 per ticket to see Oprah at one of the four stops on the 2001 "Live Your Best Life" national speaking tour. "She is one of the most personable women I have ever met," Janna told us. "She actually came off the stage, walked into the audience, talked to people directly, asked questions, sat down with them. She has such a magnificent view of life, and she is such a giving spirit that I think everybody should have a chance to meet her up close and personal. I have a lot of respect for her." Both Oprah's message and her medium resonate with Americans.

O magazine further reinforces Oprah's connection with American women by identifying themes around which to build the signature Oprah mélange of advice, information, and influence. Each issue focuses on a "mission," and these missions tap into the four emotional spaces that we have identified through our own consumer research. Missions have included Stress Relief, Health, Comfort (Taking Care of Me); Intimacy, Family, Friendship, Love, Sex, and Dating (Connecting); Adventure, Journey, Reinvention (Questing); and Success, You're Invited, and Dream Big (Individual Style). In the October 2002 issue of *O*, focused on "Stress Relief," Oprah offers her readers the following: "Taking care of yourself so you can better care for others is an idea many women I talk to still can't embrace. . . . It's the oxygen mask theory: If you don't put on your mask first, you won't be able to save anyone else. Stop. Go mindless. Breathe. Let go. And remind yourself that this moment is the only one you know you have for sure."

Oprah's ability to connect emotionally with U.S. women has resulted in a high level of influence on their behavior and thinking. When Oprah challenged American women to "Get Moving" and join in her 1995 "Spring Training" fitness campaign, thousands answered her call. "You're never too busy to exercise," one woman explained. "I learned that from watching Oprah. She's the busiest woman in the world. So if she can find the time, so can anyone." Each of the titles selected for Oprah's Book Club since 1996—and at this writing, there have been forty-six—has become a bestseller. In 1999, the National Book Foundation recognized Oprah's influence by awarding her the National Book Award for her contribution to reading and the rejuvenation of the publishing industry.

Like the books she recommends, the products that she selects for her annual holiday list of favorite things are also instant hits. Origins, a cosmetics supplier, has reported that the star seller of its holiday season was the A Perfect World intensely hydrating body cream with White Tea ($30 for seven ounces), one of Oprah's holiday 2002 selections. Similarly, Chico's, the specialty retailer of misses clothing and accessories whose $38 watch was featured on the same show, told *Women's Wear Daily* that customers overwhelmed their stores and call centers following the show—and that 75 percent of calls were from new customers. Oprah's influence has also paid off handsomely. Her net worth is estimated at about $1 billion, and her show and magazine generated revenues of about $300 million and $140 million, respectively, in 2001.

Martha Stewart's enterprise, Martha Stewart Living Omnimedia, evolved in reverse order from Oprah's, starting with the magazine *Martha Stewart Living* and then moving into television. *Living*, with 2.4 million paid subscribers, still runs a close second to *O*, and her shows, *Martha Stewart Living* and *From Martha's Kitchen*, are viewed by millions of households. Martha focuses on eight categories—Home, Cooking and Entertaining, Gardening, Crafts, Keeping, Holidays, Weddings, and Baby—and calls herself "America's most trusted guide to stylish living." Even during her difficulties in 2002, involving insider stock trading, her popularity and influence did not decline, although her company's share price did. As one woman said to us, "Martha is one of the first people who said your home is important. She gives the family validity. She is a source of comfort."

Goods and services play a prominent role in the activities of both women. Oprah's message is directed primarily at the individual; she talks about self-improvement and self-actualization, about taking care of yourself and "being worth it." Although she is less linked to products than Martha, she urges her followers to look after Spirit and Self, Relationships, Food and Home, Mind and Body—and not feel guilty about what it might take to do so. Martha is more of a social facilitator who helps people express themselves and make more fulfilling connections with their family and friends. She markets products under her own brand name, and she openly and unapologetically promotes her many commercial partners and sponsors. These two women have played a key role in the trading-up phenomenon. Oprah has said it's okay to trade up. Martha provides the how-to.

Products and services take on even more emotional meaning when they become associated with fictional characters of great appeal. About twelve million viewers tune in to *Sex and the City*, the HBO hit series about four love-seeking women living in New York and featuring actress Sarah Jessica Parker as Carrie Bradshaw, a newspaper lifestyle columnist.

The characters associate themselves with real products and activities taking place in real places (such as restaurants and retail shops), and their fears and aspirations rub off on the things they own and use. Because so many people identify with the characters in *Sex and the City*, the show has become a key influencer in certain categories of goods, particularly liquor, restaurants, clothing, jewelry, accessories, and shoes. When the women on the show started sipping pink Cosmopolitans (four parts citron vodka, one part Cointreau, juice of a lime, and a dash of cranberry juice), they catalyzed a martini craze that spread across the country and spawned dozens of variations— and increased the sales of cranberry juice at the same time. When they dined at Sushi Samba, a restaurant that combines Japanese and Latin cuisine, the company gained so much consumer awareness that it was able to expand into the Miami and Chicago markets.

The greatest impact of the show, however, is on women's fashion. *Women's Wear Daily*, a fashion magazine, wrote, "Industry observers agree that *Sex and the City* is having more influence over what young women want to wear—and buy—than any other TV show, let alone film." The show's signature fashion association is with Manolo Blahnik, creator of expensive slingbacks, pumps, and mules. "She's one of my miracle workers," says Blahnik about Parker. "People come to us and ask, 'Do you have the shoes that Sarah Jessica wore?'" Most women we spoke with for this book were aware of both *Sex and the City* and the show's influence on fashion and lifestyle. Carrie Bradshaw has done for vodka and slingbacks what James Bond did for gin and cigarettes in the 1960s.

Sex and the City is only one example of a practice that has become ubiquitous throughout popular media: product placement. James Dean made the Ace comb popular in the movie *Rebel Without a Cause* in 1955. Sales of Reese's Pieces skyrocketed when the boy lured the alien with them in *ET* in 1982. Today, product placement is hardly an adequate term to describe the infusion of branded and named goods into every vein and artery of the media. As part of its launch of the MINI Cooper, BMW placed the car in rap videos. Nike created a documentary called *Road to Paris.* Revlon launched a line of 007 makeup with Halle Berry as spokesperson. As one consumer remarked to us, "It has reached the point that it would seem strange if real brands and real products *didn't* play important roles in movies and on television. They're so much a part of everyday life. Why shouldn't they be a part of the media?"

Finally, American consumers have a large array of celebrities who provide living examples of people with fulfilling and exciting lifestyles (or so they seem). And we have them not just in movies and television, but also in every walk of life. Celebrity chefs, like Wolfgang Puck and Emeril Lagasse. Celebrity businessmen, including Jack Welch and Richard Branson. Celebrity authors, such as Stephen King and J.K. Rowling. Celebrity athletes Tiger Woods and Michael Jordan.

Thanks to incessant media exposure, we know how these celebrities live, the activities they engage in, the goods they use, and the products they endorse. We know we can't be them, and we don't really want to be. But we will take cues from them and sometimes associate ourselves with goods and services they find worthwhile. If we use the clubs they use or wear the clothes they do, a little bit of them rubs off on us.

The Four Emotional Spaces

These shifts in our society have given American consumers greater purchasing power, consuming knowledge, and a broader range of goods to buy. They feel excited by the possibilities and want to experience as much of life as they can. They aspire to live well and enjoy themselves, be healthy, and achieve prosperity for themselves and their families.

But the changes have also brought with them penalties and stresses. Americans are working longer hours, and work intrudes more into their personal lives. Relationships are difficult to maintain, and divorce is on the rise, owing in part to our work stress and intense lifestyles. Job security is rare, and employee loyalty scarce. There is so much choice, it can be dizzying. People feel pressure to compete with each other for the most rewarding jobs and most attractive partners. We fear that we won't measure up, will lose out, get sick, look stupid in front of our peers and colleagues, somehow fall into ruin, and lose it all.

Melissa, a twenty-eight-year-old training manager, told us, "If I don't do anything with the fruits of my hard work, what's the point? What's the point of not enjoying life? A lot of people in generations before ours definitely didn't have that concept of enjoying life. The mentality was you live to work, you don't work to live. I know it's a cliché, but I think people our age have gotten beyond that cliché."

Betsy, the twenty-two-year-old who told us she likes to shop in specialty grocery stores, says, "You're putting yourself through all this stress so you can afford to be exposed to comfortable, nice, wonderful, luxurious things. If you don't indulge in any of those things, you can get a little burned-out and lose sight of what you are doing it for. But then that brings me to the question: Is it all worth it?"

In addition to personal stress, our society is going through difficult times—with a slow economy and rising unemployment—as is the world, with more acts of terrorism, war, and other kinds of unrest. Accordingly, many Americans see it as a kind of civic and patriotic duty to keep spending. Kim, a twenty-six-year-old woman who lives with her boyfriend and has a household income of $80,000, says, "I think we are in scary times right now, financially and in the world. But I think you cannot stop spending money because that is just going to put us in a worse place than we are now. I want people around me to be employed. The way I look at things is: go out and support businesses. I think that helps everybody."

Consumers have always sought to engage with products, but today they ask even more of them. They seek goods that will help them make positive statements about who they are and what they would like to be and that will help them manage the stresses and distempers of everyday life. Sophisticated consumers know that possessions won't resolve their emotional struggles, but they're also candid and self-aware enough to know that goods can, in fact, help.

Through our research—which included a quantitative survey of some 2,300 consumers, in-depth interviews with hundreds of people across demographic types, and group discussions relating to specific categories with another 500 consumers—we have defined four important "emotional spaces" that affect consumer buying behavior and that are closely linked to the purchase of New Luxury goods. (These are discussed in more detail in chapter 4.)

Taking Care of Me. Most working Americans—and working women with families in particular—feel overworked and time-deprived. They are looking for ways to get a few moments alone, reward themselves after a tough day, rejuvenate the exhausted body, soothe the frayed emotions, and even restore the soul. They don't see the point of working hard, earning good money, and not spending on themselves. As one female consumer explained, "Women are more willing to spend on themselves today. They think their mothers did not get to spend on themselves because they were not earners, but they get to do that now. Such consumers say that a $9 bottle of Aveda shampoo—with its "all-natural" formula, calming aroma, and environmentally conscious image—can make them feel refreshed, renewed, and better about themselves in ways that a $2 bottle of conventional shampoo cannot. Personal care, bath and body products, spas, gourmet in-home foods, linens and bedding, and home electronics are important Taking Care of Me categories.

Connecting. Connecting is about finding, building, maintaining, and deepening relationships with people who are important to us. Connecting includes three subspaces: attracting mates, belonging with friends and groups, and nurturing family members.

Connecting is a major emotional activity and a very important market for New Luxury goods. To help attract mates, consumers buy clothing, lingerie, jewelry, accessories, and all manner of cosmetic procedures to make themselves more appealing and younger looking. To build friendships and affiliate themselves with groups, they indulge in premium wines, spirits, restaurant dining, cars, sports equipment, and travel. To nurture family members, they buy time-saving appliances, home theater equipment, gourmet foods, and cruises.

Celebrities play a role in reinforcing our feelings that connecting is difficult. "Billy Joel has a big stadium tour and a new Broadway show and 16 platinum albums," read a headline in *The New York Times Magazine*. "But all he really wants is a girlfriend."

Questing. Questing is about venturing into the world, gaining new experiences, and pushing back personal limits. It includes adventure, learning, mastery, and fun—preferably all mixed together. Accordingly, New Luxury consumers seek experiences that teach and challenge them and, not inconsequentially, help define who they are in the eyes of others. The combination of exploration and learning is worth a significant premium to most New Luxury consumers. Travel, spas, cars, sports equipment, dining out, computers, and wines are Questing categories. Questing involves real action and experience; it is also a space for fantasy and daydreaming.

Individual Style. Individual Style is about expressing personal taste, differentiating oneself from others, and demonstrating sophistication and success. It is often associated with Connecting, especially mating, because people use goods to send prospective partners signals that help communicate who they are and what they're looking for. But Individual Style also has to do with being "hip" and looking "stylish" and feeling "unique." Apparel, lingerie, fashion accessories, watches, cars, spirits, dining out, and travel are categories that enable consumers to express their style, knowledge, taste, and values.

The most exciting New Luxury goods, and the most successful and profitable over the long term, are those that address more than one of these emotional needs. For many consumers, clothing, food, and cars can touch on all four. A New Luxury car, for example, can provide moments of personal solitude (Taking Care of Me), an attractive expression of worth and values (Connecting), and an exciting activity (Questing).

Dr. Michael Ganal of BMW told us that BMW drivers "view the hour or two they spend in their cars as some of the most pleasurable time of their day. It is an environment they are completely in control of. They are comfortable in the seat. They enjoy driving. Sometimes they do not even take the most direct route to work if there is a better driving road. They have the sound system, the telephone. They feel completely at peace, protected and also invigorated in their driving environment."

There are two other elements that come into play in the emotional spaces: morality and values. We are not totally selfish beings, and we feel a strong sense of responsibility to other people, our country, and our world environment. As lawyer Emily says, "We acknowledge we like nice things, and we have an incredibly nice lifestyle. We try not to feel guilty about that, but we also try to be conscious of the fact that we're part of a broader society and community and try to make sure we give to charity and donate money."

It's important to New Luxury consumers that the goods they buy reinforce their good intentions toward the world. Judith buys premium imported foods, for example, because "European countries have stricter laws about using genetically modified seeds. They use fewer pesticides and herbicides, fewer antibiotics and hormones in raising livestock." Melissa's boyfriend does the same. "He's adamant about being socially conscious and going to the local food co-op. I very much support that, but when you're buying organic raspberries at $8 a pound, you think, 'Oh my God. We're spending $130 on groceries that would probably cost $60 somewhere else.' Yet he sees nothing wrong with that because he is making a conscious choice to be ecologically sound and also healthy."

New Luxury consumers, then, are complex creatures. They have wealth and sophistication. They are driven by fears but have high aspirations. They want it all, but they are often exhausted by trying to get it. They spend liberally on themselves, but they also believe they should do right for the world. They rocket, they trade up, and they trade down. They follow fashion and scoff at it. They buy for individual style and a little bit for status. They are highly influenced by their friends and cultural figures, but they have strong tastes of their own. They will try almost anything, but they give their loyalty sparingly. They don't believe in debt, but they don't let money stand in the way of buying what they want. They love objects, but they don't believe in conspicuous consumption.

New Luxury consumers need a lot of understanding. When they get it, they are not only appreciative, they are also likely to open up their pocketbooks and spend. They are a growing force of consumers—one to be reckoned with.

Three

The Creators and Their Goods

Who creates New Luxury goods?

Very often, they are created by a leader who is an outsider to the category. Ely Callaway spent thirty years in the textile business before he entered the wine business and then, at the age of sixty-three, created Callaway Golf. Pleasant Rowland had been a teacher before she created the American Girl doll. Fred Carl, Jr., was a homebuilder before his wife challenged him to develop a better stove, now known as the Viking. Jim Koch was a management consultant (with The Boston Consulting Group) before he created Samuel Adams Boston Lager beer.

But New Luxury goods can also be created by an established leader or industry insider who has the rare ability to *think* like an outsider. Leslie Wexner had long experience in the apparel industry when he purchased a small lingerie business and transformed it into Victoria's Secret. Joe Coulombe had been in the grocery category for almost ten years as founder and leader of a chain of convenience stores called Pronto Markets before he transformed it into Trader Joe's. Ronald Shaich was CEO of Au Bon Pain but was able to see that his acquisition, the Saint Louis Bread Company, had more potential than his original brand. Joe Foster, a senior vice president at venerable laundry-appliance maker Whirlpool Corporation, took a risk on a European-style front-loading washer-dryer combination—

long considered by industry insiders as a nonstarter in the American market—and built it into a remarkable success.

Outsider thinking is important because it enables the entrepreneur to wriggle free of that constricting assumption of the industry insider: the conventional price-volume demand curve. The industry insider is so used to the standard formula of "how many units" can be sold at "what price point" that it becomes hard for him to imagine that a premium product can move off the standard demand curve and sell at significantly higher volumes and higher margins. Outsider thinking also enables the entrepreneur to import ideas and practices from other industries and cultures and apply them to every aspect of strategy—including product development, pricing, consumer profiles, organization, and marketing.

In addition to their outsider thinking skills, New Luxury leaders have a facility for "patterning." They are keen observers who are able to analyze the elements at work in an industry and see those that are missing as well. They make connections between elements that have not been made before and then create a new frame of reference for themselves and the category. Wexner told us, "I have to see a lot of things and then somehow I just make conclusions. If I see enough stuff, get out and around, I can put it into trends and put things together in funny ways." Patterning is a back-of-mind activity that these entrepreneurs engage in constantly. Wexner told us, "My wife once asked me, 'Do you think very many people wake up and say, "I've been thinking"?' I said, 'Do I do that?' She said, 'Yeah, many mornings you wake up and say, "I've been thinking."' So I thought about that and thought I must process in the subconscious."

— When these leaders come up with "funny" ideas, they are often rejected, even scoffed at, by industry insiders, colleagues, and friends. When Robert Mondavi announced that he planned to build the first new Napa Valley winery in thirty years, he "could hear the guffaws up and down the Napa Valley," he wrote in his autobiography. "Everyone thought I was crazy." Similarly, Wexner learned to live with the skeptical looks of his friends and colleagues. "I think they saw me as kind of a mad scientist until I was about fifty," he told us. "My friends just thought I was nuts."

The difference between a mad scientist (or just a plain nut) and an entrepreneurial visionary, however, is that the idea is never enough—the entrepreneur is driven to make the idea tangible, a reality. Wexner says that people often tell him he'd be a great architect. "But I would have gone nuts being a theoretical architect," he said, "just making drawings. I have to see them work. If I really believe something, I have to concretize it and prove it or disprove it."

This description could apply to creators in many kinds of businesses, but what differentiates and distinguishes the New Luxury leader is the personal nature of his mission and the emotional connection with his company. David Neelemen, founder of JetBlue, sold his charter airline to Southwest Airlines in 1993, joined Southwest as an executive, signing a five-year noncompete agreement. But he found he hated working at Southwest, although he admired the airline, and he was so disruptive there that he was fired five months after joining. According to a *Forbes* profile, Neeleman's firing "opened old feelings of inadequacy," which stemmed from early difficulties in school. While waiting for his noncompete to expire, he began dreaming of—and planning for—a new airline, which he referred to, simply, as New Air. In 1997, he was ready to go with Jet-Blue, which was launched in 2000. There was an aspect of "I'll show them" to Neeleman's commitment to JetBlue—and he has. (Jet-Blue, like Trader Joe's, seems anomalous because of its discount price policy, but it qualifies as New Luxury because the company achieves high margins at high volumes, and it delivers the ladder of benefits, especially the emotional engagement of its customers.)

Similarly, Dr. Jordan Busch, cofounder of premium health-care provider Personal Physicians HealthCare in Chestnut Hill, Massachusetts, got the idea for his new venture when his father was diagnosed with cancer. Dr. Busch helped his father through the process of treatment. When it was over (his father died in 1999), Dr. Busch asked himself, "Why can't I treat all my patients as if they were friends or family?" Personal Physicians HealthCare charges patients a premium, so the doctors can limit their practices to three hundred patients, rather than the three thousand typical of a conventional practice. "We started very simply," says Dr. Busch. "We said, 'Let's invent the ideal practice.'"

New Luxury leaders, therefore, tend to have an abiding passion for the product itself and are hands-on managers who get intimately involved in developing their goods and in promoting them in the market. Unlike the professional manager, who argues that he could run any business, New Luxury leaders want to create and build only a specific business whose products are of great interest to them. They really love their wines and golf balls, stoves and dolls, groceries and lingerie. Edward Phillips, who developed the premium Belvedere and Chopin vodka brands, spent two years researching vodka with the intention of creating a premium entry into a category that, at that time, had none. As a result, he became knowledgeable and passionate about the category and the brand. He involved himself in the details of distilling, packaging, and promoting the brand. He even prevailed on his mother, a well-known and well-connected journalist, to lend him her Rolodex to recruit potential influential triers. Ely Callaway played golf every weekend to promote his new products and see who was playing with which clubs. David Neeleman of JetBlue takes his own flights regularly, asks fliers for their opinions, and sometimes helps unload baggage.

This emotional connection to the core of the business makes for a leader who is very different from the executive whose decisions are based on more conventional concerns—such as what will advance his career, what will most likely be approved by the board, what is easiest to accomplish, what has "always been done," what will please the analysts or press, or what will build the bottom line the fastest. New Luxury leaders are fascinating people who are as driven by their emotions as they are by a business plan. They are not always able to articulate how they accomplish their goals, but they are very clear about what they want to achieve and the things that are important to their businesses. Talking with Jess Jackson, Ronald Shaich, Leslie Wexner, Jim Koch, and the others is to listen to people who look at the world through a lens of their own making, see patterns others do not, and are committed to making their vision a reality.

A Distinct Type of Goods

New Luxury describes a class of goods that have very distinct characteristics.

	NEW LUXURY	CONVENTIONAL	OLD LUXURY
Affect	Engaging	Bland	Aloof
Availability	Affordable	Ubiquitous	Exclusive
Price	Premium	Low cost	Expensive
Quality	Mass artisanal	Mass-produced	Handmade
Social basis	Value driven	Conformist	Elitist

Old Luxury is about exclusivity. People who buy a Rolls-Royce do not wish to see a dozen other Rolls-Royce cars in the parking lot at Wal-Mart. New Luxury goods are far more accessible than Old Luxury goods, but their accessibility is more limited than conventional middle-market products. BMW sold about 213,000 vehicles in the United States in 2001, but General Motors, the quintessential middle-market carmaker, sold some 4.2 million. Similarly, Robert Mondavi sold more than 6,600 cases of its Woodbridge brand wines, at $6 to $10 per bottle, compared with 1,290 cases of its Robert Mondavi Coastal label, at $10 to $15 per bottle.

The challenge for New Luxury makers is to determine an optimal unit volume. If the goods become too available, they lose their sense of being limited in nature, and they will be unable to command a premium price. This is what happened, for a time, to Abercrombie & Fitch clothing. What started out as a New Luxury brand, with high quality and limited availability, quickly flooded the market and lost much of its cachet, especially to its original target consumer, the hip twentysomethings. When they saw the A&F logo on the sweaters and jeans of fifteen-year-olds, the emotional connection with other cool people their age was lost.

Old Luxury goods are priced to ensure that only the top-earning 1 to 2 percent of consumers can afford them and to provide a large enough margin so their makers can be profitable at very low unit volumes. New Luxury goods are always priced at a premium to conventional middle-market products—often as much as a tenfold premium—but are still priced within the financial reach of 40 percent of American households and not out of the question for 60 percent of them, those making $33,000 and up annually.

Some observers have interpreted New Luxury as a continuation of the quality revolution that began in the 1980s. New Luxury goods do, in fact, offer a high level of quality, usually higher than conventional middle-market goods and often higher than Old Luxury goods. The most basic definition of quality is "freedom from defects," and that is a guiding assumption of New Luxury goods. Traders up expect New Luxury goods to be free of faults of manufacture or assembly and to perform precisely as promised. If the product has defects or performs inadequately, the consumer expects that it will be remedied, repaired, or replaced at little or no cost and with little or no hassle. But most conventional middle-market manufacturers have also achieved high levels of quality, so freedom from defects is not enough to distinguish a New Luxury product from its traditional rivals.

Old Luxury goods, by contrast, have not always been of the highest quality, at least as defined by American manufacturing standards; rather, they have been promoted as "handmade," often by "old-world craftsmen," even if those craftsmen are assisted by machines and advanced technologies. The Rolls-Royce is largely hand assembled. Haute couture clothing is hand stitched. Superpremium wine is handcrafted. Handcraftsmanship limits the unit volume that can be produced. It also introduces variations into the finished product that offer proof of the human contribution. The limited volume and uniqueness of each piece help to justify the high selling price.

Many New Luxury goods have elements of craftsmanship, although they are not completely handmade or hand assembled, and are therefore "artisanal" in nature. There are specific steps in production that require the human touch, or the process is modeled on traditional craft methods. Olivier olives are "hand-placed" into their containers, rather than machine thrown, and they command a 50 percent premium. Mercedes-Benz says that "hand-finished laurel wood trim graces the interiors" of the C-class sedan. Belvedere vodka is "handcrafted"—distilled four times following traditions that are five hundred years old—and the bottle is stopped with a cork rather than a screw cap. Panera Bread loaves are baked in-store by master bakers. This artisanal quality allows for variation in the look and feel of the goods. The grain pattern in the Mercedes-Benz laurel trim swirls this way in one car and that way in another. The loaves at Panera Bread have slight variations of shape and color. The artisanal nature of New Luxury goods allows emotionally driven spenders to better express their individuality and personal style.

Yet this is "mass-artisanal" because the basic pattern or process does not change. The sandwiches at Panera Bread are all handmade, as is the bread, but according to a standard and unvarying recipe. (And the sandwich makers wear hygienic gloves to remove the negative connotations of handmade.) The wood inserts of the Mercedes-Benz fit precisely into openings that do not vary in size. As a result, consumers get the predictability they have come to expect and enjoy from the mass-market providers. They also make an emotional connection with the artisan involved in the creation of the product, as they would with Old Luxury goods.

Along with being exclusive, Old Luxury goods also carry a sense of elitism: the goods are meant for only a certain class of people. New Luxury goods, however, avoid class distinctions and are not promoted as elitist. Rather, they generally appeal to a set of values that may be shared by people at many income levels and in many walks of life. The Aveda customer, for example, values all-natural ingredients and simple, almost austere, design. It is this value-driven aspect of New Luxury goods that further encourages rocketing behavior; there is no sense of class confusion when a low-income earner carries a Coach bag or eats at Panera Bread. Conventional middle-market goods, by contrast, are driven by only the most obvious of shared values: convenience and cost.

With this set of attributes, it is impossible to mistake a Rolls-Royce, a fifteen thousand-square-foot mansion, or a $12,000 watch for a New Luxury good, and the successful companies are the ones that make that message clear. A marketing executive at Daimler-Chrysler says that the Mercedes-Benz brand used to foster an Old Luxury image, a brand that was like "a traditional English country club, the stuffy preserve of the elite." But no longer. Now "we want to make it more like an upmarket health club—still difficult to get into, but more modern and accessible." That is: Limited, but not exclusive. Premium, but not just expensive. A statement of shared values, rather than elitist.

Supply Side Forces That Fuel New Luxury

The New Luxury entrepreneur has been aided in the creation of this new class of goods by a number of powerful business forces.

Changes in the Dynamics of Retailing

Perhaps the most important of these changes is the rise of the specialty retailers—Crate and Barrel, Williams-Sonoma, Restoration Hardware, Victoria's Secret, and others—that have made New Luxury goods far more available throughout the country. They have achieved remarkable success by offering a limited selection of goods in a limited number of categories at premium prices. Williams-Sonoma has grown revenue 21 percent annually since 1991. Bed Bath & Beyond has achieved 29 percent annual revenue growth. These companies are makers of New Luxury goods, as well as distributors of the goods made by other creators; as much as 60 percent of the stock in these stores are private-label brands. The specialty stores are also important definers of the New Luxury lifestyle—consumers are very aware of the "Pottery Barn look" or the "Williams-Sonoma kitchen."

The growth of the specialty retailers has had the same polarizing effect on retailing as successful New Luxury goods have had on their categories. Consumers flock to the specialty stores and pay a premium for goods in categories that are meaningful to them, but in other categories, they have increasingly turned to the low-cost mass merchandisers such as Wal-Mart and Costco and the cost-focused category killers such as Kohl's, Lowe's, and Circuit City. The traditional department stores, such as Dillard's, Mays, Sears, and Federated Department Stores, have found themselves facing death in the middle—unable to match the prices of the mass merchandisers or the emotional engagement of the purveyors of premium goods.

Surprisingly, the big discounters have also become important sellers of New Luxury items in certain categories that can deliver high volume. Costco, for example, stocks a larger selection and sells a larger volume of premium wine than any other retailer. On the shelves at the Costco store on North Clybourn Avenue in Chicago we found more than thirty New Luxury items in stock—including

wines, clothing, fashion accessories, watches and jewelry, chocolates, and home goods—selling at substantial discounts to other retail outlets. Costco presents middle-class consumers with an almost
irresistible value proposition: highest quality at the lowest price.

And Costco will continue to affect the New Luxury market. The
company achieved $38 billion in sales in its 2002 fiscal year. With
412 locations, it achieved average sales per store of $92 million.
Costco serves over nineteen million members who spend an average
$2,000 per year. The company operates with net negative inven-
tory—payables exceed inventory with more than twelve net turns
per year. Costco's revenues have doubled since 1996, and product
gross margins averaged 10 percent—the lowest of all major retailers
in the world, and a good measure of its efficiency. Costco is continually pushing into new categories: it has become a major supplier of
fresh cut flowers, offering locally grown varieties at prices 50
percent to 150 percent lower than regional grocery stores or small
florist shops. Next on Costco's agenda is the "home" category—it
plans to offer premium furnishings and accessories in new free-
standing facilities of one hundred thousand square feet. Costco's entry is sure to polarize the home goods category.

The "malling of America" continues, if at a slower pace than
during its golden age in the 1970s. The trend now is toward even
larger malls, with "shoppertainment" features, including rides and
themed events, IMAX theaters, and live performances. The increase
in the number of specialty shops, the growth in the size of malls, and
the growing sophistication of the American shopper mean that
there is a steadily rising demand for New Luxury goods to fill the
shelves of America's forty-five thousand malls.

Availability of Capital

Despite a sharp drop in the amount of money raised by venture
capital funds in the years 2000 through 2002, there is no shortage of
investment capital available in the United States, and "had a hard
time raising the money" is generally not a complaint we heard from
the New Luxury entrepreneurs we spoke with for this book. David
Neeleman of JetBlue, for example, raised $130 million from five in-

vestors. "No one turned us down," he said—including George Soros, who invested $54 million in the venture.

Some of the initial financing for New Luxury start-ups comes from the founders, and the rise in income and wealth since 1970 has made more personal funds available for such early investment. Ely Callaway was one of just three initial investors in his company, and he invested $400,000 of his own money in the venture. Jim Koch, founder of The Boston Beer Company, made a $100,000 investment. David Neeleman, of JetBlue, committed $5 million.

But New Luxury start-ups usually require outside investment as well, and they benefited from the increase in venture capital activity in the late 1980s and 1990s. It was in those years that many New Luxury brands and companies were founded or expanded their operations—including Coach, Belvedere, and Viking Range. In 1990, venture capitalists provided just over $3 billion to 1,317 companies. In the year 2000, 4,608 companies benefited from venture capital investment, taking in a total of a little more than $104 billion.

After the bursting of the Internet bubble from 2001 to 2002 there was a decline in the number of investment deals done, but it did not mean that capital had dried up altogether. At the end of 2002, there was a pool of $90 billion in uncommitted capital looking for deals. Investors had been shying away from the technology sectors—including software, biotech, networking, and telecommunications. Their new focus gave an advantage to the more tangible and traditional categories that compose New Luxury, including appliances, apparel, and food and beverage.

Many New Luxury entrepreneurs do not start their companies with the intention of taking them public or selling them. Rather, they are committed to managing and building their businesses for the long haul, and many keep them private for years. Kendall-Jackson (founded in 1982) is private. Bose (1964), Patagonia (1976), Crate and Barrel (1962), Pret A Manger (1986), Sub-Zero (1945), Trek (1976), and Viking Range (1984) are all private companies.

But many New Luxury players do go public, and the last fifteen years of the last century also defined the golden age of the initial public offering (IPO). There were 109 IPOs in 1990, which raised a total of $4.5 billion. In 2000, 380 companies went public, raising

$75.8 billion, including New Luxury players Tiffany (IPO in 1987), Callaway Golf (1992), Starbucks (1992), The Boston Beer Company (1995), Martha Stewart Living Omnimedia (1999), Coach (spun off from Sara Lee in 2001), and JetBlue (2002).

Access to Flexible Supply-Chain Networks and Global Resources

The easing of international trade barriers and the emergence of global supply-chain management-services providers have enabled companies of almost every size to take advantage of foreign labor markets and put together and manage complex global networks for sourcing, manufacturing, assembling, and distributing their goods.

The major impetus for overseas manufacturing has long been low cost of labor, but there were associated risks of lower productivity, poor production quality, and high shipping costs. But manufacturers worldwide have been making gains in productivity while improving quality and still keeping labor costs low. China, in particular, has outflanked the traditional contenders—especially the newly industrialized countries of East Asia, including Taiwan, South Korea, and Singapore—as the country best able to offer quality production at low cost. This can most easily be seen by the large increase in medium- and high-tech manufactures made in China and exported around the world.

Nor is it necessary for smaller companies to maintain a presence in the countries where they manufacture, thanks to reductions in the price of global travel and the availability of global information and communication networks. The real cost of international passenger travel declined by more than 50 percent from 1978 to 2001. Low travel costs make it much more affordable for U.S. staff to travel overseas to source and oversee production. For retailers such as Crate and Barrel, this means they can do many more trips in search of new ideas and products. In the past, they would send two or three people on scouting and buying trips to Europe each year. Now they have teams traveling to Europe and Asia seven to ten times each year. The cost of shipping and distribution from overseas markets to the United States has also fallen. The real cost of Asia-to-the-United-States ocean freight declined 28 percent from 1993 to 2001, and the real rate of United-States-to-Asia shipping declined even more dramatically—by 54 percent. This makes it cost-effective to ship raw materials, components, and finished goods from around the world.

The development with the most impact on the ability of smaller and emerging companies to manufacture goods abroad is the emergence of facilitators who help create optimal supply-chain networks for their clients. This capability is most utilized by fashion retailers, including Limited Brands; Bed Bath & Beyond; and Gymboree, a retailer of children's clothing and toys.

Li & Fung, based in Hong Kong, is the largest and most successful of these supply-chain optimizers, with some seven hundred customers in 2000 and total revenues of over $4 billion. Li & Fung puts together for its customers the most effective supply chain, which may include suppliers in several countries. According to Victor Fung, a grandson of the company's founder, the company breaks up the value chain to get the best capability, cost, and schedule. Li & Fung calls it "dispersed manufacturing," and it has revolutionized the business of manufacturing in Asia for transnationals and for smaller companies based in the United States.

This "model of borderless manufacturing has become a paradigm for the region," says Fung in an interview in *Harvard Business Review*. "Today Asia consists of multiple networks of dispersed manufacturing—high-cost hubs that do the sophisticated planning for regional manufacturing. Bangkok works with the Indochinese peninsula, Taiwan with the Philippines, Seoul with northern China. Dispersed manufacturing is what's behind the boom in Asia's trade and investment statistics in the 1990s—companies moving raw materials and semifinished parts around Asia. But the region is still very dependent on the ultimate sources of demand, which are in North America and Western Europe. They start the whole cycle going."

The Li & Fung model has enabled fashion retailers to become designers, not just stockists. "Retailers are now participating in the design process," says Fung. "They're now managing suppliers through us and are even reaching down to their suppliers' suppliers. Eventually that translates into much better management of inventories and lower markdowns in the stores."

For New Luxury companies in many categories, the dispersed-manufacturing model enables them to take advantage of capabilities available only in Asia, shorten the buying cycle, and reduce costs. Pleasant Company, maker of American Girl dolls, for example, buys its famous "sleepy eye" from a factory in China because it makes the very best eyeball in the world, according to president Ellen Brothers. "The way they're put together, the material that we use, the actual hair that makes up the eyelashes. It's a more authentic eyeball." It is a technical difference that delivers an emotional benefit—the doll looks more real and feels more like a genuine character who can become a friend.

Focus on Speed and the Collapse of the Innovation Cascade

Another important factor in the spread of New Luxury—and closely related to the changes in the retail environment—is the collapse of the innovation cascade. New Luxury goods are more responsive to trends than are conventional goods and they flow in a faster stream of innovation. It takes much less time for a new style, design, feature, technology, or material to cascade from the high-end item where innovations generally appear first, to the middle-market good. The trend has affected every category. In cars, for example, it used to take several model years for a new technology to cascade from the high-end to the mid-range models. Power door locks, for example, were introduced in the 1956 Packard. By 1970 only 6 percent of all U.S. car models came with power door locks standard, and penetration reached 80 percent as late as 1990—more than twenty years for a desirable and relatively inexpensive feature to cascade to the majority of middle-market models.

Affluent consumers—especially the top 5 percent of earners—have been instrumental in accelerating the cascade, because they constantly push the upper limits of the categories in which they consume, in both price and innovation. In cars, for example, the most affluent consumers have pushed Mercedes-Benz and BMW to extend the price range of their models over $150,000, creating technology and innovation that will eventually (but in increasingly shorter time periods) cascade to the middle market.

The innovation cascade has been easiest to see in the world of fashion, where haute couture designers reveal their new clothing ideas in the European shows, and the producers of middle-market clothing interpret the concepts into lower-priced, practical street wear. Traditionally, the translation of the innovations in a $2,000 custom-made style into a $100 outfit could take a couple of years. Now it gets done in a few months, or even a few weeks. For example, Prada introduced a new material—ostrich leather—at the European runway shows in September 1999 and featured a $2,800 ostrich leather skirt in its spring 2000 couture collection. But the middle-market consumer did not have to wait two years to join in the ostrich leather excitement. Designer Bebe had a $78 ostrich-leather handbag ready for spring 2000, and Victoria's Secret previewed an ostrich-embossed leather skirt in the fall of 2000.

A key influence in the collapse of the fashion cascade has come from a small number of large retailers, who have sought to shorten fashion cycles and avoid the retailer's worst nightmare: unsalable inventory. Zara, a clothing retailer that is based in Spain and has more than five hundred stores worldwide, has been particularly successful in changing the rules of the fashion game. The industry standard lead time—the time it takes from the initial design of a new article of clothing to the moment it gets hung on a rack or stacked on a shelf—is about nine months. At Zara, the process can take as little as three weeks.

Zara is not driven particularly by the haute couture runway shows, nor does the company concentrate all activity around the traditional fashion "seasons"—fall-winter, spring-summer. Rather, Zara seeks to stay close to the market, watching for what's selling best and new trends that are emerging, and responds to them quickly. It does this by creating and maintaining a close connection between the store managers and a team of more than two hundred designers who work at the headquarters in La Coruña, Spain. When a store manager notices that a particular style is moving briskly, for example, she can order more units via a customized handheld device. The order is placed immediately and sent to one of Zara's factories, most of which are in Spain. Factory deliveries are made twice each week, resulting in about eleven inventory turns per year, two to three times the industry average. Any store manager may also make a suggestion for a modification to an existing style or propose an entirely new article or design. The designers at headquarters collect and evaluate the suggestions as they arrive, produce designs on their computers, and, when finalized, send them over the company intranet to a factory. The result is that Zara designs and produces as many as ten thousand new items every year. Although its manufacturing costs run some 20 percent higher than its competitors', Zara rarely needs to write off unsalable inventory. Profits of Zara's parent, Inditex, increased 31 percent in 2001. Zara's founder, Amancio Ortega, is the richest man in Spain.

Zara's example is provoking other retailers to respond. ASDA, a giant U.K. retailer owned by Wal-Mart, has followed Zara's lead, creating what it calls "fast fashion"—it can get new styles into stores in seven weeks and bring in new styles once a month. In the United States, too, Wal-Mart has embraced the idea of fast-moving New Luxury goods. The monster retailer sells some $25 billion in clothes and accessories each year and has expanded far beyond the blue jeans, underwear, and kids' clothing it is known for. In 2002, *New York Times* fashion writer Cathy Horyn wrote about her fondness for Wal-Mart clothing. She describes wearing a pair of sandals to a Balenciaga runway show in Paris. There she bumped into Allen Questrom, then CEO of Barney's New York, a retailer, who noticed the sandals and asked, "Are those Gucci?" "No," Horyn replied. "Wal-Mart."

We've seen the collapse of the innovation cascade across New Luxury categories—a constant flow of new styles, new ideas, new features, and new materials. In food and beverage, Starbucks regularly offers new drink concoctions and features new coffee-bean types. Panera Bread offers daily specials in its cafés, lunches featuring seasonal ingredients, and a dozen varieties of freshly baked bread, from sourdough to tomato basil, in a variety of forms including baguettes, rolls, and "bowls."

Flexibility and Speed of Manufacture

New Luxury goods often present special challenges in production. It's one thing to produce a high-quality wine, for example, in a volume of a few hundred cases per year. It's another thing to produce the same wine in a volume a hundred times as high, and have the taste, color, and nose remain consistent and worthy of the premium price.

New Luxury companies generally start producing their goods in low volume and plan for modest growth. But their success can be far more rapid than they expect, requiring them to scale up production faster than they had anticipated and forcing them to find ways to maintain their product standards at much higher quantities. This is what happened to Jim Koch of The Boston Beer Company. He hoped to sell eight thousand barrels of beer annually within five years of starting the company. Instead, he reached his goal in the first four months of production, and the company proceeded to grow at 30 percent a year. Koch could not make that much beer in his own small handcraft brewery. The solution was to control the selection of the ingredients, specify all aspects of the brewing process—which combined aspects of nineteenth-century brewing with twentieth-century quality-control methods—then outsource it and, finally, manage distribution. By choosing to control the key elements of the process without building its own breweries, Boston Beer was able to grow to 1.2 million barrels in sales by 2001 and maintain a reputation for beer that is artisanal—containing elements of handcraft—but available in far larger volumes than handmade microbrews.

Many New Luxury products contain important technical features that differentiate them from their competitors and require complex and expensive manufacturing processes. Callaway Golf, for example, uses a variety of metals in its clubs, including titanium, stainless steel, carbon steel, tungsten, and graphite, along with specialty adhesives, paints, and solvents. The ability to work with these metals, often in combination, to extremely exacting specifications is a key to the Callaway technical difference. The company subcontracts the production of certain components, such as titanium heads, to shops that specialize in what is known as "investment casting." This lost-wax molding process is very flexible and cost-effective and also has the precise dimensional control necessary to produce the close tolerances Callaway requires. Callaway does final assembly of the outsourced components—the head, shaft, and grip—in its own eighty thousand-square-foot production operation in Carlsbad, California. There it also customizes the length of the shaft and the angle of the club to create some seventeen thousand variants to suit different types of golfers with different types of swings—another example of mass-artisanal manufacture.

New Luxury Is More Than Marketing

New Luxury goods cannot be imagined, developed, manufactured, distributed, or marketed following conventional middle-market business attitudes or practices—although many businesses assume they can be.

New Luxury companies such as Coach, BMW, Panera Bread, Millennium Import, Callaway, and Kendall-Jackson are careful to keep their brand names closely connected to the product itself and to the emotional drives of their consumers. Although the brand name is of tremendous importance, it is rarely promoted without a connection to a specific product or product attribute, or to the story of the leader or company that created it. Absolut vodka, by contrast, built its brand on what became a famous advertising campaign: brilliant visual interpretations of the bottle shape. But Absolut is now little more than its famous brand name; the vodka itself has become the standard pouring brand at many bars. Belvedere and Grey Goose, in contrast, the leading premium vodkas, connect their names to specific attributes of taste, distilling techniques, country of origin, awards, and bottle innovations.

Some companies hope to create a New Luxury product by sprucing up an existing product, adding new features, redesigning, or repositioning through advertising. This is the approach that American carmakers have often taken in creating "luxury" models—they use the platform of a midrange model, equip it with the most powerful engine available, fit it with leather seats and other niceties in the cabin, and make it available in special paint options. The most notorious example is the Cadillac Cimarron, introduced in 1982, which was little more than a Chevy Cavalier with fancy trim; but there are many others, including "near-luxury" models from Oldsmobile, Buick, and Mercury. New Luxury consumers are not fooled by these superficial "new and improved" products. They seek genuine benefits and real differences.

Companies sometimes assume that the New Luxury consumer will be seduced by a high price point, but New Luxury consumers do not automatically assume that if it costs more, it must be better. They are sophisticated enough to evaluate the technical and functional benefits of a product and to trust their own emotional reactions to it. We heard over and over again from consumers that the most expensive entry in a category is not always the best. As one consumer put it, "Luxury can sometimes mean better quality and last longer, but sometimes it's cheap and flimsy."

New Luxury is much more than a marketing exercise, although marketing is, of course, a key part of the process. But New Luxury goods are not created solely in the marketing. They are created through all the management disciplines—and often through unconventional marketing methods, as we'll see in the chapters devoted to specific brand stories.

The Practices of New Luxury Leaders

New Luxury leaders and their companies follow a set of management practices that are different from those of conventional or Old Luxury goods creators. Using them, New Luxury companies have shattered conventional beliefs in nearly all aspects of product creation and distribution, including ideas about price ceilings, price ranges, brand extendibility, consumer sophistication, market stability, and the innovation cascade.

1. *Never underestimate the customer.* In every New Luxury category, consumers are more affluent, better educated, and more sophisticated than ever before. In the categories they care about, they consider themselves to be knowledgeable and even expert. These consumers appreciate traditional quality, technological innovation, and emotional authenticity. They care about the heritage of a brand and are interested in the category as a whole.

As we'll see in chapter 9, Robert Mondavi and Jess Jackson challenged the long-held assumption that the palate of the American consumer was unsophisticated and undiscerning. They believed that Americans could appreciate the more complex flavors and subtle aromas of premium wine, and they built substantial businesses around that belief. In fact, they discovered that Americans had such pronounced ideas about taste that they have helped to change the flavor of wine worldwide.

This knowledge, taste, and discernment can be seen in many New Luxury categories. Young girls take close note of the minutest details of their American Girl dolls, such as the "wigged" hair and special packing material. Bottled waters have become the topic of such interest and discussion that the Ritz-Carlton New York, Battery Park, installed a water sommelier to make recommendations of the best pairings of water and food. (San Pellegrino, for example, is rich in calcium, is a good choice for pregnant women, and ideally paired with a plate of fresh fruit.)

Consumers also have a sensitive built-in calculator that enables them to assess goods and determine whether the price is aligned with the value and how the cost fits into their entire structure of emotional needs and purchasing power. They will make a purchase at a price point that their calculator tells them is too high only if that product delivers very potent rational and emotional benefits. They will also make a purchase when the price-value calculator tells them that the price point is very low and that they are getting a bargain.

2. *Shatter the price-volume demand curve.* The masstige segment, for example, is 20 to 40 percent of many personal-care categories and growing at twice the industry average. Sub-Zero shattered the conventional wisdom that there was no substantial household-appliance market above the $1,000 price point. BMW is the most profitable car company in the world, with unit volume of its New Luxury models ten times that of superluxury cars.

New Luxury companies can also maintain their position off the traditional demand curve even as they achieve high growth. Williams-Sonoma substantially increased revenues and profits in 2002 over the previous year. BMW continues to grow unit sales while maintaining prices, as do Panera Bread and Victoria's Secret. Jess Jackson redrew the demand curve for the wine industry. He saw the potential to create a new segment in the market where higher prices and higher volume would intersect for substantially higher profits.

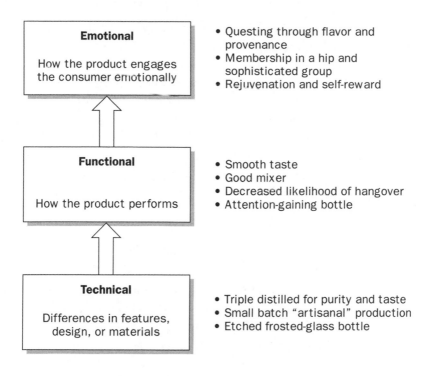

Emotional How the product engages the consumer emotionally	• Questing through flavor and provenance • Membership in a hip and sophisticated group • Rejuvenation and self-reward
Functional How the product performs	• Smooth taste • Good mixer • Decreased likelihood of hangover • Attention-gaining bottle
Technical Differences in features, design, or materials	• Triple distilled for purity and taste • Small batch "artisanal" production • Etched frosted-glass bottle

Premium vodka provides a ladder of benefits.

3. *Create a ladder of genuine benefits.* Perhaps the most important of the New Luxury practices is ensuring that the products deliver a ladder of genuine differences—technical, functional, and emotional.

The products must first succeed on a technical level, with genuine competitive differences in materials, workmanship, or technologies. Panera Bread's $6 sandwich, for example, offers bread baked on the premises, with locally grown lettuce and seasonal ingredients, which are genuinely different and perceptibly fresher than the mass-produced buns and character-free shreds of iceberg of the standard fast-food restaurant. Callaway Golf's original Big Bertha driver featured a head 50 percent larger than that of a conventional driver, but no heavier.

The next rung on the ladder is functional performance. The technical differences must translate into genuine differences in performance. The larger head of the Big Bertha driver makes it easier for the golfer to hit the ball farther. The traditional recipe and four distillations of Belvedere vodka make for what Belvedere claims is a "distinctive creamy smoothness, an aromatic nose, and a semisweet lingering finish." This is not a meaningless marketing claim, however; vodka consumers profess to appreciate subtle differences in taste and drinking style. As one vodka aficionado explained to us, "Absolut is heavier in consistency, and it definitely gets you drunk faster. Belvedere is very smooth, and it does not have this hammered-after-a-few-drinks effect like Smirnoff or Stoli. Grey Goose has a funny aftertaste to it."

— The final rung on the ladder of differences is the emotional one. For the emotionally driven spender, the greatest benefit comes from how powerfully the product connects with his needs. To find a powerful positioning, New Luxury innovators must understand the consumer's behavior, needs, and unspoken (sometimes even to himself) desires. They must also offer distinctive functional advantages that are specifically tied to the targeted emotions, as well as a technical platform that lends credibility and authenticity to the functional claims.

If the product delivers the ladder of benefits, consumers will make a connection between the technical and functional benefits and become emotionally engaged with the brand. Pet lovers, for example, buy gourmet pet food such as Nutro because it is technically different, offering added nutrients and organic ingredients. They believe that the technical differences create superior product performance—they produce, as promised, a shinier coat or a calmer disposition. Consumers find these performance differences emotionally meaningful because it seems that the product is enabling them to be more nurturing and loving. The premium and super-premium pet-food segments are growing at 9 percent compound annual growth rate, in comparison to 1 to 2 percent for conventional products, and they now account for almost one-third of the total pet-food market.

A word of caution: traditional market research will often miss the emotional underpinnings of New Luxury success, and conventional product testing may undermine the linkages between the emotional, functional, and technical benefit layers. To generate insight, innovative players typically spend more time in the market and conduct one-on-one interviews with their core customers—in their homes, at retail sites, in their domains.

4. *Escalate innovation, elevate quality, deliver a flawless experience.* The market for New Luxury is rich in opportunity, but it is also unstable. This is because technical and functional advantages are increasingly short-lived, as new competitors enter the market, and because of the relentless downward pressure of the innovation cascade. What was luxurious and different today becomes the standard brand of tomorrow. A well-established brand can't maintain an emotional position for long if the technical and functional benefits become undifferentiated.

Winners in New Luxury markets aggressively and continuously up the ante on innovation and quality, and they render their own products obsolete before a new competitor does it for (or to) them. They strive to shorten the product development cycle, make substantial investments in manufacturing improvements, and do not slavishly follow the rule that research and development should equal 5 percent (or any other fixed percentage) of sales.

5. *Extend the price range and positioning of the brand.* Many New Luxury brands extend the brand upmarket to create aspirational appeal and down-market to make it more accessible and more competitive and to build demand. A traditional competitor's highest price may be three to four times its lowest; New Luxury players often have a fivefold to tenfold difference between their highest and lowest price points. They are careful, however, to create, define, and maintain a distinct character and meaning for each product at every level, as well as to articulate the brand essence all the products share. The Mercedes-Benz range, for example, extends from the successful C230 sports coupe at $26,000 to the Maybach 62 at $350,000, a thirteenfold span. Every Mercedes-Benz model shares the brand themes of advanced engineering, quality manufacture, flawless performance, solidity and safety, luxurious comfort, and the distinctive Mercedes-Benz look and badging. But each one interprets those themes in its own characteristic and genuine way.

6. *Customize your value chain to deliver on the benefit ladder.* New Luxury creators often work outside the established value chain in order to overcome the structural barriers that stand in the way of

small producers. They put the emphasis on control, rather than ownership, of the value chain and become masters at orchestrating it. Panera Bread mixes all the dough for its signature sourdough bread at a central commissary to ensure that the quality and taste never vary. Callaway Golf assembles its outsourced components in its own facility to ensure that the "swing" is right. Jess Jackson built a disproportionately large sales team to ensure that the retailers— who were used to buying standard brands from big wholesalers— understood the Kendall-Jackson "fighting varietal" story.

7. *Use influence marketing; seed your success through brand apostles.* In New Luxury goods, a small percentage of category consumers contribute the dominant share of value. In categories with frequent repeat purchases, such as lingerie and spirits, the top 10 percent of customers generate up to half of category sales and profits. Reaching those important consumers requires a different kind of launch, involving carefully managed initial sales to specific groups in specific venues, frequent feedback from early purchasers, and word-of-mouth recommendations. Belvedere vodka, for example, was launched through tasting events for bartenders, and gift bottles were sent to cultural influencers in important markets.

Such consumers are often highly influenced by well-known advocates they admire. Jess Jackson enlisted key influencers to create a buzz for his wines. When introducing the Big Bertha driver, Ely Callaway understood that recreational golfers—many of whom are businesspeople—would be influenced by who was using the new and unusual clubs. He enlisted Jack Welch, the most celebrated CEO golfer at the time, not only to use the clubs but also to invest in his company, and he persuaded Bill Gates to appear in ads. Red Bull, a premium-priced "energy" drink, has built a $100 million business by focusing on the social environments of its core customers: health clubs, bars, and hip hangouts.

An intense, continuing focus on these core customers will yield early signs of a shifting market and ideas for next-generation variants, features, or products.

8. *Continually attack the category like an outsider.* New Luxury creators look beyond their own categories for the trends and patterns that will generate the next breakthrough. Sources of inspiration can

include Old Luxury products or services, innovations from Europe or Asia, analogues from other categories, and advice from experts and professionals. It was on a worldwide scouting expedition that Edward Phillips came across the vodka that became the prototype for the Belvedere brand. When the makers of Freschetta pizza sought to overtake Kraft Foods' DiGiorno in the premium frozen-pizza segment, they assembled a panel of five gourmet chefs from the best restaurants in the United States. The chefs, in turn, worked closely with some of the best cooking schools in Italy to develop a superior sauce and crust.

People within New Luxury organizations don't think like employees of conventional producers, and that is often because they are driven by the original outsider thinking of their founders. Ellen Brothers, president of Pleasant Company, maker of American Girls, says that the thinking of founder Pleasant Rowland still infuses the company. "If you ask any of our 1,200 employees what business we are in," says Brothers, "no one will say 'the toy business.' Every one of them will say, 'We're in the girl business.'"

The challenge for the New Luxury creator is that when she becomes successful, her outsider thinking becomes the new conventional wisdom, and competitors flood the market hoping to capitalize on it. The Napa Valley is home to many small producers who hope to follow the Robert Mondavi and Jess Jackson model but who don't have the personal vision or the commitment or the understanding of the New Luxury practices. As a result, New Luxury creators must force themselves to think like outsiders all over again. This is a rigorous lifestyle, one that Leslie Wexner of Limited Brands describes as "very lonely."

Four

Where Goods and Emotions Intersect

What drives the consumer of New Luxury?

People who trade up act in response to a relatively small set of powerful emotional drivers, both positive and negative. They are lonely, fearful, stressed, and longing for peace, but they are also hopeful, optimistic, and eager to try new things. Although they buy New Luxury goods in a wide range of categories, trading-up activity is concentrated in a small number of categories of high emotional content.

The findings of our survey of 2,300 American consumers making $50,000 or more per year—including people of all demographic descriptions—show that people are both highly aspirational *and* stressed, disconnected, and anxious. A majority of respondents "agreed" or "strongly agreed" with the statements "I am happy with my life right now" (62 percent) and "I have peace of mind" (55 percent). But their general statements of happiness are slightly belied by their responses to questions about more specific aspects of their lives. Only 39 percent agreed or strongly agreed with the statement "I have the right balance in my life"; 37 percent with the statement "I feel like a part of my community"; 35 percent with the statement "I have a lot of close friends." The statement that achieved agreement from the highest percentage of respondents (64 percent) was "My home is my castle." And 59 percent agreed or strongly agreed

Percentage of people who strongly agree or agree with these statements:	
I never have enough time	54.8
I don't get enough sleep	53.8
I don't spend enough time with friends	51.5
I worry about my health	40.1
I'm working harder than ever	39.0
I feel a great deal of stress in my life	36.6
I don't feel appreciated for all that I do	36.5
I am happy with my appearance	30.5
I'm happy in my romantic relationships	17.8

Our survey of 2,300 consumers showed that many Americans feel overworked, isolated, lonely, worried, and unhappy.

that "I'm happiest at home." These responses paint a picture of consumers who may like to think they are generally happy and connected but who feel happier at home than they do in the wider world.

These darker underlying themes become more dominant when consumers talk about specific aspects of their lives. Fifty-five percent agreed that "I never have enough time," and 54 percent agreed that "I don't get enough sleep." Nearly 40 percent said they are "working harder than ever," and 37 percent said, "I feel a great deal of stress in my life." A significant percentage of the respondents said that they don't spend enough time with their friends (51 percent) or family (35 percent), that they worry about their health (40 percent), and that they are anxious about the future (40 percent). The picture thus becomes a little fuller—of consumers who say they are generally happy, possibly because they want to believe they are, but who also feel pressed for time, stressed by work, and out of touch with people who are important to them.

The respondents told us that there is a connection between these emotional concerns and their buying and consumption behaviors. More than a third (36 percent) agree that "I love to shop," and 29 percent think of shopping as a "form of stress relief." When asked about consumption in specific categories, there is far more enthusiasm. Seventy-five percent of our respondents said they "love to travel," and 64 percent said they "love to try new foods." Sixty-five percent said that "in the areas I spend more for quality, I know all the fine details." So the complex and sometimes conflicting nature of the New Luxury consumer becomes evident: a majority of our respondents say they are happiest at home, but they say also that they love to travel. Only a third say they really like to shop, but two-thirds say they are expert in the goods they care about.

The spending behaviors in specific categories align with the emotional interests. We asked the respondents to consider twenty categories of consumer goods and indicate the ones in which they would be "likely to spend more to get a product that is better than the rest." The home or apartment topped the list, and many home goods were among the top twelve, including furniture, home entertainment, personal computers, bedding, kitchen appliances, laundry appliances, and cookware—as you would expect of consumers who are happiest at home and consider their home their castle. Sit-down restaurants ranked second. Cars, shoes, and apparel are also categories where many consumers say they will spend more.

Consumers at every income level are rocketers. Ninety-six percent of the respondents say they have at least one category they are willing to pay more for; 51 percent admit there is at least one category in which they "spend more than I should." And the spending continues, even during slow economic times: 50 percent say, "Even when the economy is bad, I'll spend on affordable luxuries." That's why New Luxury companies such as BMW, Coach, Panera Bread, Starbucks, and Williams-Sonoma posted remarkable performance gains in 2002, even during the dismal holiday selling season, in comparison to flat sales or declines for conventional producers. Consumers with the lower incomes, $50,000 to $100,000, are willing to spend more in the same categories as those with higher incomes, $100,000 and above, but they are able to rocket in fewer categories.

Although the most affluent consumers are able to trade up in every category, they don't necessarily do so—in fact, they often trade down in many categories. Richard, for example, is in the top 1 percent of earners in the United States. He owns a business that provides security to high-profile musicians when they're on tour, and he makes what he calls "quite a bit of money"—about $2.5 million a year. Although he believes in spending on things that are important to him, he also likes to "live simple" at his Texas home which he shares with his wife and two children. He's thinking of buying a Hummer for himself and a sports car for his wife, but he doesn't think it makes sense to spend money on premium clothing for the kids. "Their clothes come from Wal-Mart and Target and maybe JC Penney and Sears. We have a few clothing stores where you can buy better brand stuff, but why do that when they are going to go run around and play in the dirt?"

The most intriguing findings from our survey are about how buying certain categories of goods makes consumers feel. Respondents were asked to choose from a list of forty-four terms that describe how trading up in their category of choice made them feel. These terms "pooled" into six distinct groups which we combined into four "emotional spaces": Taking Care of Me, Connecting, Questing, and Individual Style. Each category has a dominant emotional space associated with it—personal care is primarily about Taking Care of Me, for example—but some categories, such as the home, are important in all four of them.

Taking Care of Me: Time for Myself, Convenience, Renewal, and Reward

This emotional space is the most personal and immediate and, for many American consumers, the most important. It is about goods I buy to make me feel as good as I can, as immediately as possible. It is about physical rejuvenation, emotional uplift, stress reduction, pampering, comfort, rest, and moments to myself. It includes such goods as personal-care products, spas, ice cream, chocolates, coffee, home theater equipment, appliances, furniture, and bedding.

Because these activities are so personal, they are sometimes

Taking Care of Me	Connecting	Questing	Individual Style
Time for myself	Attracting	Adventure	Self-expressing
Convenience	Nurturing	Learning	Self-branding
Renewal and reward	Belonging	Play	Signaling

thought of as selfish, self-indulgent, or guilty pleasures. Working women and working mothers, in particular, feel the most need for such comforts, as well as the most guilty about indulging in them, especially if it means reducing time spent with family or doing things for the family. However, their stresses are so high and the cultural permission has become so explicit that they are buying extensively in these categories.

Time for Myself

Working women, and especially working women with families, are in search of time for themselves. They are lucky to find a few moments a day when they are not in demand for some task and to find some place to enjoy those moments—a place where they are not at risk of being interrupted by a child's plea, a spouse's query, a business phone call, or the needs of a pet. Paula, fifty-eight, has had a life with its share of difficulties, including two divorces and health issues such as heart surgery and a bout with breast cancer, all of which she handled while raising two kids and holding a full-time job in a university library. The job pays about $40,000 a year. "It took years for me to realize that a mother is not the person who is supposed to work until dawn getting things done for other people," Paula told us. "I went to a therapist, and she would ask me, 'What have you done for yourself this week?' And I would think to myself, 'What a stupid question,' because I was not even to the point where I thought I could do something just for myself."

When women find a few moments for themselves, they like to make the most of them. Sometimes they retreat to the bathroom or in-home spa, where they can feel safe, comfortable, warm, relaxed, and reasonably certain they will not be disturbed. They are likely to take with them one of a number of New Luxury goods. They may soak in Aveda Soothing Aqua Therapy, whose "fragrant combination of Dead Sea salts, plant-based emollients, vitamin E, and beneficial essences turns a bath into an indulgence" at $34 for a 16-ounce jar. A scented candle from Yankee Candle ($19.99) may flicker on the edge of the tub. They may sip a glass of Kendall-Jackson Grand Reserve Chardonnay ($20 for the 750-milliliter bottle) or enjoy a Godiva Dark Chocolate Ganache. (Paula is especially fond of chocolate as a form of Time for Myself. "One good piece of chocolate is worth twenty-two Hershey's bars," she says.) Even in moments of such personal indulgence, moral and social values come into play. Melissa buys Aveda personal-care products because "they are very environmentally conscious. Even though I'm 'trading up,' if a company is environmentally conscious, I'm much more apt to purchase from it, and my husband has no problem with me going to Aveda and buying more expensive products there. You can buy a bottle of Suave for $2. The shampoo I buy from Aveda is $9."

Men, too, seek moments alone but are more likely to retreat to a room equipped with a personal computer, a premium sound system, or a home theater. Anna, thrity-three, bought her husband, Roy, a Sony home theater system as a Christmas gift so he could "have a room in the house that was his own personal space and getaway." With a household income of $63,000, she spent about $3,000 on a six-speaker Sony Dream System, but even so, it represented a trade down. She really wanted to buy the Bose system, but it was "just way too expensive for me."

Convenience

Taking Care of Me goods are also tools that help busy consumers leverage their time better. These include restaurant dining, premium convenience foods for consumption at home, and laundry appliances that make doing the wash easier and less time-consuming. The success of the Whirlpool brand Duet washer-dryer pair (see chapter 8) is rooted in its technical and functional differences—it is energy-efficient and easier on clothing—but is more the result of the consumer's emotional response. The Duet pair has twice the capacity of other machines so the person doing the laundry (usually mom) can make fewer trips to the laundry room to empty and reload one machine or the other. This feature, along with the ease of front-loading, makes it a convenience of great value to its owners. They make a direct connection between the performance of the washer-dryer and a decrease in the amount of time they have to devote to the washing chore. It is time they can devote instead to Taking Care of Me, or to Connecting with family members.

Renewal

The toll of stressful careers on American consumers, especially those in high-stakes professions, can lead to physical exhaustion, illness, and more. Emily and her husband, Paul, public-sector lawyers, lead a stressful life. "Paul and I both have jobs that are very stressful because of what's at stake," Emily told us. "With Paul's job, what's at stake is somebody's life. It's an insane amount of stress. If he screws up, somebody's going to jail. Or worse. For me, it's the fear that if I screw up, if I do something that makes my boss say something that's wrong and it's out in the press . . . Good Lord!" One solution for this couple is eating well. They dine out several times per month, often spending $50 or more for a dinner for two. They're not alone in this stress-management solution. Over the past decade, annual restaurant visits per capita have risen from 153 in 1991 to 178 in 2001. The total spending per visit is also on the rise, up 4 percent in 2000 over the year before.

Consumers also spend more on ingredients that they believe make dining at home more healthful, fun, and sensuous for themselves and their dining companions. Kim, twenty-six, has lived with her boyfriend for three years, and they have a high household income, $80,000, with few expenses. They seek rejuvenation and connection by dining at home. They watch the Food Channel regularly, and Kim likes to shop at a specialty grocery near her apartment in St. Petersburg, Florida, where she buys ingredients such as organic vegetables for new recipes. "I cook probably five nights out of the week," says Kim. "I love it. We feel very lucky that we can afford to shop there."

But not all trading up in food is to organic vegetables and exotic ingredients; many Americans think of ice cream as a major food rejuvenator and are eating premium ice cream at the expense of the "healthier" ice cream alternatives, frozen yogurt, sorbet, and tofu treats. They want the uplift and refreshment that come with the intense tastes of Edy's Dreamery, Starbucks, and Häagen-Dazs. Ben & Jerry's offers ice cream in some fifty flavors and forms, providing for a great deal of personal variation and individuality. As a result, the average price per pint of ice cream has risen 26 percent since 1997.

However, to compensate for the additional calories, consumers are buying the premium ice cream in smaller containers. Pints and quarts are growing in popularity while the larger sizes are growing in sales at a slower rate. These superpremium ice cream brands contribute a disproportionate amount to the profits of the entire category. We estimate that a pint of Ben & Jerry's earns about $.92 profit per pint in comparison to $.14 contributed by a pint of a typical conventional brand made by Dean Foods, whose brands include Dean's, Oak Farms, and Mayfield Dairy Farms.

Rejuvenation is also the story behind the success of spas such as Canyon Ranch. Mel Zuckerman, who with his wife, Enid, cofounded Canyon Ranch, states the mission this way: "Our mission is not selling vacations, but promoting a direct, emotional connection between what people know they should do and what they actually do every day." The goal has been to create places that can bring a "sense of safety, peace, pleasure, and warmth." Canyon Ranch combines the physical rejuvenation that comes from any respite from work with "self-discovery, health-consciousness, individual empowerment and lifestyle medicine." This "intersecting" of emotional spaces leads to a powerful personal experience.

Mel and Enid Zuckerman founded Canyon Ranch partly in response to their own need for Taking Care of Me. Zuckerman's father died at the age of seventy-six, from lung cancer, when Mel was forty-nine. Mel, a homebuilder, was overweight and overstressed, and in addition to the grief he felt at the death of his father, he felt concerned about his own health and well-being. He and his wife decided they needed to change their lives. They bought a ranch near Tucson, Arizona, and built a series of casitas—free-standing one-bedroom accommodations—on the site, as well as a fitness and exercise facility. Canyon Ranch Health Resort opened in 1979. At first the ranch attracted primarily middle-aged, overweight women. But the spa phenomenon took off in the 1980s, helped by a clientele that included prominent visitors from the arts, politics, and business. In 1989, the Zuckermans opened a second location, Canyon Ranch in the Berkshires Health Resort, near the town of Lenox, Massachusetts, a two-hour drive from Manhattan—easily accessible to the affluent and influential consumers of New York and New England. Its reputation grew.

A Canyon Ranch facility is designed to be an experience of physical, emotional, and spiritual attention and improvement. Typically, the guest starts the day with a three-mile walk at a moderate pace in attractive surroundings, followed by a healthful breakfast that usually includes fruit, decaffeinated coffee, a whole wheat pancake, and half a toasted whole-wheat bagel. Breakfast is followed by a stretching session to prepare the body for the activities of the day and then by several hours of more strenuous physical activity, such as working with weights, kickboxing, or dance aerobics. The late-afternoon yoga session is particularly popular; guests take a final stretch before dinner and often are so relaxed they fall asleep. In addition to the physical activities, there is also time for a class in pottery, watercolor, or cooking.

During the course of a weeklong stay, guests generally lose three or four pounds—thanks to low-calorie meals that include lots of fruits and vegetables—and feel renewed and revitalized. Before they leave, guests are counseled on how to "take the Ranch home." The emotional engagement is so strong that Canyon Ranch visitors become apostles. They tell their friends, neighbors, and colleagues about the "life change" they have experienced and often talk about their lives as they were "before the Ranch" and as they have been improved "after the Ranch."

Zuckerman told us that he did not understand the full potential of his concept at first. He began the business as a personal mission. He wanted to get away from the pressures of being a homebuilder in an up-and-down market and to improve his health. He also wanted to create a business where he and his wife could work together to help people and change lives.

By taking care of himself—rejuvenating his own life—Zuckerman created a hugely successful business. With 350 guests paying up to $6,000 per week, each Canyon Ranch delivers an estimated 20 percent operating margin. Sales of ancillary materials including videos, cookbooks, equipment, clothing, and cosmetics add another 5 percent to gross revenues. Now the Zuckermans are doing what all New Luxury creators do—seeking to extend their concept to serve new consumers: families, singles, teens, and short-stay travelers. They want to develop and offer new products: vitamins, nutritional supplements, and skin products. They are constantly offering new activities, including golf and skiing, and educational programs, such as a tantra workshop in sexual health.

Although the original Canyon Ranch borders on Old Luxury, the success of Canyon Ranch has transformed the category from a minor industry into a major phenomenon and helped make spas more affordable. There were close to 9,700 spas in the United States in 2001—7,200 day spas, 1,200 resort or hotel spas, 700 club spas, 300 mineral-springs spas, 200 medical spas, and 70 destination spas. Spending on spa vacations of all kinds, a segment that scarcely existed before 1970, is close to $11 billion. The fastest-growing subsegment is day spas—one-day Taking Care of Me vacations. They accounted for close to 70 percent of all spa visits in 2001, or $7 billion in revenues.

Reward

Taking Care of Me is also about indulging oneself because "I'm worth it," and pampering oneself after a tough day. As twenty-eight-year-old Melissa says, "To me, luxury means treating myself." So for many consumers—especially women—buying luxuries is no longer a guilty self-indulgence; it is their right and even their obligation to make sure they are feeling their best. As Paula puts it, "I think women need to do more to make themselves feel good. We were raised to feel guilty if we don't give the kids enough attention. And to feel guilty if we don't run around naked all the time and keep our husband's fantasies going. Women need to look at themselves and say, 'What do *I* really like to do?'"

New Luxury goods also bring a measure of comfort into a world that can be harsh and uncertain. Americans have become far more aware of the frightening possibilities that surround us—we live with heightened fears of terrorism, war, and other conflict at home and abroad. We also live with a persistent concern about the national and global economy. Will the stock market really recover, and if it does, will it ever be the same as it was? Will the Social Security Administration eventually run out of money? As we learned from the survey, about 40 percent of the respondents are "worried about the future."

But even in the face of uncertainty—especially in the face of uncertainty—Americans don't want to spend their money on bland, emotionally empty goods. They want to spend on items that bring emotional engagement, from spirits to nice sheets. Why not? As Frances puts it, "There's a part of me that feels like, 'Spend some money. Have some fun! You're going to die tomorrow.'"

Connecting: Attracting, Nurturing, and Belonging

Connecting is as important as Taking Care of Me for American consumers, and New Luxury goods are instrumental in helping to make connections and keep them strong.

Attracting

The rules and practices of dating have changed dramatically in the past twenty years; today, for many singles, dating is a marketing exercise that must be undertaken with great seriousness. Would-be connectors seek every possible advantage through the savvy use of goods.

There is a new set of dating rules, and it is mostly women who are making them up and enforcing them. But this does not mean that they're not frustrated and confused by the process. This is primarily because they are generally more interested in marriage than men are; although both women and men are delaying marriage, men delay longer. The National Marriage Project, based at Rutgers, the State University of New Jersey, found plenty of evidence to support the popular notion that "men don't want to commit." The top two reasons that men won't commit, according to the study released in 2002, are (1) "They can get sex without marriage" and (2) "They can enjoy the benefits of having a wife by cohabiting, rather than marrying."

These rather unstartling revelations, however, take on a remarkable significance when viewed in the light of long-term changes in sexual behavior. The most sexually active women are eighteen- to twenty-nine-years-old, and the great majority of them have their first experience of sexual intercourse while in high school. So, because most women (as well as men) come into their dating years with early sexual experience and because they are delaying marriage, the median time between first sexual encounter and marriage has dramatically increased, from 1.3 years to 8.1 years. That means the period of active dating is very much longer than it used to be.

Even though the window for "hookups" is longer, the pace of the dating game has not slowed, and the business of finding a lover who might become a suitable mate seems as fraught as ever. This is partially because of the greater sophistication of the dating "consumer"—people are seeking the best possible companion available, and thanks to the popular media, they have a much larger pool to evaluate, at least virtually. It's also because everybody is so pressed for time—working harder, doing more, trying to cram more of everything into life.

Accordingly, the dating process has been streamlined and facilitated via a number of new methods, including dating services and Web dating. Janna, forty-five, lives in Hollywood and works in real estate, earning about $80,000 a year. She has never been married. "I am not averse to marriage at all," she says. "It just has never come up. I have been engaged three times and just realized it was not the right person. I am more selective now. I would rather find the right one instead of finding a lot of wrong ones." She has tried two Web dating sites, where she has met a number of "geeks" as well as a number of "really great men." Janna calls herself a chronic dater, but she is in no rush to commit to a long-term relationship. "I think you have to weed through a lot of idiots before you meet a good one," she says.

Because daters are so pressed for time, a new method called "speed dating" has emerged. Speed dating is an organized activity in which participants pay a fee in order to meet a large number of eligible members of the opposite sex in one evening. Each couple gets three minutes together, during which time they talk and try to determine whether there is any interest in furthering the relationship beyond the evening. At the end of the session, the participants exchange contact information with those who interest them.

Suzy, a single twenty-three-year-old member of our research team, volunteered (more or less) to explore the speed-dating phenomenon for us. On the night she attended, she was introduced to thirty men, most of whom were between thirty and forty years of age, reasonably successful, and college educated. Most of the men there confessed they had tried speed dating before; most women said they were there just to "check it out." Most left the evening feeling disappointed with the results. Many said they would be reluctant to admit to their friends that they had attended. Suzy told us she would not be repeating the assignment. "Even three minutes can seem like an eternity when you're talking with someone you know you have no interest in," she said. The key finding of this field research is that the process of searching for, evaluating, and selecting a partner can be a business of singular intensity. It is therefore not surprising that people look for ways to make the process work more effectively. One way to do so is to use goods to send prospective partners signals that help communicate who you are and what you're looking for.

But "sending signals" is not simply about showing off wealth, as it might have been in years past. The National Marriage Project reports that men are put off by women who overemphasize material goods: "They resent being evaluated on the size of their wallet, their possessions, or their earnings." However, many daters don't mind signaling the size of their income in subtle ways. Alvaro, a twenty-six-year-old administrative assistant earning $35,000 annually, says that when you call for Ketel One vodka, "you might as well hold out your dollar bills and fan yourself with them."

More often, however, the language of goods in dating is about signaling our taste and knowledge, achievements and values, and those qualities are the very basis of New Luxury things: the liquor we order, the lingerie and clothing we wear, the jewelry and accessories we display. But it is not only a language of display; it is also the New Luxury objects and experiences we talk about—from a description of a wine we like to describing a trip we took. It is very unlikely that conventional middle-market goods will be referenced in dating conversations. "I really love to drink Gallo jug wine" or "I wear Sears chinos" may be telling statements, but they're not very impressive.

For many consumers, however, the display of goods is not enough. They fear the dating and mating game has become so fraught and competitive that they will be unable to compete because they are physically at a disadvantage—they look wrong, have some defect, are too fat, or look too old. As a result, there has been a remarkable growth in products and services designed to improve our appearance. Americans underwent about 8.5 million cosmetic procedures in 2001, spending nearly $9 billion. The industry has been growing at a compound annual growth rate of 42 percent since 1997.

The growth in cosmetic procedures has come about because of the emergence of a number of new, more affordable, and minimally invasive procedures that focus on reducing wrinkles, improving skin, and removing unwanted hair. These include Botox injections, chemical peels, collagen injections, microdermabrasion, and laser hair removal. These procedures avoid the three barriers that have kept people from the traditional forms of cosmetic surgery that involve the use of the knife—money, fear, and embarrassment. The average nonsurgical procedure runs about $500 in comparison to $3,300 for surgeries such as liposuction (fat removal), breast augmentation, and eyelid and nose jobs. They are less invasive, less risky, and thus less scary. And they have become acceptable; the media influencers are always reshaping themselves, and magazines are filled with stories and advice about them.

Another major change is that patients are opting for cosmetic work at a much younger age. The thirty-five- to fifty-year-olds are looking to forestall the aging process while they still look good; they want to avoid having a radical redo when they're older. They never want to hear the gasp when they step into the street at age seventy, when it is more obvious what they have had lifted or tucked. The under-thirty-five crowd selects procedures that will make them look different—and "better"—rather than younger. They wish to reshape the nose, chin, or breasts.

Gloria, forty-eight, told us about her difficult choice: a new van or a new face. She wanted both, but at $20,000 for a van and $18,000 for a face-lift, she could afford only one. She chose the face. "I had met about twenty women who had had the surgery," she told us. "And it seems like everybody I know is getting something done. A little collagen to get rid of the wrinkles or whatever. I wanted to do something about my neck, in particular. A surgeon was offering a free consultation, so I went to talk to him. He said the surgery would do what I wanted and that it would last for fifteen years. He offered me a discount—$4,000 off the regular price—so I did everything. The eyes, the face, and the neck." Gloria was not pleased with the results for about two months after the surgery, but now she feels more relaxed, healthier, and younger looking. "My husband likes it. Women think I'm ten years younger than I am. I'm glad I did it. Now I'm thinking about going for the permanent eyeliner."

Less dramatic procedures include teeth whitening (strips, toothpastes, and laser whitening) and hair loss treatments. Teeth whitening is now a billion-dollar business, and fifty million American men have spent more than $1.5 billion on various methods of hanging on to their thinning hair. And all kinds of new and more exotic cosmetic procedures are gaining in popularity, including nipple enhancements and belly button reshapings.

New Luxury goods and body enhancements are tools of attraction not just for young daters and those in the marriage market for the first time; they are also sought by people who have divorced or suffered a breakup. As Carrie Bradshaw, the lead character of *Sex and the City*, puts it, "Breakups: bad for the heart, good for the economy." Today, the likelihood of such breakups is higher than ever. Dating couples say they are less likely to stay together for very long if the relationship is "not the real thing" and on the road to marriage. For married couples, the likelihood of divorce within the first ten years of marriage increased from 20 percent in 1973 to 33 percent in the year 2000. In 1996, the lifetime probability of being divorced for a twenty-five-year-old was 52 percent.

Newly single consumers, whether separated, dumped, divorced, or playing around, tend to be ardent consumers. If they feel wronged, they may become revenge spenders. Women spend on apparel, jewelry, cosmetics, spirits, and dining out. Men tend to spend on electronics and cars. But sometimes after a breakup, the spending habits change permanently. "As a kid, we used to go for quantity, not quality," says Melissa. "Now, with my parents' being divorced, my mom has changed a lot in terms of her views toward luxury and what she's willing to buy for herself. She definitely indulges more than she ever did before." When people are hurting, especially after something as intense as a romantic breakup, goods bring solace, comfort, reward, revenge, and some measure of self-esteem.

Nurturing

The use of goods to facilitate connecting continues even after marriage, and among all members of the family, including the children. The primary reason is time.

In many families, family members may find very few moments to spend together. They want to be sure the experience is as rich and rewarding as it can be. As Nicole, a twenty-eight-year-old lawyer, says about the time she spends with her doctor husband, "We love to experience restaurants. We like to get to know a chef and follow him around. We drive a Honda Civic. We will not drive a BMW. But we like our entertainment, and that is a priority. And we like to travel. In the end it is all about the memory for us."

When family members cannot spend time together, goods can act as a compensation, even a substitute for the lost moments—sharing a cup of Starbucks coffee, eating a gourmet take-out meal, spending time in front of the Sony home theater, or listening to music on the Bose Wave radio. Dorothy, forty-five, has never been married and has no kids, but she is very close to her eight-year-old niece. They spend a lot of time together, reading and attending cultural events. But Dorothy also likes to buy nice things for her niece, such as clothing and lunches out. Next year, they plan to go to American Girl Place in Chicago (they live in Indiana) to buy a doll and accessories. "Because I have no children and she is my niece and the only one I have, I am willing to spend that amount of money for something special," says Dorothy, who earns $55,000 as a librarian. "I think every little girl should be able to experience that one time in her life. That's what aunts are for."

Belonging

New Luxury goods also provide a way for consumers to align themselves with people whose values and interests they share—to join the club. "When buying things that are just for myself," says Jack, a business supervisor earning $70,000 a year, "I can easily trade down if I have to. I don't really have to buy DiGiorno. I could easily go generic. But when it comes to social things where I'm out with a group of people, it would be a lot harder for me to say, 'Well let's not go to Panera because it's too expensive. Let's go to Subway.' That would be harder for me to give up." Charles, a fifty-five-year-old real estate developer, agrees. "One of the reasons I buy wine at $80 a bottle, and we do buy a certain amount of that—I have one hundred bottles downstairs that will fall into that category—is because we have some friends who will look at and value that if we serve it."

A search for Belonging sometimes overlaps with the expression of Individual Style. Miguel, thirty-one, works for a nonprofit organization in Colorado and earns $70,000 a year. He is single, owns a home, and has already saved more than $100,000; he has no credit card debt. "Both of my parents come from very poor backgrounds, with very large extended families," he told us. "But they wanted a different life for their kids. They understood the pains of not having an education and all the troubles that can go with that." Miguel was born in Mexico, but his parents moved to the United States, and he and his siblings were brought up in a predominantly white, middle-class environment. His parents worked hard to make sure that Miguel had the clothing and accessories that would help him fit in with his new group. "If I wanted the fancy-cut jeans or the fancy Guess? shirt, I could get that, and it would not be a problem. We took vacations, and my dad always had a really nice car. Those luxuries were important for my parents and for us kids, so we would not feel that much different and we could fit in and do the things the other kids did." Miguel is still conscious of fitting in and will buy premium goods—including clothes, cologne, watches, and other personal accessories that he purchases at stores such as Dillard's, Neiman Marcus, and Saks Fifth Avenue—to show that he belongs to the ranks of the successful and has good taste.

The need to belong to the "club" (whatever it might be or however it is defined) and to succeed in it is also a reason for some people to undergo cosmetic procedures—especially men. Although women undergo the great majority of all cosmetic procedures—88 percent of all procedures are conducted on female consumers—men are starting to join in, especially ambitious men who are looking for a competitive edge and want to fit in. *The Wall Street Journal* reports that "growing numbers of salesmen and lawyers, bankers and stockbrokers are fixing their facial expressions with Botox." Why? Botox not only reduces wrinkles, it freezes parts of the face, making it less likely that a high-powered professional will betray the wrong emotion at a crucial moment in a business deal or a big trial. According to the article, one investment banker was laid off and was having trouble getting a new job. Finally, an executive recruiter told him why the interviews weren't going well: his facial wrinkles made him look angry. Nobody wanted him as part of their business club. A few shots of Botox and, two weeks later, he was back among the ranks of the employed.

Questing: Adventure, Learning, and Play

Questing is the emotional space that has emerged the most strongly in the past several years. It is all about those goods and services I can buy that will enrich my existence, deliver new experience, satisfy my curiosity, deliver physical and intellectual stimulation, provide adventure and excitement, and add novelty and exoticism to my life.

Travel is the key category for Questing, but it has many less-active forms as well. Many people think of eating, for example, as a form of Questing—trying out new flavors and new restaurants. Many wine drinkers also think of their hobby as a form of Questing, as do some car drivers. Robert, sixty-one, lives in Texas, where he works as a technical writer and has a household income of about $105,000. He and his wife, Carla, think of wine as their hobby. "We enjoy finding new wines," he says, "and discovering the tastes and seeing how a wine from the same winery can vary year to year. We like to visit the wineries and get to know the winemakers. We are friendly with some winemakers here in Texas."

Questing is about venturing out into the world, experiencing new things, and pushing back personal limits—and travel is the most popular way to do so. Seventy-two percent of the respondents to the survey told us they "love to travel," and as we've seen, Americans are traveling more than ever before, primarily to Europe and Asia. But the focus on Questing means that the nature of travel has changed: New Luxury consumers want to experience travel that does more than give them a rest and a getaway. Seventy percent of our respondents also said that "knowledge is the greatest luxury." They want to combine travel with knowledge gathering, acquiring new skills, and collecting memorable experiences.

This has led to the rise in adventure and experiential travel. What else could explain the popularity of what *Newsweek* calls "authentic holidays"? Consider, for example, a camping visit to eastern South Africa, hosted by a group of native people, where dinner is a stew of pumpkin leaves and dumplings and the entertainment is listening to tribal folktales around the fire. Although beach vacations are still the most popular, the World Tourism Organization predicts that sport- and nature-based vacations to new and lesser-known destinations will have the most growth. They project a threefold rise in total trips worldwide between 1995 and 2020, with the greatest growth in trips to East Asia, Africa, the Middle East, and South Asia.

In our interviews, travel was a recurring theme and topic of enthusiastic discussion. Barbara and her husband, James, with a household income of over $200,000, travel extensively from their home base near San Francisco. "I like to go to countries where I do not feel like I would be real familiar with the lifestyle," says Barbara. "In Belize, we went into the rain forest and tubed five miles down the river through lots of caves. We swam with manatees and sharks and stingrays and did a lot of adventurous things." Miguel regularly travels for business, and "that has encouraged my desire to travel for fun and for pleasure as well," he says. "I think there is a certain air about traveling, a sense that it is a little bit of a privilege. Not everyone gets to do it. It gives you a little bit more of a worldly perspective. It gives you a sense of being refreshed, and it is almost like a badge of honor that you can wear when you come back. When you get back to the workplace, people are buzzing about your trip, wanting to know what it was like and what you did." Craig, a thirty-five-year-old who earns less than $40,000 a year, talked about his trip to Thailand. Janna has visited every continent and is looking forward to a trip to Bhutan.

The interest in Questing has brought dramatic change even to a travel category that has long been the epitome of Old Luxury: cruises. Today cruises are becoming an affordable luxury for middle-market consumers. Almost seven million North Americans took a cruise in 2001, up from just over three million in 1988. Half of all cruisers had household incomes of $65,000 or less. During the 1990s, cruises grew twice as fast as all other types of vacations, achieving a 6.2 percent compound annual growth rate since 1988. The popularity of cruising has risen because cruise operators, such as Carnival Cruise Lines, have successfully slashed the average cost per day of a cruise by nearly 30 percent and have added nearly 7 percent capacity each year. They are also offering more short cruises, making the real cost of a voyage even lower.

But most important, the cruise operators are striving to connect with the emotional needs of their customers. They have incorporated services and activities that relate to Taking Care of Me. Orient Lines, for example, offers a spa experience that emphasizes relaxation and pampering with treatments that include steam wraps, Swedish and shiatsu massage, seawater therapy, and foot massages on deck. Royal Caribbean International ships offer a well-equipped fitness club. While onboard, cruisers can use weight machines, free weights, stationary bikes, stair steppers, treadmills, a sauna, a whirlpool, a steam room, and thermal suite.

As Jack said to us, "The idea of a cruise never really appealed to me until recently. I've seen commercials for a cruise line where it's not just about sitting there and doing nothing. They have all of these activities to do on the boat—rock climbing and in-line skating. Knowing that's available, I'm more apt to consider a cruise."

Cruises are also about Connecting. *Conquest*, Carnival's largest "fun ship," has twenty-two bars and restaurants to explore, providing plenty of opportunities and options for meeting and evaluating potential partners and playmates. With some 3,000 passengers aboard, it's like a four-day speed-dating event with 1,500 candidates to choose from.

Cruises traditionally have been about food, but food in the Old Luxury tradition—indulgent, not particularly healthful, and "sinful." In fact, eating was the main activity of most cruises. Although food is still a central part of the cruise, it is less about gluttony and more about exotic, gourmet, or healthy dining—about Taking Care of Me, Connecting, and Questing. The Nautica Spa aboard the *Conquest* offers a "healthful, low-fat" menu. Seabourn Cruise Line offers menus designed by "celebrity chefs" such as Charlie Palmer, chef of Aureole in New York.

Cruises are also becoming Questing vacations. Carnival runs discovery-and-adventure cruises that include opportunities for "snorkeling in the breathtaking coral areas of Aruba, mountain biking through Curaçao's beautiful, unspoiled parks, or sport fishing in Mazatlán." Royal Caribbean ships have skating rinks and rock-climbing walls onboard.

The rise in travel has also catalyzed a wealth of travel-related New Luxury services. For example, SkyMeals is a service that offers custom-prepared gourmet meals and delivers them to your home or office prior to your flight. You take your orange-and-blue SkyMeals bag aboard, open the foil-lined container, and enjoy a meal of flash-seared ahi tuna with Gorgonzola polenta at $32.50 or a charcuterie platter at $36.75. SkyMeals argues that its offerings are not only tastier than airline fare, they also help solve some of the many problems associated with air travel. "Medical research suggests the timing of meals could be a key factor in reducing the effects of jet lag, stress, and even possibly air rage," says its Web site. "Certainly, it is important to maintain the same number of hours between meals. Bringing your own meal means you can eat on your schedule and not on the airline's." The traveler who takes the trouble to bring a gourmet meal aboard the flight is signaling her devotion to style and good taste and her knowledge of the limitations of airline food.

When New Luxury tourists travel, their eyes are open to goods, services, styles, and tastes they might not encounter at home, and collecting interesting and meaningful goods is very important to them. As Nicole puts it, "What really drives me, and my husband too, is feeling part of an underworld of stories. Like, 'Oh, we got that piece when we were traveling here, and we got that piece in the night market in Hong Kong.' We love to do stuff like that because it is cool."

This influx of "hand imports," as well as stories and ideas shared with friends about goods sampled abroad, has a tremendous influence on the market. People become interested in goods that capture the essence of foreign and exotic places, especially places they have personally visited. Barbara, for example, likes to incorporate her travel experiences into her cooking. "We buy sauces and seasonings every time we travel. I'll use some sauce that I bought in Belize for a dinner party I'm having for friends of mine who really enjoy hot foods. I am re-creating a typical dinner from Belize, with the same types of side dishes and a jerk main course."

Individual Style: Self-Expressing, Self-Branding, and Signaling

Although New Luxury consumers are not driven primarily by a desire for status or empty infatuation with a brand name, that does not mean they care nothing for the messages that goods and brands deliver about their Individual Style. "Luxury is good," says Rebecca, "because it allows people to express themselves." Consumers know they can say a lot about themselves through their choice of specific brands and types of goods. As Dennis explains, "One of the characteristics of luxury brands is that the consumers, maybe not all of them, but certainly a better than average chunk of them, go to some extra trouble to educate themselves about the brands and what they offer." So, rather than purchase *because* of the brand name, New Luxury consumers often purchase specific attributes that cause them to appreciate and stick with a brand.

In some categories, such as cars, brands are extremely important to expressing Individual Style. This is partially because the advertising messages contained within each brand have been sharply defined and repeated a million times over. Even if we don't exactly believe in what the advertisers tell us, we are aware of the messages and know that others know them, too. For those brands where the advertising messages connect with the reality that the consumer experiences, the brand identity can become exceptionally strong. BMW, for example, has established itself as the "ultimate driving machine," which may sound innocuous until it is analyzed in the context of competitive models. The BMW brand is all about driving, which is an activity involving mastery and adventure, and not about comfort or luxury. And the emphasis on the "machine" reinforces the primacy of the BMW engine, which is the soul of the brand and has been since its inception. (For more on BMW, see chapter 12.)

Brands play an important role in creating an Individual Style that sends messages to all kinds of people—including potential employers, colleagues, friends, lovers, and family members—and is, in this way, closely associated with Connecting. Brands provide a reasonably reliable, efficient, and consistent method for signaling others about who I am or who I would like to be. These signals tend to be most important in brands that are mobile, whether worn or carried: goods such as shoes, clothing, spirits, fashion accessories, and watches.

Self-branding through association with brand names can be tricky because of the speed of the fashion cycle. Messages can change quickly, and brands can become distorted in meaning. Kathy told us, for example, "I do not care about the brand name with clothes as much as I do with makeup or with accessories. With accessories, I value the brand. But fashion comes and goes. I could cut back in that area and buy more things that I like rather than just the most expensive items."

New Luxury consumers are very careful to align themselves with brands that they have a genuine affinity for and that are a good match for their own Individual Style. Jake took note of our own set of Callaway golf clubs and, after watching our first drive, remarked, "Those clubs are too good for you." Because consumers can be so expert in deciphering the messages contained in brands, the consumer risks appearing superficial or foolish in basing an Individual Style on an inappropriate brand, or buying a name brand that he knows little about.

However, when consumers purchase brands that are meaningful to them and align with their own activities and values, the combination can be powerful. Martin, a scientist earning more than $100,000 annually, enjoys hiking, skiing, trekking, and other kinds of adventure travel. He wears premium Patagonia clothing, not only on his adventures, but also to his office and to social events. For those who know Martin and admire him, the devotion to Patagonia clothing does not seem silly: it seems an endorsement of the brand by an appropriate apostle. It is very much a part of his Individual Style.

The home is a place for status purchasing, and it's an important expression of Individual Style. Nadyenka's parents, with a household income of $80,000, are Sony apostles. "My mom is very conscious of spending money on certain stuff," says Nadyenka, "yet she would have no problem spending $3,000 on a large-screen Sony television. She sees Sony as the epitome of quality and the only brand of electronics to have. Anything else you would buy, she would look down on you. Maybe it is a lot driven by her friends. When you buy Sony you are showing that your living standards have gone up and that you can spend that much money on electronics. She has a Sony television, a Sony DVD, a little Sony television upstairs, and a Sony VCR. She pretty much has a Sony everything."

A New Luxury kitchen often has a six-burner cooktop, griddle, triple ovens, warming drawer, side-by-side or walk-in refrigerator, wine refrigerator, and more from companies such as Viking, Sub-Zero, Gaggenau, Jenn-Air, and others that consumers value for their look, features, and values. They are expressions of Individual

Style as much as they are tools for living. Some 75 percent of the
Viking cooktops that are installed are never used, but the owners are
proud of them and think of them as expressions of their interest in
Questing, as well as good investments.

Goods As a Language of Social Dialogue

Any "map" of human emotional needs is simplistic; ours is meant as
a tool to help consumers and creators of New Luxury understand
the key impulses behind most purchases.

The emotional spaces are closely related and do not have sharp
boundaries between them. The woman soaking in the bath is not
only taking care of herself, she may also be preparing for a moment
of Connecting—wanting to feel, look, and smell good before a dinner with friends or a date.

Sometimes the spaces are in conflict. When a parent spends a
disproportionate amount of the household income on a new car for
himself, satisfying his need for Questing and Taking Care of Me, he
may feel guilty about spending too much on himself—perhaps he
should have spent less and had more to spend on Connecting with
the family.

New Luxury goods are more than simply objects of consumption. They have become a language, a nonverbal method of self-
expression and social dialogue. The language enables consumers to
say, "I'm intelligent and discerning," in many different and individual ways. In a country as large as the United States, encompassing
great regional differences and composed of people from many cultures with many different languages, it is not surprising that we have
sought to unify ourselves through the common language of goods.
There is more complexity, interest, variation, and subtlety in New
Luxury goods than in conventional products (an ordinary washing
machine, a Budweiser) or even in Old Luxury goods that often call
more attention to themselves (a Gucci handbag) than to their owners. For sophisticated and discerning spenders, New Luxury goods
provide a rich and broad vocabulary with which to speak—without
saying a word.

Part Two

The Leaders

Five

The World Is a Sexy Place

Looking and feeling sexy is a powerful emotional space for New Luxury. The sexual revolution—widely acknowledged to have begun in the 1960s and catalyzed by the antiwar movement and the introduction of the birth control pill—continues four decades later. Americans are getting married later; the median age at first marriage has risen from 20.8 years in 1960 to 25.1 years in 2000. They are having sex at a younger age—two-thirds of all women have had intercourse by the time they are eighteen. The combination of earlier first intercourse and later marriage means that the "dating window"—the time Americans spend dating, hooking up, and looking for mates—has increased dramatically. In 1960, the average dating window was 1.3 years; by 1997 it had widened to 8.1 years. Today the average American will have had about ten sexual partners prior to marriage, versus about half that number in the 1970s. Men and women are ever more demanding and explicit about their sexual behavior, attitudes, and expectations. And our popular culture seethes with sexuality.

The new sexual attitudes and practices are, as expected, most striking among younger Americans. According to one report on sexual behavior: "among all young adults twenty to twenty-nine, eight in ten agree that it is common for people in their age group to have sex just for fun without any expectation of commitment. This view is more strongly held by those with higher levels of educational attainment." In one survey, 46 percent of women respondents aged eighteen to thirty-five claimed to have a "booty-call" partner (someone they can count on for casual sex). Author Erica Jong, whose *Fear of Flying* was published in 1973, says, "I look at my daughter and her friends in their twenties, and they are genuinely reveling in their sexuality. I told my daughter, 'your generation does it; my generation just talked about it.'"

Not surprisingly, a similar revolution surrounding the goods used for seduction has followed the social trends. One man has been instrumental in this latter revolution: Leslie Wexner, a visionary merchant who introduced attainable sophistication, aspiration, and entertainment into the world of women's intimate apparel.

Born to Sell

Leslie Wexner was born in 1937 to Bella and Harry Wexner and spent his childhood immersed in the retail apparel industry. His father, an immigrant from Russia, worked as a store manager for a small apparel business and his mother was a buyer for F&R Lazarus, now part of Federated Department Stores. In 1951, the Wexners opened their own women's clothing shop. Young Wexner dreamed of becoming an architect but was discouraged by his father and instead went to Ohio State University to study business and law. Although he had vowed never to join the family business, he dropped out of Ohio State in 1961 to work with his parents.

The arrangement was short-lived. Wexner's ideas for helping the business grow—focusing on the bestselling women's sportswear segment instead of low-turn, low-profit dresses and outerwear—were poorly received by his parents. "I thought it would improve business if we just sold sportswear, because it was the only profitable thing. My idea was to be a specialist, not a generalist. The world values specialists, not generalists. I wanted to have a focused, well-edited, concise point of view—to really stand for something and own it." Like Robert Mondavi, who broke away from his family's Charles Krug Winery, Wexner set off on his own with a combination of pride and conviction that he could improve on his family's existing business model. He borrowed $5,000 from his aunt and set out to start his own business.

In 1963, Wexner opened The Limited—named for its limited assortment of women's sportswear—in a 2,500-square-foot space in Columbus, Ohio. The new store sold moderately priced, casual women's sportswear. His ambitions were modest. "The primary goal was to not go broke, because I did want to pay back Aunt Ida. I wanted to have a new car every three years. And someday make $15,000 a year."

Wexner brought a distinct point of view to the world of fashion retailing. "It was a lot about my taste as a young man and the women I was dating. I had a clear vision of what they wanted. Women want things they haven't seen. And whatever it is, women see it as sexy. When women are wearing loose Levis and loose flannel shirts, for whatever reason, it's sexy. And if they're wearing tight jeans and tight T-shirts, it's because it's sexy. Apparel, for men and women, has a lot to do with sex appeal. The world is a sexy place. It's primal."

Wexner focused his merchandising on sportswear with a "fashion forward" point of view. In its first year, The Limited achieved $160,000 in sales—about 60 percent more than he had expected. A year later, he opened his second store, and by 1970 he had eleven stores. His parents soon closed their shop and joined the board of The Limited. With the malling of America, Wexner saw the potential for a national rollout of his specialty concept. "It was in that period of the 1960s and 1970s that the central business district began to come apart. People moved to the suburbs. Shopping centers were created. I saw the potential of something very large."

In the early years, The Limited practiced fashion arbitrage. The prevailing wisdom at the time was that the European fashion cycle was always two to three years ahead of American adoption, and that the heart of the country was another two years behind the fashion trends introduced in New York, Los Angeles, and San Francisco. The assumption was that the middle-American customer was less sophisticated and inherently slower to adopt new fashion ideas. Wexner saw it differently. He believed that middle-market consumers had the potential and aspiration to be just as fashion forward as their European counterparts or the sophisticates in New York.

The problem was one of accessibility rather than one of taste. He built his business by bringing European fashion to the United States more quickly than any other retailer.

The Limited went public in 1969, enabling the company to finance its expansion. By 1979, The Limited was operating 318 stores, and Wexner was beginning to think about branching out to new brands.

— In 1982, he acquired a small retail business called Victoria's Secret. The concept would become the growth engine for his retail empire over the course of the next two decades. Since 1985, Victoria's Secret has delivered compound annual sales growth of 25 percent, while the number of stores has grown 16 percent annually. Gross margin per square foot (one of the better measures of store productivity) is far above the specialty retail norm, and operating margins are well above those of most retailers. Today, Victoria's Secret is one of the most successful specialty retailers in the world, a $3.5 billion multichannel brand built on the emotional connection between women and their lingerie.

Victoria's Secret is a quintessential New Luxury story. It demonstrates the importance of a visionary, hands-on leader. It illustrates the role that patterning can play in developing a vision and staying ahead of the competition for a sustained period of time. It underscores the necessity of constant, relentless innovation, even when a brand is on top. It testifies to the results that can be achieved when a brand builds advantage on all three benefit layers, aligning its technical and functional benefits to support a powerful emotional position.

Origins of the Victoria's Secret Brand

In the early 1980s, Wexner was visiting one of his Limited stores in San Francisco when he noticed a small store nearby called Victoria's Secret. He stopped in and found a retail operation very different from the Victoria's Secret of today. "The shop sold sexy lingerie in a bawdy way," Wexner told us. "It was business on a G-string." The store was one of four, all located in San Francisco, owned by a man named Roy Raymond. The stores, along with a Victoria's Secret catalog operation, had annual sales of about $4 million. It was eccentric, even a little perverse, in its obsession—and on the verge of bankruptcy.

But Wexner was intrigued. Despite the almost sleazy nature of the stores and the poor financial condition of the company, Wexner had a sense that the lingerie category was important and had tremendous unrealized potential. Most of all, he believed that the category had a great deal of emotional content, largely untapped. He bought the business for about $1 million in 1982. For the first couple of years he did little with his acquisition. He simply let it operate and watched it carefully, studying the category, seeking to develop a vision of where it might go. His other businesses, The Limited and Express, were growing and consuming most of his energy.

While he took time to develop his vision for the brand, Wexner was quick to determine what was wrong with the Victoria's Secret business model. The former owner had believed that men buy lingerie for the women in their lives, and he had decorated the stores to appeal to men, with lots of leather and dark colors. More fundamental, the male customers bought garments that they thought were sexy, but women generally found their choices unappealing and uncomfortable. As a result, women were not Victoria's Secret fans. Wexner wanted to change the orientation of the store to become a place primarily for women and to offer better quality, higher emotional appeal, and a feminine point of view.

Patterning European Luxury Lingerie

Wexner patterned the market by immersing himself in his subject, combining field research with data gathering. As an outsider to the lingerie category, he was free to invent a new way of approaching the products. He visited American department stores and European lingerie boutiques. He studied the European market and the European consumer. A bachelor at the time, he talked about lingerie with the women he dated. He became convinced that he could create a brand with $1 billion or more in sales and operating margins of 10 percent. His view of what Victoria's Secret could become was based on four observations:

Observation #1: European women's attitudes about lingerie were different from those of American women. From his patterning of retailers, brands, and consumers in Europe, Wexner realized that European women tended to wear lingerie every day while American women tended to wear underwear every day. He believed that if American women had access to the same kind of quality, sophisticated, aspirational lingerie as their European counterparts—presented in the right kind of feminine, pampering environment—they would want to wear it for both special occasions and every day. "Women need underwear, but women *want* lingerie," he said. "I like to be in the want business. The margins are better than in the need business."

Observation #2: There was a void in the American market between high-aspiration and high-volume brands; he saw the opportunity to be both. In the mid-1980s there were three pricing segments in the lingerie market: exclusive superpremium (bras priced at $75 or more), department store brands such as Warner's (with bras typically priced between $10 and $15), and mass brands (with bras priced from $3 to $10). No important competitor had claimed the masstige price position in the gap between department store brands and the exclusive superpremiums. Wexner was captivated by the quality, taste, and sophistication of La Perla, a world-renowned Italian lingerie brand in the superpremium segment. He saw the potential to create a "La Perla for the mass market" and break the compromise between aspiration and accessibility. Given the choice, he believed American women would trade up to beautiful quality lingerie at premium, yet affordable, prices.

Observation #3. The lingerie category in the United States was stale and not sexy. When Wexner began his research, lingerie was an unexciting category. It had little growth and was sold primarily at a discount and through promotions. In 1990, half of all bras were sold on sale. The conventional belief was that there was no substantial volume potential in the price segments above $20. The market was divided into two types of wear: functional undergarments, such as Playtex 18-Hour bras, for everyday use, and special-occasion lingerie, which women bought to wear for special, often romantic, events. The selection in both segments was dull and lacking in innovation. Even so, consumers were loyal to their favorite bras. Once a woman found a bra that fit well and felt comfortable, she would buy the same brand over and over again, often waiting for a sale to stock up. As a result, the leading underwear brands, including the Warnaco Group's Warner's and Olga lines, held stable share positions from year to year.

Observation #4: Shopping for lingerie was a dreadful experience. Department stores had long dominated the lingerie category, particularly at the higher price points. Although the lingerie department was an important destination for the female shopper, it was usually relegated to a dimly lit corner of an upper floor, and the products were hung in dense clumps in utilitarian displays. The sales associates had little knowledge of the category and did almost nothing to merchandise or romanticize the products. Wexner believed that an inviting, intimate, feminine store environment—one that fulfilled a fantasy of glamour and luxury at the point of sale—could elevate the category and transform the experience into something special.

Lingerie for the Most Beautiful Women in the World

On the basis of these observations, Wexner developed his vision. He would create beautiful, European-inspired products, made of the best fabrics and with the best methods of construction, and offer them at prices most women could afford. He would use vivid colors and distinctive prints and link his innovations in lingerie to the hottest trends in other fashion categories. He would develop a romantic and intimate store environment, with a far more appealing visual presentation, which would engage the emotions of his customers. He aimed high: he wanted to create a store where the most beautiful women in the world would shop for their lingerie. And, once they did, every American woman would aspire to be a member of the club.

To bring his concept to life, Wexner invented a story about Victoria, the fictional founder of the brand. Victoria was a worldly and glamorous model of English and French descent; although she was sophisticated and a women of taste, she also pushed the boundaries of sexiness. She created a store on fashionable Sloane Street in London to offer European-inspired lingerie. Wexner used the story and character of Victoria, her values, and sensibilities, to provide edit points for the brand. Employees referenced Victoria as they made decisions about everything from product development to marketing to store design. "It was like the making of a movie or telling a story to children," said Wexner. "You go around the room and ask, 'Does everybody understand that Victoria's Secret is about sexy?' And everybody says 'yes.' And then you say 'But which sexy is it? Are you imagining a Britney Spears sexy, or is it a Sharon Stone sexy?' And you have a big debate about the essence of sexy as it relates to the Victoria's Secret brand. The story was so believable and engaging that our marketing people, merchandising people, store people, and store designers could get involved in it and tell it themselves."

Victoria became the arbiter of the brand, helping to define the attributes of sexiness, good taste, European heritage, sophistication, and femininity. The Victoria story enabled Wexner and his colleagues to develop a clear brand concept and refine the concept as times and fashions evolved. "The fashion business is a business about change," says Wexner. "So what sexy are we talking about today?"

Managing the Brand

Defining a brand concept with richness and clarity is one challenge. Making it real, translating it throughout a big organization, and getting the right kind of detailed execution is another. In the early 1990s, Wexner began to think more deeply about the notion of brand leadership. He was intrigued by the fact that brands outperformed businesses and that great brands not only have great concepts but also have great execution that fulfills a promise to the consumer. He realized that his own brands lacked consistency and precise execution. So he developed a new proprietary brand-leadership process to raise the quality and integrity of brand execution, and he applied it first to Victoria's Secret. His goal, as he put it, was to "take the brand to 'Next.'"

Although not as consistent as Wexner wanted, Victoria's Secret became a well-established and successful brand. In 1995, sales had reached $1.9 billion (nearly one-third of which came from catalog sales), and the company operated 670 stores. The brand had a strong emotional franchise, a unique store concept, and had executed several successful product launches, including the Miracle Bra and the Second Skin Satin line. But although Victoria's Secret lingerie had a reputation for being fashionable, Wexner and his team had not paid enough attention to the technical and functional aspects of the products. As a result, the brand had not yet achieved Wexner's goal of breaking the compromise between everyday wear and special-occasion lingerie. Victoria's Secret could not yet claim to be the "sexy, high-fashion everyday lingerie." For most customers, Victoria's Secret was still a ²⁄₇th brand; a woman would wear it two days a week, usually on the weekend, and it occupied only a quarter of her underwear drawer. The challenge remained: to make Victoria's Secret lingerie comfortable and functional enough that women would want to wear it every day, but sexy and appealing enough that they would pay a premium for it and wear it on special occasions.

Wexner decided to focus on the bra as the pièce de résistance of the Victoria's Secret brand. "The item of apparel that women wear with the greatest loyalty to brand is the bra," said Wexner. "They have even more loyalty to their bra than to their brand of cosmetics." He believed that if Victoria's Secret could become known for fashionable bras that were also of high quality and that fit well, the company could build a much stronger following for the brand and draw customers into associated purchases of panties, hosiery, sleepwear, and beauty products. "We couldn't become *the* lingerie brand if we didn't have credibility in bras," he said.

To that end, Victoria's Secret launched two new bras in 1997: English Lace and Dream Angels. English Lace was launched as "Possibly the most beautiful bra in the world." The launch buzz drew customers into the stores, but although the bras looked beautiful, they still did not fit as well as everyday wear. The Dream Angels line also got high marks for its luminescent colors and fabrics, but the bras had a coarse feel and mediocre fit. Although the launches helped focus attention on Victoria's Secret as a maker of bras, the emotional claim was not backed by meaningful technical and functional benefits. Both lines were eventually dropped.

In 1998, the company tried again. Angels 2000 was launched as a high-tech line of lingerie with a bold promise: "The Future of Lingerie Is Here Today." Angels 2000 was a flop. Not only was the product a failure, the advertising did not fit with the founder's story. The ads featured supermodels, clad in silver lingerie, emerging from a spaceship to proclaim the future of lingerie. This was a very different kind of sexiness and fashion from the one espoused by Victoria of Sloane Street. The ads were laughable, not aspirational, and were widely mocked in the press and by late-night television comedians.

Although the launch of Angels 2000 was a failure, and the line was eventually discontinued, it proved to be an important turning point. Wexner realized that he needed to refocus his entire team on the fundamentals, especially product design and construction. He charged his designers and merchants to create dramatically better products that would offer technical and functional advantages. And to improve the brand's emotional positioning, Wexner directed his chief marketing officer, Ed Razek, and the staff of the catalog operation to elevate the quality, taste, and sophistication of the brand's marketing materials. He also directed the store team to improve the store design and visual presentation to create more Wow!, and make the stores even more intimate and appealing.

A breakthrough came in March 1999, when Victoria's Secret launched Body By Victoria. The product line was developed as the result of competitive and consumer intelligence that showed a significant shift in the market toward seamless bras. Unlike traditional bras, which have a seam at the center of the cup, seamless bras use a stretchy fabric molded into shape. They give a smoother, more flattering look, especially under the clingy fabrics and tighter-fitting clothes then coming into fashion. Not only was the Body By Victoria bra seamless, it was also made from better fabrics and padding than other bras on the market. At $34, it was more than twice the price of the average department-store bra.

Body By Victoria was a blockbuster success. In its first four weeks on the market, it sold more than 2.5 times the sales volume of any Victoria's Secret bra previously launched. Customers liked it so much they flooded the company with approving comments. "I bought one, and after the first time I wore it, I went out and bought six more," said one consumer. "The only other brand of bra that I've found comparable to these are La Perla, which are much more expensive," said another. "It is the best bra I've ever bought," said a third. At last, the consumer was experiencing what Wexner had envisioned from the beginning—that Victoria's Secret was the premium, European-style, emotionally engaging, everyday lingerie for the middle-market consumer.

Body By Victoria delivered on all three benefit layers. On the technical layer, the product was soft, seamless, and smooth. Functionally, Body By Victoria fit well, was extremely comfortable to wear, and delivered a flattering silhouette that looked better under clothes. And emotionally, the product gave women a sense of confidence, a feeling of being well put together. Body By Victoria made everyday lingerie sexy in the way only Victoria's Secret could. Six weeks after launch, the products were almost completely sold out.

The Thirty-Second Ladder

Just as important as the product breakthrough was the corresponding breakthrough in marketing. Razek, the chief marketing officer, put emphasis on higher production values and a higher level of taste and sophistication. He also created a rarity in television advertising, the thirty-second ladder. Marketers say that it's difficult to communicate more than one benefit in a thirty-second television spot effectively, yet Razek managed to do it. The ad told women that the Body By Victoria bra was seamless (a technical benefit), and that the technical benefits delivered the functional advantages of contouring and shaping curves. Most important, the ads expressed a particular kind of sexy appeal, a combination of curves and confidence.

The ads featured supermodels wearing Body By Victoria bras, posing and stretching before a minimalist modern backdrop. Some wore classic white button-down shirts, opened to reveal the lingerie beneath. The voice-over narration, spoken by a woman, was simple and to the point. "Victoria's Secret Body By Victoria. A devastating collection of lingerie. It's as seamless as it is sexy. Wear Body By Victoria and all you'll see is curves."

Body By Victoria did what all New Luxury products that deliver on all three benefit levels do—it shattered the traditional price-volume demand curve. At more than twice the price of the average bra, it now sells more units than any other bra in the United States. The success of Body By Victoria pointed the way for the brand and validated Wexner's fundamental belief in the trading-up strategy. He wrote in the 1999 annual report that the new brand leadership process was "paying dividends. The recent 'Body By Victoria' launch was, really, the first integrated product launch that used the brand process start to finish."

Victoria's Secret continued to up the ante in the lingerie category. In 2001, the company launched a new line of lingerie called Very Sexy. It, too, delivered on all three benefit layers while projecting different facets of the Victoria's Secret brand of sexiness, and it was another major success. Razek continued to challenge competitors in marketing. He hired the best photographers in the world to create still imagery and world-renowned movie directors to develop television campaigns. Even the most elite fashion brands could not top the production values of Victoria's Secret communications media. Rezak continued to associate the brand with the most beautiful women in the world. Their fashion show moved to prime time and attracted more than twelve million viewers. Grace Nichols, the CEO of Victoria's Secret Stores, kept up the competitive pressure by driving brand consistency and product innovation.

In just three years, Wexner had dramatically repositioned the Victoria's Secret brand. It was more sophisticated, of higher quality, and more aspirational. Prices were higher, and so was volume. The entire brand, just like the Body By Victoria line, had moved off the demand curve for the category.

"In 1995, Victoria's Secret did no advertising, except promotional items attached to the catalog and sales signs in stores," Wexner said. "Margins were in the mid-thirties, and bras sold at around $14.98. Victoria's Secret was composed of independent businesses with no coordination of styles or marketing efforts. There

	1997	2002
Average unit retail price	$15	$26
Premium over department store brand	5%	75%
Volume index	100	160

A focus on the Victoria's Secret brand dramatically improved the company's performance.

was really nothing beyond the common name that connected the businesses. We thought it was sound enough. Now, the average bra sale is over $30, margins are in the mid-forties, and the strategy is to make sure that Victoria's Secret stands for an integrated world-class brand, internally and externally."

The strength of the repositioned brand enabled Victoria's Secret to extend into related categories, such as fragrance, just as Wexner had intended. It took Estée Lauder almost ten years to build its bestselling fragrance, Beautiful, into the top prestige fragrance in the United States. Victoria's Secret overtook that position in less than two years with the launch of Dream Angels Heavenly. Victoria's Secret Beauty is now a $600 million category of its own, with an objective to grow to over $1 billion in five years. Beauty products occupy 3,200 square feet in the flagship Victoria's Secret store at Thirty-fourth Street and Broadway in New York, and there are twenty make-up artists serving customers.

At the heart of the growth and success of Victoria's Secret is its leader's drive for quality and innovation and ability to embrace change. Wexner cites the influence of one of his mentors—Arthur Cullman, a marketing professor at Ohio State University—in his appreciation of flexibility. "Cullman said that change is a habit and you have to get in the habit of it. If you don't, you will find yourself losing the ability, just as you can lose physical skills. You have to keep your mental muscle loose. You have to keep stretching it." It is largely as a result of this ability to change with the fashions and remain a relevant and powerful aspiration to its customers that Victoria's Secret has long since exceeded Wexner's original predictions for the brand's sales and profit potential.

Like other New Luxury leaders, Wexner is always considering new ideas and revolutions. "I like taking an idea, playing with it, thinking about it, rethinking it, tinkering with it. And not being daunted by the size or scale of the project or the bold differences."

Lessons from New Luxury Lingerie

1. *Never underestimate the customer.* Wexner believed that the American woman would want to wear sexy lingerie every day and be willing to pay more for it if given the opportunity to do so. Over the past twenty years, the brand has traded up its customers to higher levels of taste and aspiration across multiple categories. The brand took its customers from bland department store staples to more fashionable foundations. And then Wexner traded them up again to a $34 functionally superior, emotionally engaging bra, which became a bestseller.

2. *Shatter the price-volume demand curve.* Victoria's Secret markets all top ten bras in the country. Even a bra that performs poorly at Victoria's Secret outperforms a department store bestseller. The average unit retail price of a Victoria's Secret bra is about $10 higher than its department store counterpart. Victoria's Secret operates on a different scale than the rest of the market, achieving significantly higher volumes at significantly higher prices.

3. *Create a ladder of genuine benefits.* Brands are able to draw emotional responses but only when there is a level of quality that serves as a tangible and relevant foundation. Body By Victoria offered a compelling, tightly linked ladder of benefits, and it was a blockbuster success that dramatically increased the strength of the brand. But it took time, and a number of failures, to get the ladder right.

4. *Escalate innovation, elevate quality, deliver a flawless experience.*

"Constant innovation is the thread that ties our brands together and produces success," says Wexner. "Those who expect to win in today's environment must have brands with speed, flexibility, and agility—brands that can maintain relevancy as customers are exposed to new ideas at lightning speed. Fashion brands are about change. It's about constant evolution and constant rethinking of what you do." Wexner continues to pattern the market continually, traveling to Europe at least four times a year to visit stores and gather new input. Wexner used his approach to brand leadership to elevate the brand and ensure that it was precisely executed in all its elements. He was never satisfied with better-than-average performance.

5. *Extend the price range and postioning of the brand.* Today the entry level price for a Victoria's Secret bra is $22, and the highest-priced bra in the Manhattan stores is $600, thirty times more. By steadily increasing the upper price limit, the Victoria's Secret brand has increased its average unit retail price for bras by almost 200 percent in five years. In addition to the wide price range, Victoria's Secret uses well-defined subbrands to extend the reach of the brand without diluting its essence.

6. *Customize your value chain to deliver on the benefit ladder.* From the beginning, Wexner understood that owning his own stores created an enormous competitive advantage. Using color and visual display, he could generate excitement around the product and create a different kind of shopping experience for the female consumer—more intimate, feminine, and engaging—and build a lasting relationship with her. The power of this branded channel of distribution made it possible to launch products more rapidly and on a larger scale than any other competitor could.

7. *Use influence marketing; seed your success through brand apostles.* The most important brand apostles for Victoria's Secret are the supermodels. They wear the lingerie and are brand advocates. They create the aspiration of joining a club of the most beautiful women in the world.

8. *Continually attack the category like an outsider.* Although no competitor has seriously challenged Victoria's Secret, the brand

keeps topping itself. New, innovative bras make earlier products obsolete. New, premium fragrances upstage the previous generation of scents. By continually patterning the needs of the consumer and evolving the definition of sexiness, Victoria's Secret constantly reinvents itself.

Today, Victoria's Secret virtually owns the emotional space of feeling and looking sexy for American women.

Six

Eating As an Emotional Experience

Americans love to eat and always have, but the eating habits and preferences of middle-market eaters are changing. People are trading up from the traditional quick-service restaurant (QSR) such as Burger King, where a sandwich costs $3 or less, to a whole new category of restaurants called "fast casual," such as Panera Bread and Chipotle, where a sandwich costs $6 or more. When Americans visit a full-service restaurant (with table service and an average check of $15 or more), they are trading up to places that serve untraditional "imported" fare in a themed environment, such as The Cheesecake Factory and P.F. Chang's. And when they shop for ingredients for a home-cooked meal, they are increasingly stopping by a specialty grocery, such as Trader Joe's, to pick up exotic ingredients they can't find at the conventional supermarket.

Wherever they go for their food, middle-market consumers think of eating as more than an exercise in satisfying a hunger or filling up. Fifty-five percent of the respondents to our survey told us they rocket in the food category—they are willing to pay a premium for food that tastes better, looks more appealing, is served in a pleasing environment, and engages them emotionally. These consumers seek adventure and surprise in the aisles of a specialty food boutique. They drive out of their way for a latte. They wait in line for an hour or more to share coconut-and-lime shrimp with friends at their favorite sit-down "fusion" cuisine restaurant. They're hungry for an experience as much as for the food itself, and when a company delivers it, price is not an issue.

Increasingly, middle-market consumers prefer to eat away from home. Most Americans feel they have less time to shop than ever before, and because they have been exposed to better and more diverse cooking in their travels and through the media, they feel less secure in their own cooking skills. As a result, spending on away-from-home food service has risen dramatically in the last thirty years, from 37 percent of total food spending in 1972 to more than 50 percent in 2002. In our survey, a sit-down meal away from home was the second most popular category for trading up.

The growth in single-person households has been a major driver in the rise of away-from-home eating, because singles don't want to bother with cooking for themselves. Forty percent of American households are either single-parent (a mom or dad with one or more kids at home) or single households (a person living alone). "Why should I try to cook for one?" said Phyllis, a sixty-eight-year-old widow. "My time has value. When you add up the shopping time, cooking time, and cleanup time, how can I justify it? When my husband was alive, he did the cooking. He liked it, but I never did. Besides, I don't have to cook—there are twenty-five places to eat within five miles of my home. They have wider variety, better quality, and they're faster than anything I could do at home."

Eating out touches on all four emotional spaces. According to our survey, eating out is primarily about Taking Care of Me—it makes people feel "pampered," "happy," "comforted," "less stressed out," and "uplifted." It is also about Individual Style—respondents told us that a good restaurant experience makes them feel "accomplished" and like a person "of style and taste." In our interviews, many people talked about eating out as a Questing experience—"I love trying new tastes and combinations," they told us. It is also about Connecting with important people in their lives. Many consumers tell us they spend the largest percentage of their discretionary cash on going out to eat with friends, family, colleagues, and lovers. Eating out provides a chance to talk and connect without having to focus on food preparation or worry about a companion's evaluation of one's cooking. For parents, it is a break from the routine and work of cooking. The kids can choose different items, and if the meal is unsatisfactory, they can send it back to the kitchen. At home, rejecting mom's prepared meal may mean an alternative as basic as a can of soup or a bowl of cereal.

The more Americans eat away from home, the more sophisticated their tastes in food become. They crave new alternatives to fast food and seek innovative food experiences. And restaurants respond with more complex dishes, more frequent menu changes, regular specials, and more elaborate menu descriptions of the food and its origins: The sea bass is Chilean; the beef is from Kobe, Japan; the cheese is three-year-old Parmigiano-Reggiano from Parma, Italy.

Americans do still eat at home, of course, but they don't spend a great deal of time or expend much effort in doing so. The average two-parent family with kids has only one sit-down meal together each week. Even then, consumers say they want the meal to be "quick and easy"—about 40 percent of consumers say they spend less than ten minutes on preparation when they cook a meal! They typically use fewer than eight ingredients, serve fewer side dishes than they did five years ago, and are increasingly making single-dish meals, such as chili or stir-fry. They are, however, incorporating bolder flavors and more diverse textures in their home-cooked meals—creating dishes with the tastes of Cuba, Argentina, Indonesia, Malaysia, India, and Thailand, as well as the more traditional Mexican, Chinese, and Italian fare.

The Rise of the Fast Casual Restaurant

Although we have seen a significant rise in dining out over the past three decades, the trend began just after World War II. From then until about 1990, much of the away-from-home food spending was on fast food—burgers and fries, pizza, Chinese and Mexican takeout. McDonald's took early leadership and defined the QSR offering— meals at a guaranteed speed, with consistent quality, and at a low price. When Ray Kroc, a former Mixmaster salesman, acquired the chain from the McDonald brothers, he built it out at a breathtaking rate. Today, McDonald's operates 12,500 stores across the United States, and achieves an average $1.6 million in annual sales per store.

The chain still holds the lion's share of the QSR market, and each McDonald's store outsells rival Burger King outlets by 50 percent. And the McDonald's french fry—made of Idaho Russet Burbank potatoes and cooked for three minutes and thirty seconds in a proprietary mixture of hot oils, sugar, and salt—is the best in the industry.

But in recent years, the QSR business has stagnated. The growth of the large chains—McDonald's, Burger King, Pizza Hut, and Taco Bell—has slowed. The market is saturated with outlets, thanks to easy availability of financing for a new burger joint or pizza parlor and the relative ease of opening and managing one. Consumer demand is flat, and competitors are engaged in a price war. American consumers still make more than fifty million visits to QSRs each day, but more and more they are bored by fast food, feel little loyalty to the restaurants, and are looking for a different kind of eating experience.

This was confirmed by research we did for a restaurant chain. We accompanied many families on what we call "shop-along" research—getting in the car with them on a weekday evening as they set off to choose a restaurant for dinner. We found that the decision-making process is haphazard at best; determining factors include traffic conditions, previous experience with the restaurants they pass, how much money they have in their pockets, how close they are to their credit card spending limits, how many days until the next payday, and, very often, the preferences expressed by the loudest and most persistent voice in the car.

Even so, the family will often drive past the Taco Bell and Burger King and seek out a fast casual restaurant, where a meal costs under $15 per person and can be ordered, delivered, and eaten in less than forty-five minutes. In comparison to the standardized food offerings of the quick-service chains, the fast casual restaurant makes sandwiches and meals to order, using fresh, sometimes seasonal and even locally produced, ingredients of better quality than those of the QSRs. It also pays more attention to the physical environment—including the decor, lighting, seating, and traffic flow—to create a more comfortable and attractive setting that is consistent with the superior taste profile of the food.

Two companies, Panera Bread and Chipotle, have emerged as the fast casual leaders, but there are many others—including Atlanta

Bread Company and Pret A Manger (a made-up French phrase meaning, roughly, "ready to eat")—that are getting attention and growing in sales. There are also many start-ups in this segment, but the competition is intense, and failure rates are high. Consumers are very willing to try a new place, but they commit to and revisit only the ones that deliver on the ladder of benefits.

Fast casual appeals most strongly to four types of households: affluent singles, affluent empty nesters, dual-income households without kids, and dual-income households with kids. Of these, the households that frequent fast casual establishments the most are those that are populated with working women—women who don't have time to shop for, prepare, and clean up after a meal. They rise at 5 A.M. to get the family ready for school and work. They work all day themselves. As the dinner hour approaches, they often turn to an "agent of convenience"—a restaurant that will help them save time while providing a meal of greater taste and interest than they could prepare themselves. Another piece of research we did for a major food supplier who wanted to encourage consumers to do more cooking at home showed that only 10 percent of working women with children at home had a dinner menu in mind by 4 P.M. on a typical workday; that's scarcely enough time to plan a menu, buy the ingredients, and cook the meal. "After working all day, especially when I haven't already taken something out of the freezer that morning to prepare for dinner, I want a quick, healthy alternative to fast food," says Kathy, a thirty-two-year-old mother of two. "It's not that I want to be served. It's all about time. I only get about one and a half hours to spend with the kids every night. I'd rather spend it helping them with homework, or just hanging out, rather than preparing a meal. Besides, I want them to have a better meal than I have the energy to cook. And I want them to try new things and experience new foods."

In addition to these changes on the demand side—including the rise in the number of working women, increased time pressures, higher household incomes, and the need for emotional engagement—the rise of fast casual has been fueled by important supply-side factors. Food delivery systems have improved dramatically in the past two decades, so there is a greater variety of quality ingredients available from all over the world. New technologies and cooking processes have enabled restaurants to deliver more complex dishes, with richer flavors and more consistent quality, without the need for highly skilled labor. And real estate developers have been enthusiastic about partnering with fast casual chains to help them expand rapidly—an ambitious chain can create one hundred new restaurants each year. As a result, the fast casual segment is growing at 15 percent per year, while the $111 billion QSR segment and the $140 billion full-service segment are both flat.

Panera Bread: An Eating Experience Built Around Bread

As with New Luxury businesses in every category, the creation of a successful fast casual enterprise depends on the emergence of an entrepreneur who has the vision, creativity, experience, taste, and skill to create a business that can transform the category—and Ronald Shaich, CEO of Panera Bread, is such an innovator. Panera is a bakery-café whose ethos centers around freshly baked bread, and whose stores offer custom-made sandwiches on a variety of breads, served in a well-designed and inviting environment.

The Panera Bread on Chestnut Ridge Road in Woodcliff Lake, New Jersey—located in a strip mall along with a Pottery Barn, a Victoria's Secret, a Banana Republic, and an Apple computer store—is typical. At 12:30 P.M. on a warm August day, there is lots of noisy chatter from the customers, mostly twenty- and thirtysomething office workers and suburban shoppers. Although the store is crowded, people move quickly through the line, ordering sandwiches, salads, soups, coffee, and desserts. All the tables are filled, and the lunchers are engaged in animated conversation. Most of them finish every bite of their meal and then linger for a while to chat and relax. A few customers, full trays in hand, wait impatiently for a table to clear. As soon as a party leaves, Panera crew members swiftly clean the table and return the chairs to order. The store has the pleasant smells of freshly baked bread and freshly brewed coffee.

The Panera Bread experience has its roots in the Saint Louis Bread Company, a bakery restaurant founded in 1987 which built a strong reputation and a loyal following in St. Louis, where it operated nineteen stores in the early 1990s. Saint Louis Bread Company

Ronald Shaich is cofounder, chairman, and CEO of Panera Bread.
Photo courtesy of AP/Wide World Photos.

was famous for its signature bread: a sourdough made from a San Francisco recipe that had been lovingly transported east by company founder Ken Rosenthal. In 1993, Rosenthal sold his company to Au Bon Pain for $24 million.

Ronald Shaich, CEO of Au Bon Pain, studied his two brands carefully. He knew that Au Bon Pain occupied a niche in its urban markets. Each store operated in a high-traffic location and was designed to maximize customer throughput, but the service was impersonal, and the eating environment was uninteresting. Consumers visited Au Bon Pain to get a quick sandwich, often to take out.

Shaich found a different story unfolding at the Saint Louis Bread Company stores. They offered an authentic and respectful alternative for people who were looking for good food in a special atmosphere, and consumer reaction had been so positive that they had expanded their sales beyond the traditional breakfast and lunch periods into new areas that Shaich eventually dubbed "chill out" and "daytime talking" spaces. On one store visit, Shaich observed a group of businesspeople from a nearby corporation huddled in a corner. "We don't have a good place to talk at the office," they told him. At another table, a teacher sat alone, drinking coffee and writing a lesson plan. At another, a worker was reading the sports pages and listening to his Walkman. "I just needed a place to chill," he told Shaich. "I don't want to go home. And I don't want to go back to work."

Shaich concluded that Saint Louis Bread Company offered what he called a "gateway into the suburban marketplace"—because many in-town workers who ate there lived in the suburbs—that could enable the chain to expand quickly. He believed that the Saint Louis Bread Company had greater potential for success than did Au Bon Pain and that it could become a nationally dominant fast casual brand.

Shaich knew that his vision would require management focus and substantial resources, both financial and human, to become a national success. In 1998, he proposed to his board of directors that they rename the company Panera Bread, sell off all the Au Bon Pain units, and put all their efforts into building the new company into a national leader with one hundred stores. It was a bet-the-company idea, and it took the board until May 1999—seven months of debate— to approve it. But the bet paid off handsomely. By the end of 2002, Panera had grown to 505 stores in thirty-two states, with sales of about $750 million and a market capitalization of over $1 billion. The company expects to reach $1 billion in retail sales by the end of 2003.

Just as it was at the Saint Louis Bread Company, bread remains the platform for the Panera Bread concept; the company's motto is simple and primal: "Fresh bread makes friends." According to Shaich, bread is "how we root ourselves in the consumer's mind." The company employs a "master artisan baker" whose job is to focus on standards of artistry and quality, research and development of new bread products, and training. The dough for the signature sourdough bread is prepared at a central commissary to ensure consistent quality and is delivered fresh, not frozen, to stores each day. At the store, the bread is baked in a specially designed oven with a stone deck that produces both heat and steam. The result is a bread that has a crispy crust and a moist interior. Bread that is not sold during business hours is given to charity at day's end. The ingredients are fresh and the best available. The soup offerings vary from day to day, and there are many seasonal specialties—visible proof of freshness. A sign that reads "No preservatives" is prominently posted in every store. The company has begun a program to make a wider variety of the artisan breads available in every store. Panera Bread wants to offer the best bread in the country—and make it available in great quantities. That is a sign of New Luxury: artisanal quality at middle-market quantity.

Panera's organization is structured to support the mission—everything is designed around the importance of bread, rather than for speed of production, customer throughput, or convenience. Panera Bread has more in common with a full-service, casual dining chain such as The Cheesecake Factory or Olive Garden than with a QSR. The employees at a fast-food restaurant typically report to the store manager, who inevitably focuses more on production than on the customer. At Panera, the bakers report to the corporate baking supervisor, who is responsible only for the baking process, not the store experience.

Panera Bread has achieved its success by delivering on the New Luxury ladder of benefits. The technical differences are many. There are fifteen sandwiches on the menu, including three grilled panini and seven signature sandwiches with combinations that can be made quickly—including an oven-roasted roast beef sandwich with smoked cheddar, lettuce, tomato, red onion, and creamy horseradish sauce served on an Asiago cheese minibaguette. Five soups and six salads are also available daily. The Tuscan chicken sandwich at Panera is composed of slices of hot white-meat chicken, with two slices of tomato, fresh basil, melted mozzarella, and a mild chipotle mayonnaise—but the baker will make it with whatever ingredients the customer requests. The sandwich is served on fresh slices of onion-and-rosemary focaccia bread that have been toasted on the grill. These technical differences—in ingredients, available combinations, and selection—deliver functional benefits: the sandwiches taste fresher and more complex, and they are more healthful than offerings from QSRs and other fast casual chains.

Panera Bread also delivers emotional benefits in all four spaces. It is a place where consumers feel they can Take Care of Me—a small self-reward in a nice sandwich. "When I go to Panera," says Mary, a twenty-eight-year-old administrative assistant living in New Jersey, "I feel like I am in a little bit of Italy for twenty-five minutes. I get fresh food prepared just the way I want it. I can have something different every time I go." Because the atmosphere is pleasant and relaxing, a meal becomes a Connecting experience. "The crowd here has more people that I would be interested in talking to," Mary adds. "We have something in common." For many, Panera is also about expressing Individual Style. Julia, a twenty-eight-year-old information technology manager at a university, says, "When I first ate at Panera, my thought was, finally a place that's worthy of me." And for others, Panera delivers a form of Questing—a place to try new tastes. "The bread is incredible," says Tony, a sixty-five-year-old retired public administrator. "I sneak over every morning for their bakery and coffee." These are not comments you would hear about a Burger King.

As a result, Panera creates apostles. Julia, for example, is more than willing to spend $7 on lunch because, as she says, "It's worth it. True, sometimes I think, 'Whoa! That lunch cost a lot more than $4,' but then I remind myself that I'm not getting $4 food!" To create apostles, Panera—like New Luxury players in every category—has created a detailed story for its consumers and for its store associates. They are able to articulate what makes Panera special and unique, talk about why it was founded and its mission (beyond profitability), and what the individual store manager (known as an owner) is particularly passionate about. Sometimes the story also defines an oppositional positioning—exactly what the restaurant is *not* and why. All successful fast casual chains have a set of creative building blocks to tell their story, including print materials, Web sites, activities, and events; these blocks can be used in a variety of ways, but they deliver consistent messages.

Panera Bread stores produce healthy profits, and the company is experiencing strong growth. The average check is $6.19, and that delivers earnings before interest and tax (EBIT) of 11 to 14 percent. At a QSR the average check is $4.34, with an EBIT of 7 percent. The raw materials cost more at Panera—20 percent higher per meal than at a QSR—but the revenue is 40 percent higher. The average Panera store delivers $1.75 million in sales, half of which comes from lunch—nearly 10 percent more than the average McDonald's and almost three times as much as the average Starbucks. It costs about $800,000 to build out a typical 4,500-square-foot Panera that seats 110 customers—fewer than a Burger King store that produces half the sales volume. As a result, Panera has more than four hundred stores and aims to have 1,500 within five years. The company is a top performer in the Standard & Poor's Small Cap 600.

As with other categories, the success of Panera Bread and its close rivals in defining the fast casual segment has produced a rush of competition. In its efforts to diversify its base, provide more upscale offerings, and leverage its considerable operating skills, McDonald's has taken an ownership position in two fast casual chains, Pret A Manger and Chipotle.

Pret A Manger, which began in the United Kingdom, offers high-quality prepared sandwiches—thirty to forty different kinds, wrapped, and displayed in coolers. The restaurant offers speed, with an average checkout time of ninety seconds, and freshness. The menu is constantly changing—if an item doesn't sell, it isn't offered again. Pret A Manger has expanded from its London base, where it has a dense network of stores, to locations in New York and Hong Kong.

McDonald's other fast casual acquisition, Chipotle, was founded by Steve Ells, who, like Ronald Shaich, wanted to create a simple, fresh alternative to fast food. He trained at the Culinary Institute of America, then decided to apply his skills to creating a new style of Mexican peasant food. Ells modeled the menu and store on the Mexican "taquerias" in the Mission district of San Francisco. A taqueria is a step up from street food—a small storefront offering a very limited menu, manned by the owner-operator making custom tortillas behind a stand. Ells calls his concept "a gourmet experience you can enjoy in fifteen minutes."

The first Chipotle Mexican Grill was an eight hundred-square-foot restaurant near the University of Denver campus, and it achieved $1 million in sales in its first year. Today, Chipotle is known for its giant flour burritos and tortillas, stuffed with a choice of black beans, grilled peppers, grilled onions, rice, salsa, cheese, sour cream, beef, pork, or chicken. The simple, focused menu allows the company to concentrate on perfecting its operations and using only the highest-quality ingredients—fresh lime juice, cilantro, roasted chiles, fresh avocado. The company has doubled its sales volume each year since 1998, when McDonald's acquired its stake.

"Chipotle's philosophy is summed up in its name—a chipotle pepper is a jalapeño pepper that has been smoked and dried, elevating it from something ordinary to something extraordinary," says Mats Lederhausen, president of McDonald's Development Group, the business unit responsible for Chipotle and Pret A Manger. "That's what Chipotle has done for fast Mexican food. They use the finest ingredients, such as free-range pork from Niman Ranch, and gourmet cooking techniques, so that their burritos and tacos go beyond fresh to be food with integrity."

Chipotle has 230 restaurants in twenty-three U.S. cities, and McDonald's believes it can grow it to more than 2,000 restaurants in the United States. Chipotle appeals most to higher-income young adults aged twenty-five to forty-four who are dining alone or with friends and coworkers.

"The large portions, atmosphere, and quirky advertising help foster Chipotle fanatics—more than half the customers eat there four times or more per week. This past Halloween, sixteen thousand customers around the country were willing to dress like burritos to get the food they craved for free. And a recent episode of MTV's *The Osbournes* featured Ozzy's weeklong diet of nothing but Chipotle burritos," says Lederhausen.

Pret A Manger is different. It's fast—as fast as a customer can choose from the handmade sandwiches in the grab-and-go case— but the offerings are more aspirational, have higher integrity and a fresher feel, than traditional sandwich places. "At Pret, sandwich making is an art. Customers will find oriental tuna, crayfish and rocket; and hummus and red pepper; as well as a selection of sushi, espresso drinks, and decadent desserts," Lederhausen told us. "Pret revolutionized the sandwich market in the United Kingdom, where we have 124 shops. We believe there is great potential around the world. Pret has thirteen shops in New York, five in Hong Kong, and five in Japan. Pret's slogan is 'passionate about food,' and the sandwich chefs strive to adapt offerings to each country's local tastes, while minimizing the use of chemicals, additives, and preservatives."

Lederhausen maintains that both Chipotle and Pret A Manger have the potential to significantly help the parent company grow and improve profitability.

The Cheesecake Factory: Around the World in a Meal

A step up in price above the fast casual restaurants takes the trading-up away-from-home diner to one of the fast-growing sit-down restaurants built around a theme—such as an unusual fusion of different cuisines, a special decor, or a unique philosophy of eating. This casual sit-down restaurant—with a dinner check of $15 and up—is the favored dining spot for upper-middle-market Americans, including affluent singles, affluent empty nesters, and especially dual-income couples with no kids. DINKs have plenty of money to spend, are generally short on time as a result of their work schedules, have no children to attend to or spend money on, and have a yearning for education, travel, and adventure.

The Cheesecake Factory is one of the fastest growing of the casual sit-down restaurants—a $500 million chain with a 27 percent compound annual growth rate from 1996 to 2001. Others include P.F. Chang's, Outback Steakhouse, and Carrabba's Italian Grill. The Cheesecake Factory has succeeded by ignoring the conventional industry wisdom that says a restaurant should simplify its operations by limiting the number of menu offerings and changes and realize purchasing economies by rationalizing the number and types of ingredients required. Instead, Cheesecake lists two hundred items on a typical menu—including forty different kinds of cheesecake.

David Overton, the CEO of The Cheesecake Factory, is a typical New Luxury entrepreneur—he loves everything about his product. "This business works because I am on a continuous food adventure. I want to bring the world to my customers." His customers seem more than happy to accompany him on his global culinary journeys. "I come here once a week with my girlfriends," said Madeleine, a thirty-two-year-old Chicago single. "It's fun. It's loud. We get three or four appetizers, three or four entrees, and a couple of slices of cheesecake. We start our meal in Thailand, go to the Caribbean for the main course, and then end up in Wisconsin for dessert. And it doesn't break the bank."

The business began in 1949, in a very small way, when David Overton's mother, Evelyn, made a cheesecake for her husband's boss. The boss loved it and asked Evelyn for more cakes that he could give as gifts, and soon she had a basement business—and it continued for twenty years. David, after spending time as a drummer for various musicians, including Jimi Hendrix, joined his parents to open their first bakery in Los Angeles, in 1978. It offered an eclectic menu with large portions and the cheesecake as its signature. The Overtons opened a second restaurant in 1983 and had five by 1991. In 1992 they went public and began to grow more quickly, adding stores in Chicago, Houston, Boston, and Boca Raton, Florida. In 1999, the company opened the Grand Lux Cafe, a twenty-four-hour restaurant at the Venetian Resort Hotel Casino in Las Vegas and did a whopping $18 million in sales its first year.

Overton is a hands-on leader who is passionate about his company. "I love to eat and it shows," he says as he pats his substantial belly. "Each of my restaurants reflects me and my tastes." Overton attends each of The Cheesecake Factory's store openings and supervises the major menu overhaul the company does every six months. In making menu choices, he allows himself to be guided by his instincts for what his customers will want. "No item makes the menu until I certify it offers comeback quality," he says. Gerald Deitchle, Cheesecake's CFO, says, "Sometimes the numbers don't explain everything. The numbers are not the business—they are symbols of the business."

A Cheesecake Factory restaurant is a destination, an experience; and strangely enough, an important part of the experience is the wait. Consumers in line at the Cheesecake restaurant on Michigan Avenue in Chicago talk enthusiastically about the chain's technical and functional differences—the breadth of variety, wonderful tastes, consistent quality, and big portion size. For example, the "mile-high" meat loaf sandwich, at $9.50, includes meat, potatoes, and onion rings, and although not actually a mile high, does loom up an impressive ten inches. Appetites at Cheesecake are big. One party of three consumes a double order of burgers called "roadside slide," an appetizer of firecracker salmon rolls, and entrées of Chinolatina chicken, shepherd's pie, and Jamaican black-pepper shrimp, tamping it all down with a slice of chocolate tuxedo cream cheesecake and two slices of tiramisu cheesecake.

The average Cheesecake Factory delivers a mammoth $11 million per store on sales of $1,000 per foot. That's more than three times the average for a fast casual chain and the highest space productivity in the restaurant industry. The average per-person check is $15.70, 50 percent higher than the category average. Compare Cheesecake economics to those of another fast casual chain, Applebee's. The average Cheesecake store delivers a 34 percent higher check average, 98 percent higher per check earnings before interest, depreciation, taxes, and amortization (EBIDTA), 350 percent more visits per store, and seven times the EBITDA per store.

For its apostles—and there are many—a visit to The Cheesecake Factory is mostly about Connecting and Questing. Cheesecake's relentless innovation cycle—a full menu revision every six months—continuously provides consumers new ways to explore the world of food in an atmosphere rooted in hometown America.

Trader Joe's: Questing in the Supermarket Aisle

Although America's eating trend is to away-from-home meals, there is another small, but fast-growing segment of middle-market consumers who do their food Questing in a very different way. These consumers say their favorite shopping experience is at the specialty market, gourmet shop, or organic food store. Shopping in these stores makes them feel "knowledgeable," "intelligent," "adventurous," and "inquisitive."

Joe Coulombe did not have the benefit of such research when he founded his first Trader Joe's store in Pasadena, California, in 1967. His mission was to make difficult-to-find gourmet items more accessible to American consumers. "I started Trader Joe's on the premise that the number of educated people would grow, and that is what has happened," he says. "I wanted to appeal to the well educated and people who were traveling more. Nobody was taking care of them." As the ranks of these consumers grew, he reasoned, so would his business opportunity.

Today, Trader Joe's operates 177 stores and takes in an estimated $2 billion in revenues. It is a specialty food empire built with virtually no broadcast advertising (save the occasional radio spot) and everyday low pricing (but rarely a sale). Analysts and competitors estimate store productivity at $1,000 per square foot—two to three times the industry average. Although Coulombe sold Trader Joe's in 1979 to the Albrecht family for $6 million and turned over the CEO reins in 1989, the company still follows his business practices.

Coulombe had a clear vision of his target consumers: well educated, well traveled, and underpaid. They were working professionals such as schoolteachers, engineers, and doctors—budget-conscious consumers with sophisticated palates. Or, as one spokesperson put it, "the unemployed Ph.D." With this customer in mind, Coulombe set about engineering what would become his signature, iconoclastic grocery concept. To evoke the romance of travel that would appeal to his target, he derived the name Trader Joe's from the book *Trader Horn*, which chronicles the adventures of Alfred Aloysius "Trader" Horn, a nineteenth-century ivory trader in Central Africa. Coulombe began by traveling the world in search of boutique wines, then added gourmet foods, because he believed that wines must be tasted and evaluated in connection with food. Knowing that his customers would value education—that they would read labels and seek information about the products they chose—he selected clever and whimsical names for his private-label items, such as Trader Joe's "Prelude to a Quiche." He also created *Fearless Flyer*, a newsletter designed to be "a marriage of *Consumer Reports* and *MAD* magazine," with content that could never be communicated in a thirty-second television spot. *Fearless Flyer* offers stories on the origins and distinctions of new and featured products, and information on what enabled the low price—replete with Victorian illustrations and puns that are as likely to be in French, Italian, Latin, or Chinese as in English. (Example: One seal says to another, "So I said to myself— *Crabé Diem*—Go ahead and seize that fresh-packed crab!")

Trader Joe's is an intriguing New Luxury player because it offers low prices, while most New Luxury goods are offered at a premium to their conventional counterparts. However, Trader Joe's real competitors are not Wegmans and Kroger, but rather the mom-and-pop groceries, gourmet shops, and organic food stores. Trader Joe's stores, at ten thousand square feet, are much larger than these competitors and generate much higher volume.

In addition, Trader Joe's is essentially a private-label store—

about 85 percent of its items are private label, and many are unique, with no national-brand counterpart. This makes it difficult to compare Trader Joe's prices with those of other specialty shops or conventional supermarkets. What makes the chain a New Luxury player is that it maintains higher margins than the industry average and has higher volume than its true competitors. Trader Joe's proves that New Luxury doesn't always have to be more expensive than conventional goods. Sometimes it can involve higher quality, taste, and more interesting products cascading to the middle market.

Trader Joe's maintains high margins by carefully managing its costs. It locates its stores outside central shopping districts, where rents are lower. A typical Trader Joe's carries a carefully edited assortment of about two thousand stock-keeping units, or SKUs— roughly 5 percent of the selection in a conventional grocery. Products are sourced by buyers who travel the world in search of "interesting products at an exceptional value." Once products are sourced, Trader Joe's purchases them directly from its suppliers, thus eliminating wholesalers. The company participates in designing packaging that saves space and cost, and it makes large purchases to achieve scale; it always pays in cash, so there are no carrying charges. Rather than stock many sizes of the same or closely related products, only the most popular sizes of a product are carried—or alternatively, sizes are selected to optimize cost. And, rather than commit valuable shelf space to loss leaders, the company constantly removes the poor performers. When costs change, so do the prices. In this way, Trader Joe's is able to preserve margins.

Finally, Coulombe insisted that the company be "outstanding" in whatever it sold; if someone else could do it better or cheaper, Trader Joe's would not offer it. As a result, the chain does not sell cigarettes and carries only a few national brands, and a store manager can tailor her assortment to local-market tastes, rather than follow a corporate planogram.

Very important to Trader Joe's customers, values strongly inform the company's decisions about product development and assortment. Frozen chickens are "floor-raised" (not in cages), without the use of antibiotics or hormones. Since 1987, only fish and shellfish that have not been treated with sodium tripolyphosphate or sul-

fites—chemicals used to retain water before freezing—have made
the cut. And when customers began campaigning against genetically
modified ingredients in 2001, the company responded with a promise that all new products would be certified free of genetically
engineered ingredients, and it set a goal to reformulate existing
products within one year toward the same end. (This goal proved
more difficult to achieve.)

The store experience has been carefully designed to support and
express the sense of adventure contained in the product. The
Hawaiian-shirted "crew members" are visible, friendly, and well
versed on the products. We visited the Trader Joe's in Glenview, Illi-
nois, on a Sunday afternoon, and we found a crew member cooking
up hamburgers for all to sample, and tasting stations offered sips of
San Pellegrino Limonata, a sparkling beverage from Italy, nibbles
of biscotti (double chocolate with almonds and hazelnuts), and bits of
Trader Joe's Organic White Corn Chips. "We do lots of demos to
give people an opportunity to taste and feel—we try to do demos
seven days a week," the store manager explained. "People here are
more hesitant to try new things than in California where I'm from,
but we're changing that—it's our goal."

The strategy is working. A twenty-nine-year-old librarian visiting the Glenview store for the first time commented, "At first it was
a little overwhelming, but it was fun. I was just amazed at some of
the prices—they have a lot of things that I would be interested in
trying once at a price that made me willing to try it. I bought lots of
things I've never tried before—Kashi cereals, natural peanut butter,
refrigerated pulled barbecue pork, wine, artichoke ravioli, frozen
fish, frozen peaches."

Trader Joe's delivers on all three benefit layers. Technically, the
chain delivers unique, healthful, and interesting products. Functionally, the store delivers value and an interesting, unusual shopping experience. Most important, customers talk about the experience as
one of adventure, discovery, and fun. "It's surprising and incongru-
ous," remarked Linda, a fifty-four-year-old social worker who has
been visiting the Wayne, New Jersey, store about once a month for
the past three years. "You're not sure what you're going to find—
there are unusual things—you look around and find surprises."

The Trader Joe's operating model has paid off richly: company overhead is reportedly a lean 2 percent of sales, about 50 percent less than the typical grocery chain. And although the closely held company does not discuss profitability, former CEO John Shields once remarked that the company was able to expand eastward in 1996 without any outside funding because the Trader Joe's West Coast stores were a "cash cow," adding that the approximately fifty stores that resulted from this expansion were also "very profitable." In an environment where grocery retailer margins are typically 1 to 2 percent, Trader Joe's has invented a novel way to profit from Americans' propensity to trade up to higher levels of quality and taste.

The Winning Practices of New Luxury Food Suppliers

1. *Never underestimate the customer.* The conventional wisdom in the retail grocery and QSR industries is that customers are too busy, too lazy, or too uninterested to go out of their way to shop for food or travel any distance for a better bite to eat. Customers of Trader Joe's and Panera Bread have proved that when offered a higher-quality and emotionally engaging alternative to the norm, they will go out of their way for the experience, and they'll happily pay a premium for it.

2. *Shatter the price-volume demand curve.* The growth of the fast casual segment suggests that there is plenty of volume to be had at high prices—so long as the benefit ladder stays intact. While the away-from-home-eating demand curve is still in the early phases of being redrawn, Panera Bread—whose premiums are 100 percent and higher relative to fast-food alternatives—is well on its way to rendering the traditional price-volume trade-off largely irrelevant.

3. *Create a ladder of genuine benefits.* Among its peers, The Cheesecake Factory wins on taste, menu variety, and portion size. These functional advantages are based on real differences on the technical level, including foods made from scratch on the premises—from high-quality and fresh ingredients—rather than outsourced, two major menu changes per year, and an environment characterized by an upscale and contemporary design. These benefit layers support the emotional Wow! factor for which tourists and regulars alike will obligingly queue up for one to two hours.

4. *Escalate innovation, elevate quality, deliver a flawless experience.*
Panera Bread employs its master artisan baker to ensure the quality of
its bread and develop new offerings. It also employs a "senior vice
president of consumer experience." Through these employees' efforts,
Panera has introduced new tastes (artisan breads, pesto mayonnaise,
garlic-roasted portobello mushrooms), new forms (panini), and imported ingredients to the standard lunch fare. And Panera gives customers a stream of new products that can deliver "adventure in
minutes." What's more, it does so in an environment with pizzazz—
replete with classical music, natural lighting, leather couches, and real
silverware and china. Suddenly, $6 for a sandwich seems like a bargain.

5. *Extend the price range and positioning of the brand.* Rather than
rest on its laurels, The Cheesecake Factory is expanding its franchise
to include the upscale Grand Lux Cafe, a full-service restaurant
whose price range extends further than that of The Cheesecake Factory. (Appetizers range from $4.95 to $10.95, versus $3.75 to $9.95 at
Cheesecake; entrées range from $6.50 to $28.95, versus $6.50 to
$24.95; and desserts range from $4.95 to $6.95, versus $3.95 to
$6.95.) The first location, a twenty-four-hour restaurant at the Venet-
ian Resort Hotel Casino in Las Vegas, debuted in 1999 and quickly
became the company's largest restaurant. Grand Lux's first-year
sales topped $18 million, nearly twice the already impressive per-
restaurant average of the company's flagship concept. A second location opened in Beverly Hills in 2001, and a third in Chicago in 2002.

6. *Customize your value chain to deliver on the benefit ladder.* Joe
Coulombe developed his business in this order: First, he defined his
customer's functional and emotional needs. Second, he envisioned
the concept that would meet them. And third, he devised a unique
value chain that would enable him to deliver on those aspects critical to delivering on the benefits. He defied conventional practice in
grocery retail—and built a lean, profitable enterprise that contra-
dicted most aspects of prevailing industry wisdom.

7. *Use influence marketing—seed your success through brand apostles.*
Tony, the retired public administrator, told us, "I tell anyone and
everyone about Panera. Now we've got our son and daughter-in-law
hooked." Carol, the administrative assistant, claims that she loves
taking first-timers to Panera Bread. Word of mouth enabled Trader

Joe's to build a $2 billion retail franchise despite the out-of-the-way store locations and lack of broadcast advertising.

8. *Continually attack the category like an outsider.* Like Robert Mondavi in the wine industry, Panera Bread CEO Ronald Shaich was not an outsider to the category he transformed—he had co-founded Au Bon Pain in 1981 and led its acquisition of the Saint Louis Bread Company in 1993. Yet he used his position as an insider to understand the opportunities presented by the shortcomings of the status quo. He saw Panera Bread as a clean slate that would enable him to devote himself entirely to building on his vision of an emotionally engaging brand that offered "specialness" at a premium. He resisted the urge to hang onto Au Bon Pain—a business that had been successful but, he decided, lacked a concept big enough to generate exceptional growth.

On the Menu for the Future

The appetite for New Luxury eating is far from satisfied. The need for new, well-managed, moderately priced food for the single-household family on-the-go will grow. The winners will be authoritative and expert in their ingredients, finished goods, and product and service delivery systems. But even today's winners have no assurance of success in the future, because food is a fashion business—tastes wander, and consumer fads come and go.

The grocery retail business, too, is ripe for a New Luxury transformation—waiting for an entrepreneur who can break the current trade-offs between variety and price, convenience and specialness. Those who trade up in groceries tell us that they split their shopping between several types of food providers—milk, bread, and eggs from the conventional retailers; produce, meat, and specialty items from retailers such as Trader Joe's and independent ethnic markets. Conventional players are experimenting with new formats to tap into the trading-up opportunity (for example, H-E-B's European-style Central Market). Yet it remains to be seen who will be the first innovator to crack the code of how to serve customers in the market to Take Care of Me, Quest, Connect, and reflect Individual Style as they pick up a gallon of milk and a box of diapers.

Seven

Only the Best for Members of the Family

The 1950s American family—composed of mom, dad, and two kids—is now almost an anomaly (only 24 percent of adult Americans are married and have children living at home), but that does not mean that consumers do not care about family or don't want to strengthen connections among family members. It's just that they are redefining what the family is and how they go about Connecting.

As we've seen, today's families have fewer kids and the parents have less time to spend with them, so they sometimes turn to premium goods to enrich their time together. Twenty percent of the respondents to our survey said they spend on goods that "make them feel like a good parent." In many single, nonfamily households, of which there are thirty-five million, pets have become the new children. There are 136 million dogs and cats in the United States, compared to forty-eight million children under the age of twelve—and the pet owners, both single and married, lavish attention, and premium goods, on them as if they were their kids.

Kids and pets are important drivers and recipients of New Luxury spending; the role of American children is particularly interesting because they are sophisticated consumers in their own right. They are exposed—often more exposed than even their parents are—to the marketing messages contained in every form of media. Kids in their "tweens" (ten to twelve) and early to mid-teens (thirteen to seventeen) are particularly savvy about the messages and meanings of certain categories of goods. As they make the transition from childhood to being full-fledged members of society, they become concerned about self-branding and aligning themselves with people and things they deem to be "cool" and of value.

American kids also have more disposable income of their own. They are spenders in ways that their parents and grandparents were not. Younger teens, especially, are willing to put most, if not all, of their cash into goods that they believe will improve their looks and heighten their status with other kids. As one eighteen-year-old put it, "Ninth and tenth graders—that's where the money is."

Today's kids have a very different view of material needs than do their parents or grandparents. The many activities of the "overprogrammed" American child often require specialized goods, and the children—often far more than their parents—are eager to gain status through their possessions. School clothing, sports equipment, stereo gear, CDs, televisions, computers, phones, furniture, travel, health care, medicines, gourmet foods, food supplements, dentistry and cosmetic surgery—kids are major consumers in many New Luxury categories. It is not unusual for young American consumers to have their own phones, electronics, and premium sports equipment, and to have traveled widely during school vacations.

American children also have significant influence over many of the purchases made in the household, from the clothing dad wears, to the car mom buys, to the food the family eats, to the destination of the next family vacation. In some cases, it is the kids who will catalyze the parents' trading up. They prefer to go out for a family lunch at Panera Bread or Chipotle rather than Burger King. As we'll discuss in chapter 14, the next generation of consumers are sure to be even more discriminating and demanding purchasers of New Luxury goods and to trade up even further.

The Girl Business

We have seen that women are important New Luxury consumers; girls are, too—and girls, aged seven to twelve, are a special group. They are old enough to be readers and learners but still young enough to be strongly influenced by their families and their peers. They are educated enough to be interested in history and society, but still young enough to enjoy playing with dolls. And unlike girls of earlier generations, they are surrounded by messages that encourage them to be strong young women and succeed in whatever endeavor they choose. But they are also bombarded with messages from the popular culture about the excitements of being cool, dating, competing, and winning. Barbie, the biggest-selling doll in the world, is all about dressing up, going out with boys, and being a hip teenager.

But Pleasant Rowland, creator of American Girl dolls, believed there were many young girls who were in no particular hurry to grow up and start competing and plenty of mothers and fathers who felt the same way. These girls, she believed, were still more interested in dolls than in boys, and they wanted dolls that looked like they did—like girls.

The result of Rowland's conviction has been the emergence of American Girl: a $370 million brand of premium dolls that has sold seven million dolls since 1986 and eighty-two million books (not one of which features a first-romance plot) and claims 650,000 subscribers to its magazine. At $84 each, the dolls are more than $60 pricier than a typical Barbie. And while most other tween brands are driven by short-term trends, American Girl has introduced only five new dolls to its core American Girl Collection line since 1986.

What's more, over 80 percent of the brand's sales are direct-to-customer sales, meaning that while the creation of higher quality and greater original content may entail higher cost, American Girl is able to capture more of the value than competitors who sell through nonproprietary retail channels.

Many of our trading-up stories begin with a founder's vision, and Pleasant Rowland's is one of the most vivid of all. In the fall of 1984, Rowland, then forty-four, accompanied her husband to Colonial Williamsburg for what she thought would be a vacation. "Instead," she told *FSB* magazine, "it turned into one of the seminal experiences of my life." As a teacher and history buff, she loved everything about Williamsburg—the sense of the past, the costumes, the homes, the accessories. She described "reflecting on what a poor job schools do of teaching history, and how sad it was that more kids couldn't visit this fabulous classroom of living history. Was there some way I could bring history alive for them, the way Williamsburg had for me?"

The "way" became clear to her the following Christmas, when she went shopping for gifts for her two nieces, then eight and ten years old. It was the year of the Cabbage Patch Kids, which Rowland found ugly; she was similarly unimpressed by Barbie. "Here I was," she told *FSB*, "in a generation of women at the forefront of redefining women's roles, and yet our daughters were playing with dolls that celebrated being a teen queen or a mommy. I knew I couldn't be the only woman in America who was unhappy with these Christmas choices." Then a vision "literally exploded in my brain." She imagined "a series of books about nine-year-old girls growing up in different times in history, with a doll for each of the characters with historically accurate clothes and accessories with which the girls could play out the stories."

Like many other New Luxury founders, including Ely Callaway, Jim Koch, and Jess Jackson, Pleasant Rowland funded her idea largely with her own money. She had saved some $1.2 million from textbook royalties and decided that she would risk $1 million of it on her idea.

In a single weekend, she developed the first three characters— Kirsten, Samantha, and Molly—their clothing, and the stories that would surround them. They would all be bright and interesting girls, each living in a different time period and with a detailed personal story. Samantha Parkington, one of those first dolls, is still the most popular. She is, according to the Web site description, "a bright, compassionate girl living with her wealthy grandmother in 1904. It's an exciting time of change America, and Samantha's world is filled with frills and finery, parties and play. But Samantha sees that times are not good for everybody. That's why she tries to make a difference in the life of her friend Nellie, a servant girl whose life is nothing like Samantha's!"

Rowland had no experience in doll making, but knew she wanted a very different product from the conventional molded-plastic dolls that flooded the mass market at the time—and still do today. She

Hair is "wigged" rather than rooted.

Facial expression is
stenciled on.

Historically authentic clothing—this
is a middy dress popular in 1904—
is created by high-fashion designers.

High-quality textiles with superb
construction details in cut and
stitching.

American Girl dolls have genuine differences in design and construction that translate into long-lasting performance and emotional engagement spanning generations. Photo of Samantha courtesy of the Pleasant Company.

wanted to create quality figures with a lot of character that would have expressive faces and beautiful clothing and would last through many hours of play—she did not mean these dolls to be placed in display cabinets or kept on the shelf. She located a doll maker in Germany who could turn her vision into a reality, and—as many other New Luxury leaders have done—outsourced all the production of her dolls to him. The accessories were outsourced to a manufacturer in China.

Rowland then turned to the marketing channel. She knew that Samantha would be unable to compete with Barbie on the shelves of mass-market toy retailers such as Toys "R" Us. The American Girl offices were not far from Lands' End, a direct-mail clothing retailer, and she decided to apply its strategy to her product by reaching out to girls through direct mail. In the fall of 1986, Rowland sent out five hundred thousand catalogs—far more than her direct-mail contractor advised her to send. From September 1 through December 31, 1986, the company sold $1.7 million of American Girl dolls—

the first $1 million of revenue coming in the first three months of business. Within four years, American Girl had grown to $77 million in sales, and it grew to $300 million in the five years following.

In 1998 in Chicago, American Girl Place was opened—a retail and entertainment environment that includes a theater and an original musical revue, a café, shops, a bookstore, and a variety of events and programs designed to bring the dolls and their stories even more alive for the visitors. It has become the highest-performing retail store on Michigan Avenue, Chicago's main shopping thoroughfare, and it generates $40 million in revenue each year.

Girls go to American Girl Place for "fun and fancy dining." Birthday parties include three-course lunches featuring "Savory Toast Points," "Tic-Tac-Toe Pizza," "Frittata Quiche," and "Chocolate Pudding Flower Pot." In addition to lunch, there's the Circle of Friends: An American Girl Musical. And there are after school teas, cooking classes, book signings, and the American Girl photo studio, where any child's picture can be placed on a souvenir copy of *American Girl* magazine.

The store has become a mecca for little girls, attracting more than 1 million visitors per year. Young girls beg their parents to take them to the Chicago store in much the same way that others yearn for Walt Disney World. We visited American Girl Place with Alison, the eight-year-old daughter of a close friend, and during our visit she told us about her favorite doll, Samantha Parkington. "I love Samantha," Alison said. "She is my friend. I know where she grew up and that she made it through tough times. I love to dress her and care for her. I even have clothes that match hers, so that we can dress alike." By the end of the visit, we had succeeded in spending $300—for a doll, two extra outfits, one matching outfit for Alison, two Samantha books, and a photo of Alison reproduced on the cover of *American Girl* magazine.

In 1998, her dream realized, Pleasant Rowland sold her company to Mattel, makers of Barbie, one of the catalysts of her original vision. Many observers found the sale ironic, but Rowland felt a "genuine connection with Jill Barad"—who was then CEO—"the woman who had built Barbie." She saw in Barad a woman not unlike herself: a "blend of passion, perfectionism, and perseverance with real business savvy. During the same thirteen-year period that I built American Girl from zero to $300 million, Jill built Barbie from $200 million to $2 billion." Ellen Brothers, current president of Pleasant Company, maker of American Girl dolls, continues the girl business that Rowland created. "It is not products we're selling," Brothers told us. "It is stories. It is incredibly powerful. The daughter aspires for the dolls, and the mother endorses them."

The dolls succeed on all three levels of the benefit ladder. First, they offer genuine technical differences in design, features, and methods of manufacture. Alison's mother quickly ticked off the distinctions of an American Girl doll: "They have wonderful hair, sewn seams and real buttons, shoes that tie, outfits that are authentic to the historical period, and bodies that are anatomically correct and realistic."

The hair is a particularly important characteristic of American Girl dolls. "Most dolls in the world today have rooted hair," Ellen Brothers told us. "Rooted hair is the kind you sew on a sewing machine, and it is very cheap to get that done in the factories of the world. You pick up a doll and pull back the hair and you can see the little dots. You'll see the sewing marks. From day one, Pleasant said, 'I'm going to have wigged hair.' This hair is much more expensive to manufacture, but it is the difference between night and day."

The American Girl books are as carefully created as the dolls themselves. They are produced in China, elaborate and in full color, with extensive illustrations, photographs, and special features. *Samantha's Ocean Liner Adventure*, for example, tells the story of Samantha's trip to Europe aboard the SS *Londonia*, and includes reproductions of many of the items Samantha might have enjoyed on her journey, such as the dinner menu in first class, a dance card, a game, and a luggage tag. Lots of information is contained in a charming story.

The package of beautiful dolls and rich books delivers functional differences in how girls play with the dolls. Clarissa, a seventeen-year-old, remembers playing with the dolls when she was about nine. "My friend and I made story lines based on the essential character of each doll, but we brought them into the present day, though sometimes they traveled in time to visit each other. I remember fondly starting a story in my friend's room and ending it somewhere in the far corner of her yard. The assorted outfits and accessories traveled with us; we couldn't let Samantha meet her friends for the evening in her *morning* outfit!"

Alison discovered an important functional difference in American Girl dolls when her brother threw Samantha out the window, causing an amputation. Alison's mother called the company and was told to send the doll to their "hospital," where she would receive "treatment" from an American Girl "doctor." Samantha was returned home, good as new, with a patient's bracelet around her wrist. Alison cried at the sight of her. "We can offer a 100 percent guarantee on our dolls," says Ellen Brothers. *American Girl* magazine is a critical link between company and consumer. The magazine provides a sounding board for problems the girls are facing. One writes, "My parents recently told us that they are getting a divorce. I'm really scared. Nothing helps." Another adds, "Both of my best friends are moving. I never had a best friend move before, and I don't think I can handle it. I cry just thinking about it! What should I do?" "Thank you for your wonderful magazine. I can't keep my eyes off of it. When I grow up, I want to help American girls make their dreams come true. Just like you do for me," another girl writes. An older girl adds, "You really do celebrate girls yesterday and today. You've changed my life with my mother. Every time I received an issue, our bond between mother and daughter became closer." Most important—as with all New Luxury goods—is the strong emotional connection that girls (and their mothers) make with the dolls. "Our market research says there is so much emotion wrapped up in these characters," Brothers told us, "that moms want to hand them down to their daughters. They're not put away on a shelf. As soon as I have a daughter, I want it to be hers. That's different from the collector's mentality. They don't want to open the box, because it's worth ten times more on eBay with the original box and packaging. That's a Barbie phenomenon, but it's not the American Girl phenomenon."

Much of the emotional appeal, especially to parents and grandparents, stems from the expression of values. The American Girl dolls are about civility, generosity, caring, respect for diversity, and ambition. Josefina, a Hispanic girl living in New Mexico circa 1824, hopes to be a healer. Addy, an African American girl, escapes from slavery in 1864 and learns the true meaning of freedom. Kaya, a Nez Percé Indian of 1764, shares stories with her blind sister and hopes to become a leader of her people one day. The dolls may play to classic themes, but they are not presented as stereotypes. Brothers says that they believe in the "authentic replication of anything of a historical nature." Kaya's moccasins, for example, have a little flap on the back just as traditional Nez Percé moccasins do. "One of the tribal members said to us, 'Wow! How did you know to do that?'"

For American Girl consumers, the dolls touch on three emotional spaces. They are, when playing alone, a form of Taking Care of Me—moments of quiet play and exercising of the imagination. They are also a key form of Connecting, as Clarissa attests. The dolls enable girls to connect with each other through stories and characters and to connect with their parents, especially mothers. Finally, little girls do a lot of Questing through their dolls—learning about historic times and exotic places and creating scenes and stories in which they are vicariously the heroines.

As Alison's mother told us, "I found out about American Girl from another mother. Now I'm telling all of my friends that there's a doll available that comes with a history lesson. If you want your child to read, and if you want your child to have perspective on her place in the world, then get her an American Girl doll and the books that go with it." That's word-of-mother marketing.

The American Girl vision is clear: provide girls with a wholesome, inviting way to learn through fantasy about everyday heroes and give them role models that survive and prosper under difficult conditions with respect, kindness, and appreciation. As a business, American Girl commands premium prices and earns extraordinary brand loyalty. It offers customers a continuous stream of new products supported with extensions that build on the original product idea.

"We're in entertainment *and* education," says Brothers. "It's about empowerment. It's about being the best you can be. Every character has a different passion, and there's always a moral. A lot of emotion is wrapped up in these dolls, and they become heirlooms."

Even as part of Mattel, the outsider thinking of founder Pleasant Rowland has continued. "If you ask any of our 1,200 employees what business we are in," says Brothers, "no one will say 'the toy business.' Every one of them will say, 'We're in the girl business.'"

Pets and Their People

Mothers of girl children are no more indulgent of their daughters than are owners of beloved pets. Mona, a twenty-seven-year-old single professional, had been considering adopting a cat for some time. She lives alone in a studio apartment in a city, and although she's in a long-term relationship, her boyfriend works in a different city, so Mona spends her nights alone more often than she would like. Still, she wasn't sure she wanted to take on the responsibility of caring for a pet, nor did she think it was fair to make a pet spend long hours alone during the day.

But after September 11, she took the plunge and adopted Chloe, a five-year-old tortoiseshell that is, she told us, "the most beautiful kitty in the world." Mona cites two reasons for bringing Chloe into her life. "First, and I know this sounds melodramatic," she said, "if there is a catastrophe here like there was in New York, I don't want to die alone. I'd feel much better if Chloe was with me. Second, I really felt the need for more companionship post–September 11. There's only so much solace you can get from talking with your boyfriend long distance. And seeing colleagues during the day or friends in the evening is not the same as having a fuzzy fellow creature living with you and hanging out on the bed with you watching television."

Soon enough, Chloe had become not only a fixture in Mona's life but also a major focus of spending. "She will eat nothing but premium Iams cat food," says Mona. "I often get her special kitty treats from the Three Dog Bakery around the corner. And I bought her a $120 pet carriage so when we stroll to the vet for a checkup she doesn't have to be confined in one of those tiny, cramped carriers. Spoiled enough?"

Americans love pets—62 percent of America's 105 million households are home to a pet. In addition to the 136 million dogs and cats sharing their lives with us, there are untold numbers of other creatures, including such exotic companions as fish, birds, turtles, frogs, geckos, rabbits, iguanas, chinchillas, hamsters, gerbils, rats, squirrels, opossums, snakes, prairie dogs, and an increasingly popular type of lizard known as a skink.

Although the pet population has remained fairly stable over the past decade, growing in size at a modest 1 to 2 percent annually, spending on pets has grown at a much faster rate—a compound annual growth rate (CAGR) of about 8 percent. Nearly half of all pet spending is on food; not surprisingly, the premium and super-premium brands—including Diamond Pet Foods, Eagle Pack, and Bil-Jac Foods—are growing at a 10 percent CAGR, outpacing the big makers of conventional foods, which have been growing at just 1 to 2 percent annually. The other half of pet spending is on a range of supplies and services, many of which sound remarkably human, including health care, grooming, spas, bakeries, insurance, day care, swimming lessons, psychotherapy, travel and hotels, and bedding.

The reason for this flood of pet-related spending is that Americans no longer think of their dogs and cats as pets, but as members of the family and as friends. A poll by the American Pet Association shows that humans welcome dogs and cats into their homes because they want "someone to play with" and "companionship." Thirty percent of those polled said that they were as attached to their dog as they were to their best friend, 14 percent said they were as attached to their dog as to their children, and 10 percent felt as attached to their dog as to their spouse.

Although there was a rise in pet adoptions after the September 11 attacks, the fundamental drivers behind pet spending are the ones we have been discussing throughout this book—people are seeking ways to take care of themselves and make connections with others, whether human beings or animals. More and more Americans are living alone or as couples without children and feel the need for a live-in companion. Young childless couples, married or not, think of having pets as a way to "test the waters" of parenthood. Empty nesters see pets as a partial substitution for the children who now live away from home. Young single women and divorced women get a pet to provide protection, companionship, and solace.

(Forty-five percent of women aged thirty-five to fifty-four who have been divorced, separated, or widowed own a pet.) And, in addition to companionship, pets provide seniors with an activity that can fill their time and bring meaning to their lives.

Pets have been humanized in American society, and as a result become subject to the same benefits of trading up as human beings. Affluent and sophisticated consumers want the best for their dogs and cats and they seek to make the most of the important emotional connection they have with them. This emotional need has led to the rise of New Luxury pet goods and the growth of the companies that create them.

The change began in the mid-1990s, when there was little differentiation among pet food brands. Consumers bought these mediocre offerings out of necessity and resignation, but they were becoming ever more frustrated by their inability to provide for their pets as well as they wanted to. Increasingly, pet owners see themselves as nurturers and caretakers of their pets. According to a survey by the American Animal Hospital Association, some 83 percent of pet owners call themselves "Mommy" and "Daddy" when talking with their pets (up from 55 percent in 1995), and almost two-thirds celebrate the pet's birthday. But the products available did not align with this emotional model.

Then a few small companies began to make technical changes in their products, making the recipes more healthful and improving the flavor and aroma; and they detailed each product to the pet owner's most trusted advisers: veterinarians. The companies formulated foods to meet the specific dietary needs of different breeds of pets. They created "life stage" diets, designed for the requirements of animals of different ages. They offered a wider variety of food forms, including moist, dry, biscuits, cookies, pizzas, and more. They developed foods for animals with special needs and owners with particular requirements –foods that promoted shiny coats, did not upset sensitive stomachs, strengthened joints, or reduced the likelihood of hair ball formation. The makers incorporated a variety of higher-quality ingredients—including real meat, organically grown vegetables, cheese, and garlic—as well as special supplements that improved product taste or promoted wellness, such as glucosamine for better joint health. And they marketed foods that aligned with religious, moral, and social values, including kosher pet food, "holistic" formulas, and "USDA inspected and approved" pet foods.

These technical benefits delivered performance benefits. Pet owners believed their dogs were healthier, looked better, were less picky in their eating habits, and were living longer or likely to do so. Most important, pet owners who treat their companions to premium foods and gourmet snacks feel they are developing a more loving relationship. They feel satisfied that they are taking good care of another being and at the same time taking care of themselves. Many owners also feel a sense of Questing in their pet ownership—they are learning the professional touch in pet management, providing their pet with all the benefits of foods developed, used, and endorsed by breeders, trainers, and other animal experts.

For these benefits, New Luxury pet-food brands can command a healthy premium. The Eukanuba Advanced Stage Veterinary Diet–Canine sells for $29 for a 16.5-pound bag, or about $1.75 per pound. Compare that to Iams Chunks at $17 for a 20-pound bag, or $.85 per pound, or Purina Kibbles and Chunks at $11.49 for a 20-pound bag, or $.57 per pound. Although New Luxury providers spend more to create their products, both in cost of goods and in marketing and distributing them, they are also able to achieve significantly higher margins. We estimate that a typical mass-market pet-food company achieves a 16 percent operating margin, while the smaller specialty brands can earn margins as high as 31 percent. The premium brands represent 20 percent of the sales volume in the pet food category, but earn 55 percent of the profits. As a result, pet food has become an important New Luxury category, at about $12 billion in annual sales, growing—all segments combined—at about 4 percent per year.

The success of the small New Luxury pet-food companies has provoked changes in marketing and channel strategy for many players in the category. Mass merchandisers are carrying more high-end products and offering their own private-label products. This category is not immune from the trading-up and trading-down phenomena. Wal-Mart's Ol'Roy is a product for frugal pet owners, and it has grown to nearly $1 billion at retail. Meanwhile, pet superstores are gaining ground as "category killers," offering a broad range of food and nonfood products and services (including medical services and training). Ninety percent of food sales at Petco are premium products and brands. The losing channels are supermarkets that continue to carry primarily conventional products at middle-market prices.

We expect that the pet care category will continue to grow in sales and profits faster than the pet population, with new players emerging and transforming additional segments of the category. As the number of nonfamily and singles households increases, it is likely that owners will devote even greater resources to their non-human companions, and the pets will gain even greater stature as family members.

As Mona told us, "Chloe's great-grandpa sent her a birthday card this year. Her great-aunt sent her a new bowl. Her godmother brought her some organic catnip from Oregon. Chloe is not just part of my family—she is becoming the axis around which my family revolves."

Eight

Inside the New American Home

The changing character of the American home is one of the clearest indicators of major shifts in our society. The home reflects not only our sense of economic well-being but also our attitudes about living, raising a family, social interaction, personal style and taste, and accomplishment. Among the thirty categories we have studied, the home ranks at the top of the trading-up list by a substantial margin—Americans distort their discretionary spending toward their home more than any other category. "The American Dream" is not only alive and well as an aspiration, it has become the emblem of our identity, the physical expression of our heart and soul.

Homes and home ownership have changed substantially over the past fifty years. In 1950, the average size of the American home was 983 square feet, and about 55 percent of households owned their homes. Two decades later, the average house had grown to 1,500 square feet, and 63 percent of households owned their houses. By 2000, the average American home was over 2,200 square feet, having grown by over 10 percent in the 1990s alone. And—thanks to years of low interest rates and greater accessibility in the mortgage markets—more than 68 percent of households owned their home in 2001. In new construction, New Luxury amenities have become almost standard. From 1970 to 2000, the share of new homes with at least 2.5 bathrooms rose from 16 percent to 56 per-

Photo copyright H. Armstrong Roberts/Corbis.

The average 1950s kitchen (top) cost about $9,000 (real 2002 dollars); today it costs more than $57,000. Photo copyright Brownie Harris/Corbis.

cent, two-car garages from 39 percent to 83 percent, and central air-conditioning from 34 percent to 85 percent.

Equally dramatic, however, has been the change in the floor plan and layout of the house. Today's homes are more open and less formal than ever before—an emphasis on an easy flow from room to room has replaced compartmentalization. Traditional living and dining rooms are giving way to larger, more open kitchens with breakfast rooms and big multipurpose family rooms, the centerpiece of which is the entertainment center or home theater, rather than the traditional fireplace. Ceilings are higher. Foyers and stairways are grander and more spacious. The master bedroom has become the master suite, complete with a spa-at-home bathroom, a sitting area, and walk-in closets. Also, the larger footprint of the house takes up a greater share of the lot. From 1985 to 2000, the ratio of average lot size to average house size fell from 10-to-1 to 5.8-to-1. It's a reversal of the traditional idea of a modest home surrounded by lots of lawn and open space; today's houses crowd the lot but open up space on the inside.

Suzanne, a stay-at-home mom with two kids (aged two and four) and a household income of about $75,000, describes the trend well. "I love my home," she says. "My husband and I built it from a blank piece of paper. We wanted a very, very open floor plan. We can watch the kids more. We love to cook and entertain, and we can have more people in one space. We eliminated the formal living room and dining room. We have just one big eating area. We have two islands, one for cooking, one for hanging out. My husband and I both like to cook. We have all stainless-steel appliances in the kitchen and a collection of brands—mostly Thermador and Sub-Zero. The quality of our appliances represents us."

Behind this trading-up phenomenon in the home lie powerful economic, demographic, and emotional drivers. Declining and low interest rates have made housing more affordable, bringing new buyers into the market and inducing existing owners to trade up. The housing affordability index, which measures the ability of a household with the median income to afford the median home price (at 100 the two are equal), has risen over 50 points since 1980, from an index score of 80 to 130. Rising equity values created a wealth effect that allows consumers to increase their spending and investing. The average homeowner today has $50,000 in unrealized gains in his home; households making more than $75,000 have over $100,000 in economic value. It's like a leveraged-buyout opportunity for the average Joe. Those who put 10 percent down on a house in 1995 earned a return on equity value of over 200 percent by 2001; those who were more conservative and put down the more traditional 20 percent earned a return on equity in excess of 100 percent. Nearly 70 percent of this equity that is tapped through home equity loans has been reinvested in the home.

Reinvestment in the housing market has shown remarkable resilience in the United States. Through the down market of 2001, new home sales and housing values remained at near-record levels. A correction may yet come; the market may be overheated and overextended. The low end of the market—the majority of first-time homeowners—is highly vulnerable to shifts in the economy. Yet any forthcoming cyclical adjustments should not be confused with longer-term trends. The fundamentals of the housing market will remain strong for the foreseeable future because they are both economic and emotional. Spending on the home has the double benefit of giving emotional pleasure today and earning a return tomorrow.

The emotional connection Americans have with their home is powerful, deep, and complex, touching all the emotional spaces. The home is an important statement of a person's personal brand—her style, taste, sophistication, priorities, and values. The homeowner tends to personify the house, talking about its heart, soul, intelligence, style, grace, and beauty almost as if it were an extension of herself. The home is also a means of "living your best life," to borrow a phrase from Oprah Winfrey. It is about Connecting with family and friends, nurturing and nostalgia, safety and security, and Taking Care of Me. It also taps the emotional space of Questing—in creating and enriching their homes, consumers find adventure, learning, and self-improvement.

In our study of consumer spending behavior, the home had the most powerful combination of high emotional intensity and a broad base of consumers trading up. More than 55 percent of respondents indicated a strong propensity to trade up on home-related spending.

The events of September 11 contributed to a trend that had been building for years. More and more people are turning inward for emotional fulfillment, to the comfort, warmth, connections, and security that lie within their castle.

Spending more on the home category to get the very best makes you feel . . .	Percentage who strongly agree or agree
Happy	78
Safe	72
Successful	61
Like I'm taking care of myself	60
Family oriented	58
Confident	57
Like I'm improving myself	52
Better about myself	52
Accomplished	50
Like I'm living my best life	48
Smart	46
Like someone of style and taste	42

The richness and complexity of this emotional response can be seen in the way consumers relate to the various rooms of the new American home.

Take the kitchen, for example. Once separated from the flow of household traffic, the new American kitchen has become the heart of the home. For the past five years, kitchen remodeling has topped the list of home improvements, with over 65 percent of all projects in 2000 involving a kitchen renovation. The new kitchen is the primary space for Connecting—the command center of family interaction and coordination. For many, the kitchen has also become the nexus of entertaining and social interaction with friends. As one consumer put it: "When you have a party, everybody ends up hanging out in the kitchen. That's where you spend so much of your time, whether you're cooking, eating, or sitting around and yakking." That helps explain why professional-grade appliances like Sub-Zero refrigerators, Miele dishwashers, and Viking ranges—and corresponding interpretations from Whirlpool, General Electric, and Jenn-Air—have grown so quickly in popularity. They are showpieces in the Connecting space. Even those who can't cook, or don't like to, want the badge of sophistication, accomplishment, intelligence, and authenticity that these appliances supply. Says Russell Morash, creator of the television program *This Old House*, "We've moved away from well-mannered out-of-the-way appliances to in-your-face kitchen as theater."

Next on the remodeling wish list is the new American bathroom, the master bath in particular. The master bath taps a different emotional space than the kitchen. It's less about Connecting and more about Taking Care of Me—my time, my space, my personal sanctuary—a refuge of escape, renewal, bliss, and well-being. It appeals fundamentally to an intense need to reduce stress and get a few moments alone, particularly for working women. Top-end amenities include his and her vanities, heated floor, a Jacuzzi bath, high-end ceramics, marble and stone, towel warmers, European-style fixtures, and precision spray showerheads. In response to the growing demand for "bathroom retreats," suppliers have upgraded their product lines and expanded the range of offerings across a wider range of prices. At Sears's Great Indoors, for example, the shopper finds a wall display (interactive: push a button and activate the spray) of more than one hundred showerheads, priced from $13 to more than $450, a thirty-four-times range. Similarly, prices for toilets at Lowe's range from $44 to $731 for a top-of-the-line Kohler model, a sixteen-times range.

The family room—or "adventure center"—comes next. Like the kitchen, it's a place of Connecting, as well as a space of Questing for escape, adventure, and learning. In past generations, the focus was on comfort and style, and the fireplace was the hub. Today the focus is on experience, whether it's replicating the experience of a movie theater or taking a virtual tour of the globe via the Internet. Factory sales of home theater components and systems grew from $8.2 billion in 1996 to $12.5 billion in 2001, an 11 percent annual growth rate. Home theaters had an estimated household penetration of 25 percent in 2001, and personal computers can be found in more than 67 percent of American homes.

Both categories exhibit high participation rate and high emotional involvement. At the emotional core lies a need for adventure, learning, and experience (similar to the emotional underpinning of the rapid growth in travel), and the convergence of this need with new technological capabilities is bringing entertainment and personal computing together. John Sculley, former chief of Apple Computer, calls the iMac an enabler in "the democratization of filmmaking." Use your digital video camera to capture memories and experiences, edit the material on your personal computer, overlay some cool music, press your own DVD, gather family or friends, and presto—you're a film director, movie producer, entertainer, and entertainment complex all in one. Or store your entire library of audio CDs on your home computer, create playlists for different moods or occasions, and connect to your sound system. You become your own DJ. Technology brings this democratic form of New Luxury to the middle market at a rapidly accelerating rate, just as more and more consumers are looking for a greater sense of experience and adventure in their lives. Prices for a new entertainment technology often fall by 30 to 70 percent in the first year or two on the market. In 1997, the average price of a DVD player was about $400; today, you can buy one for under $100.

Winners and Losers

The trading-up phenomenon in the new American home has created three groups of winners. "Enablers" like Home Depot and Lowe's have helped create and sustain home improvement activity. "Democratic arbiters of style" have helped consumers trade up to a more sophisticated sense of style and expression. "Appliance innovators" have helped consumers to make a statement about their skill or to learn and explore, or enabled them to spend less time on boring chores and more time on interesting and emotionally engaging pursuits. The major losers are the "old retail" stores that got stuck in the middle, failed to evolve, or never understood the powerful aspiration behind the trading-up movement. The traditional hardware store, for example, was based on the assumption that Americans tinkered with and fixed their homes when necessary. These stores were not positioned to tap into—and inspire—the bigger, bolder dreams that helped the big-box retailers and specialty stores like Restoration Hardware grow so quickly. Most department stores, which once had a strong business in home furnishings, stood still as home category after category was attacked by specialty players with more sophistication and expertise— and a far more exciting, compelling consumer experience.

Battle of the Titans: Home Depot and Lowe's

The growth of Home Depot during the 1990s was nothing short of spectacular. At the beginning of the decade, the retailer had $3.8 billion in sales. By 2000, sales exceeded $50 billion, and market value was above $120 billion. With low prices and a vast assortment of goods, it was a place where home improvers could both economize and splurge. One woman told us, "I come to Home Depot just to dream. My husband and I come here twice a month. Sometimes we buy things. But mostly, we dream, and we plan our future. We have a series of projects we want to accomplish over the next five years."

Lowe's is an aggressive challenger to Home Depot. While it is also a warehouse store focused on value, consumers tell us it is cleaner, more logically organized, and more female-friendly than Home Depot. It has better displays and stocks goods at a wider range of prices. The retailer has also achieved the "Costco effect" in home improvement: the ability to attract a broad demographic group and sell premium products in a discount format. In Lowe's 2001 annual report, CEO Robert Tillman described his version of the trading-up strategy:

Another important merchandising and store operations initiative is our "Up the Continuum" strategy. Today, more than ever, our homeowner customers are spending more time in, and money on, their single most valuable asset . . . their home. And for the most part, they think of their expenditures as investments, which provide both current enjoyment as well as financial return.

Up the Continuum is simply recognizing the consumer's migration to quality when it comes to investing in their home. Customers tell us they want, and are willing to pay for, quality, brand-name merchandise that's unique, consistent with their lifestyle and tastes, and lasts longer and performs better. Lowe's merchants are shifting the product mix away from our historical dependency on opening-price-point merchandise on one end of the continuum to a more balanced mix within the middle and upper end of the lines, by profiling and marketing our assortments differently. We're not abandoning our opening price points, just focusing more of our resources (floor space, inventory investment and advertising) from the "Good" merchandise to the "Better, Best and Premium" products.

During the 1990s, Lowe's grew from just over $2.8 billion to almost $20 billion, creating $35 billion in market value. As the retailer refined its positioning and concept, it gained momentum. Sales grew 18 percent per year from 1997 to 2001. In the down market from 2001 to 2002, sales from comparable stores—a key barometer of retail strength—rose a healthy 6 percent, while total sales jumped 20 percent and earnings rose 43 percent. Compared to Home Depot, Lowe's has similar sales per square foot, but a higher gross margin per square foot (a better measure of retailer productivity) and a higher operating margin. In this competition, Lowe's appears to be winning.

Arbiters of Style, Taste, and Sophistication

Building or renovating the home is just the starting point for trading up; a home also needs warmth, character, elegance, personality, and a sense of style. It must reflect the values, lifestyle, and aesthetic taste of its owner. And thanks to New Luxury arbiters of style and taste, middle-market consumers have more access than ever to a broad array of sophisticated, higher-quality housewares and home furnishings. One designer has called the trend "massophistication." The innovators include Gordon Segal (Crate and Barrel), Chuck Williams (Williams-Sonoma), Martha Stewart (Martha Stewart Living Omnimedia), and New Luxury designers such as Philippe Starck and Michael Graves.

Gordon Segal is a pioneer in defining the New Luxury home. He opened the first Crate and Barrel store in 1962, and by 1990 his company had grown to $135 million. In 2002, sales surpassed $850 million on the strength of consistent annual growth rates of 18 percent or more for most of the 1990s. The company specializes in providing high-quality European-style housewares and home furnishings at an attainable price point and great value—the sweet spot of the masstige segment. In stemware, for example, Crate and Barrel offers seventy-five styles of glasses priced from $2.50 to $11.95 per piece, well above most economy brands but still below the super-premium segment. The European-inspired designs are clean, modern, distinctive, and artistic, appealing to a broad range of tastes and useful for many different occasions. The stores are visually appealing and warmly engaging. The company's mission is clear and succinct: "To inspire people to think of their home in new ways."

Like many New Luxury enterprises, Gordon Segal's business was born of an epiphany—this one the result of life circumstances, international travel, and cultural exposure. "Crate and Barrel was a store that started because of the experience Carol and I had when we got married," Segal told us. "When we went to register for wedding gifts, I was really frustrated by what we saw. At that time, you had a choice between the really expensive items like Baccarat crystal or cheaper stuff that didn't have much style or quality. On our honeymoon in the Virgin Islands, we found a little store selling beautiful Scandinavian tabletop and kitchenware. The prices were amazingly affordable. We were amazed at the quality and value. We talked to the owner to find out how he did it and he told us he worked directly with suppliers from Denmark."

Segal was equally influenced by the two months he spent living in Europe after college. He not only experienced a different way of living, but saw a different world of products: beautiful glassware and stemware, tabletop, and other home furnishings made by local artisans and craftsmen and sold at reasonable prices. He said to his wife, Carol, "This is the way I want to live my life." Segal's vision was to bring the quality, style, and taste he experienced in Europe to the American middle market. He calls it "the democratization of style and taste." He thinks of the Crate and Barrel style as very different from Old Luxury, which he considers "almost wasteful. We're selling lifestyle, a way of living. It's like a nice bottle of wine. Not the $300-a-bottle kind. More like the $20 or $30 kind. Wonderful taste and quality, but something many people can afford."

Segal built his business on five principles:

Principle 1: Break the wholesaler-importer-retailer value chain. Segal saw the opportunity to work directly with artisans and smaller factories, eliminating the markups of the importers and wholesalers that were standard at the time. By working directly with designers and factories, he could invest more in product quality and deliver these premium products at a price that was accessible to many. He could also bring to market a broader range of more interesting, unique designs—different from his competitors' and distinctive enough to let people express their individual sense of style. This enables Segal to sell goods at up to 50 percent lower prices than department stores and provide highest-quality goods at the low prices.

Principle 2: Maximize the advantage in global sourcing and design. From the beginning, global sourcing was a core competitive advantage for Crate and Barrel. Over the years, Segal continued to build his company's global reach and capability. "In the 1970s, we used to make two big trips to Europe with a small merchant team. But the cost of doing business internationally has fallen dramatically, and that has allowed us to really extend our reach. International travel costs a fraction of what it used to. Faxes and the Internet make it much easier to conduct business internationally. Now our merchant and design teams go to Europe every couple of months and are in constant contact with our partners. We want to visit more unique locations, and find more interesting items. Europe is still the center, but we are all over the globe now. We work very closely with our team of American and European designers to make sure the products live up to our high standards of design and quality. Once we get something we really like, we buy it in big quantities. We take risks."

Principle 3: Maintain an unrelenting, maniacal focus on quality and style. Gordon Segal is a perfectionist with purpose. From the beginning, he built his brand by delivering superior quality and unique design at a "tremendous value." "You have to work really closely with your suppliers. You have to know the product, the way it's made, the particular way the glass is blown, the quality level. It has to be genuinely better. We are extremely demanding of our manufacturers, but we're also good partners." He has instilled his sense of values throughout the organization: "We are very self-critical, very open-minded, always seeking perfection. We set a very high standard."

Principle 4: Create a magical, captivating retail experience. Among major retailers, Crate and Barrel is one of the best at delivering a differentiated, exciting, emotionally compelling store experience. Visual presentation includes dazzling displays of color, light, and reflection. Glassware is meticulously presented in creative, open displays. The store layout is clear and easy to navigate. Merchandise is presented in "vignettes"—clusters of products that complement one another and are logical to the consumer. Management thinks of visual merchandising not only as an art, but as a core capability and competitive advantage. In-house architects design every store so it fits with the special characteristics and nuances of its location. Inside and out, neatness is rule number one. "We're neurotically neat. We say it takes three years to make a store manager neurotically neat enough to run things." Glassware and tabletop items are carefully wiped before being displayed and then wiped again at the register before being packed for the customer. Store associates constantly dust and refresh the displays. Store managers undergo extensive training.

Principle 5: Build loyalty, build the brand. Some would argue that the pace of Crate and Barrel's store expansion leaves much of its market potential untapped. Several large markets still do not have a Crate and Barrel store, and several competitors have expanded much more rapidly. But to Gordon Segal, growing too quickly runs the risk of undermining the level of consistency and control over the brand that is required to maintain the Crate and Barrel standard. "It's more about a belief and a mission than growth," he says. His objective is to build brand loyalty with an uncompromising focus on the fundamentals and a sustainable growth rate. Given his model, he does not see a need for broadcast advertising—customer advocacy, store expansion, and catalogs and the Web are his main vehicles for building the brand.

Segal sees the trading-up pattern clearly. "People are traveling more, seeing the world more, becoming exposed to culture and taste in many different ways. There's an awareness of quality, maturing of taste and growing sophistication of the middle and upper middle class. They're reading more, broadening their exposure. Whether it's California wines, better restaurants, travel to London or Paris— tastes are getting more refined. You see it especially in young people. Young chefs travel the world. They train with the very best. They bring taste and sophistication back home. I remember Boston in the 1970s. I used to lament that if you wanted to experience a truly world-class restaurant, you would have to get on the shuttle to New York. Now there are six or eight truly world-leading restaurants in Boston." The big winner, Segal believes, is the American consumer: "Consumers are immensely better off. Sophistication and taste are within reach of the middle class."

The Williams-Sonoma story is very different from that of Crate and Barrel, but it is a variation on the trading-up pattern. In 1947, Chuck Williams moved to Sonoma, California, with the dream of building homes. An avid cook, he traveled to Paris in 1952, where he gained his first exposure to classic French cooking techniques and equipment. It was eye-opening: "Cookware stores like E. De-hillerin or the housewares section of Bazar de l'Hôtel de Ville in Paris were unlike anything most Americans had ever seen. I was completely fascinated not only by the vast array of kitchen tools and accessories, but also by how they were displayed. Pots and pans in every conceivable shape and size, all out in the open." Returning from Europe, he decided it was time to modify his dream. In 1954 he bought a hardware store in downtown Sonoma, and within two years he had converted it into a specialty store for French cookware. He emphasized not just the merchandise but the experience of being in the store—through the fixtures and the cues of authenticity, and by telling rich and compelling product stories. Like Gordon Segal, Williams developed innovative techniques for dramatic visual merchandising and presentation. He designed and crafted his own fixtures and shelving systems to showcase each cookware piece both individually and as part of an overall collection. He recalls that "cookware and tools and things weren't displayed before. They were just piled up and never very attractive."

Williams operated just one store throughout the 1960s, constantly refining and improving his business. He launched the Williams-Sonoma catalog and incorporated his company in 1972. Shortly thereafter he opened a second store on Rodeo Drive in Beverly Hills, followed a year later by stores in Palo Alto and Costa Mesa. Then, in 1978, an entrepreneur named Howard Lester visited the Williams-Sonoma store in Beverly Hills and saw an opportunity to grow the business to a much larger scale. He convinced Chuck Williams to sell him the company and remain on as "merchant visionary," and stylistic leader. The two proved to be a powerful team. Williams focused on creating coherent, distinctive presentations of style and taste, while Lester took charge of building out the retail concepts on a large scale. In 1986, Williams published his first book, *The Williams-Sonoma Cookbook with a Guide to Kitchenware*. It was the first in what would become a series of publications about cooking and entertaining, including over one hundred titles, the bestselling cookbook series of the 1990s, and *Taste* magazine, which launched in 2000. Lester focused his attention on growth and retail execution. During the 1980s, he helped leverage the company's skill and sophistication into other segments of the home, first with Gardeners Eden in 1982 (later divested), followed by Hold Everything in 1983, and the acquisitions of Pottery Barn in 1986 and the Chambers catalog in 1989. By 2001, Williams-Sonoma had grown to over $2.1 billion from $287 million in 1990, and to nearly $2.4 billion in market value. The stores generate high productivity (over $600 per square foot) and high operating margins.

Williams and Lester built their success by focusing on quality, taste, and expertise while at the same time providing the customer with a sense of experience, authenticity, and adventure. Their brands were aimed at the emotional space of Individual Style, both self-expressing and signaling style, sophistication, and discernment. They also satisfied the Questing need for learning and adventure. Williams did this through the art of storytelling and romancing his merchandise. Almost every product in the store is presented with a sense of place, history, culture, or adventure. These are excerpts from the Williams-Sonoma catalog that provide context and romance to their home products:

> Legend has it that fondue was created by a shepherd in the Swiss Alps who was inspired to heat his nightly dinner of wine and cheese in a pot. Our Ruffoni Copper Fondue Pot, crafted by artisans at the Ruffoni factory in the Italian Alps, is ideal for making classic cheese as well as chocolate and meat fondues.

> *Deruta Serving Bowl.* This magnificent serving bowl is hand painted in Deruta, an Italian ceramics center that has been famous since the sixteenth century. Using the same methods that have been employed for centuries, local artisans create the pieces by hand and decorate each bowl with the classic Derutan scrolls and foliage.

> *Alziari Extra-Virgin Olive Oil and Fallot Dijon Mustard.* When lightly dressed in vinaigrette, fresh, leafy greens are transformed into an appealing first or final course. For a classic dressing, combine this extra-virgin olive oil and Dijon mustard with your choice of vinegar. The oil, ideal for cooking as well as for vinaigrettes, is produced at the 134-year-old Moulin Alziari, the last olive mill still operating in Nice, in the South of France. Alziari selects the best ripe olives and then cold presses them within twelve hours of harvesting to ensure a low acidity level. The mustard is made at a factory near Dijon in Burgundy, where traditional millstones are used to crush the mustard seeds.

At one of the nearly two hundred Williams-Sonoma Grand Cuisine stores, these stories come alive in a "retail as theater" setting. The consumer finds a broad array of cooking-related merchandise at premium—but not prohibitively high—prices, presented with imagination and romance. At the center of the store is a full-service kitchen for cooking demonstrations and food tastings. The experience transports the avid consumer into a world of global culture, refinement, and culinary enjoyment.

Williams and Lester applied their formula to other retail brands with excellent results. When they bought Pottery Barn from the Gap in 1983, the store had no clear point of view or market advantage. Williams and Lester transformed it into a $1 billion home-furnishings brand by giving it a strong sense of style, original design, better quality and value, and an engaging consumer experience. They took a largely American concept and infused it with a blend of European and American style. They positioned it in masstige territory—premium but attainable—and imbued it with emotion. Their catalog reads: "Each [product] has a story—here are just a few of our favorites."

Manhattan Chair. Many of our most popular furnishings take their inspiration from classic European designs. The origins of the Manhattan club chair, for instance, can be traced back to the Parisian nightclubs of the 1930s and later the New York clubs from which they derive their name. We came across this chair at a Paris flea market some years ago. Our designers updated the look and feel—wrapping it in full grain leather and giving it a higher back and deeper seat—but the chair remains an homage to another era.

Charlotte Quilt. We often find inspiration in our country's rich history of design. A good example is the classic American quilt. Every season we introduce a collection of exclusively made designs based on American motifs, like the Log Cabin and the Lone Star. The centerpiece of this series is our annual Collector's Quilt, which features dozens of hand-stitched and embroidered holiday icons.

Napoleon Chair. Italian artists shape Napoleon chairs out of solid beech, staining and sanding each piece by hand to bring out its individual character. Of course there are easier and less time-consuming ways to make a chair, but part of the reason people love Pottery Barn is the attention to detail that goes into every item we offer.

Martha Stewart has been a central force in the trading-up phenomenon. At the height of her influence in 2001, she was generating 88 million consumer impressions each month through her magazines, television programs, catalog, retail business, and Web site. At the core of her success was a highly aspirational brand premise. "I wanted to be comprehensive, expansive, all encompassing. I wanted to take a subject, not a brand. I took the subject of 'Living.'" Her influence on the middle market was profound: she inspired millions of Americans to reach for a richer, more tasteful, more sophisticated lifestyle. She was called the "mentor to the masses," an icon as influential as Oprah Winfrey. She said: "Oprah is a preacher. I'm a teacher." She had an abiding belief in the aspiration and latent potential for the middle market to trade up.

Martha's brand premise allowed her to build a business extending across a wide set of categories and a price band of ten times or more from low to high, from Martha Stewart Everyday at Kmart to the upscale Martha By Mail catalog. Her upscale customers didn't seem to mind that she had a line for a mass merchandiser, as the two lines grew together in parallel worlds of style. In the eyes of the market, her brand stood for the best possible quality and style for the price, regardless of the retail segment. At Kmart, her Martha Stewart Everyday line was priced at a 30 to 200 percent premium to the traditional Kmart merchandise. But it provided the consumer with much higher quality and a superior value. In creating the line, she was a relentless, passionate, forceful advocate for the consumer. She demanded higher quality and, through the force of her hands-on leadership style, created a class of merchandise that did not exist in the marketplace. She educated the Kmart customer on thread counts in sheets and types of cotton in towels. She brought her sophisticated color palette and design aesthetic to the middle market. As an outsider, she was unencumbered by the arbitrary segmentation of the market created by unimaginative manufacturers. She redrew the boundaries, creating a business at Kmart that grew from zero to $1.5 billion in three years.

Her line continued to grow in 2002 even after the onset of her personal troubles. Enmeshed in controversy, she was nevertheless the only bright spot for a struggling, poorly run retailer.

If Martha had a major shortcoming in building out her vision, it was her ignorance of retail. She signed an exclusive distribution agreement with the worst possible retail partner. She failed to understand the importance of the experience to the consumer. Her products looked beautiful and tasteful, but the presentation resembled a garage sale—no elegance, no grace, no Wow! factor. Her products were frequently out of stock, which frustrated the consumer. Martha Stewart, an avowed control freak, gave up a critical element of control over her brand. To make matters worse, her royalty arrangement captured only a small sliver of the value she created. Had she partnered with Target, Martha Stewart Everyday might have grown to twice its current size, and the brand would have been enhanced rather than threatened.

As New Luxury has cascaded to the mass market, more and more designers who are used to designing superpremium goods have joined the movement. Being democratic can be more hip than being exclusive, and more challenging as well. Philippe Starck, described as "the man who sets the bar for cool," is a leader in this new generation of iconoclasts. He has a remarkable record of accomplishment in high design, including the interiors of the Paramount, Royalton, and Hudson hotels in New York, the Delano hotel in Miami, the famous Café Costes in Paris, the private apartments of the Elysée Palace, and a series of sophisticated, exclusive furnishings, including bathtubs, desks, and small appliances.

Yet Starck's greatest joy in life, the one that brings him the greatest sense of accomplishment, is creating designs that put quality and style within the reach of everyday people. In 2002, he launched the Philippe Starck line of products at Target, an assortment of goods for home, office, kitchen, bath, and baby. "Working with Target has helped me to fulfill a dream that I've had all my life. My goal in this democratization of design is to make possible the most joyful and exciting things and experiences for the maximum number of people. Today, we don't need more design, more pretensions—we need more happiness and magic available to everyone. I want everyone to have the best. . . . The new modern elegance is multiplication. That means if you are lucky enough to have a good idea, you have a duty, with generosity, to try to give this good idea to the maximum number of people." Starck takes everyday items like toothbrushes and baby bottles and gives them flair and special-ness. "I want to try and inject them with intelligence and humor. Objects should be long-lived and honest." He also injects them with quality and value by constantly looking to remove all unnecessary costs. He simplifies production by simplifying design and making the most efficient use of resources. As an example, he has reduced the production cost of his signature Café Costes chair from about $550 in 1984 to $29 today.

Appliance Innovators: Sub-Zero, Viking, and Whirlpool

The final group of winners in the home sector has been the manu-facturers of premium appliances. These higher-end appliances have become the centerpieces of home improvement, and their growth has consistently defied expectations. The combination of innova-tion and consumer needs has created a resegmentation of the appli-ance category, shattering conventional beliefs about price ceilings and price-volume relationships. Even in the down market of 2001 and 2002, the premium segment sustained its growth and share gain. In refrigerators, for example, the premium and superpremium segment (units over $1,000) grew from 18 percent of units sold in 2000 to 26 percent of units sold in 2002, with an annual growth of 15 percent. For the most part, the innovation underlying this trading-up activity has been driven by category outsiders who have challenged and redefined the market, or by established players re-sponding to their actions.

Sub-Zero created the trading-up revolution in refrigerators by reconceptualizing the appliance and the role it played in the kitchen. This category outsider began as an industrial refrigeration shop back in 1945, serving primarily University of Wisconsin laboratories and national vegetable processors. In the mid-1950s the company built its first in-home unit at the request of a wealthy Milwaukee-area family who wanted a refrigerator to blend in with the rest of the kitchen.

Sales grew slowly and steadily throughout the 1960s, 1970s, and early 1980s, mostly on endorsements by celebrity cooks and home designers. By the mid-1980s, word of the Sub-Zero name had spread, and sales accelerated dramatically, growing from $50 million in manufacturer sales in 1985 to over $250 million by 2001.

Coming from a commercial orientation, Sub-Zero brought many technical innovations to the category, including dual compressors (one each for the refrigerator and freezer), precision temperature controls, tighter vacuum seals, the highest energy efficiency, and cantilevered drip-proof shelves. As architect James Kruhly said, "When you close the door on a Sub-Zero, it just has a completely different sound. It's like when you close the door on a Mercedes." Perhaps Sub-Zero's biggest breakthrough, though, was in design and customization—the ability to build the refrigerator seamlessly into the aesthetic look of the kitchen. With the same twenty-four-inch depth of most kitchen cabinets (traditional refrigerators are twenty-eight inches deep), Sub-Zeros looked like part of the cabinet furniture or even the walls themselves. At $3,500 and up, they made a powerful statement of taste and sophistication. Eventually (though remarkably slowly), the mass-market makers caught on and began developing better products for the emerging premium and superpremium segments. The premium segment grew quickly, with products like the GE Profile Artica and Whirlpool Conquest.

A similar story played out in ranges and cooktops. This time the innovation came from Fred Carl, Jr., a fourth-generation home designer and builder in Greenwood, Mississippi. In the mid-1970s, he dropped out of the School of Architecture at Mississippi State University to help in his father's construction business and raise a family. As he and his wife began building their first home, he looked for a restaurant quality stove for the kitchen. He found none on the market, partly because the large manufacturers had not seen the opportunity and partly because no one had figured out a way to master the high heat output and safety requirements in a residential appliance. "I found it unbelievable that there was nothing like this and that no one recognized the need," he said. "I knew the product needed to be created." In his spare time, he developed the design for his dream stove and took it to manufacturer after manufacturer.

"They all said, 'We can't do this.'" In 1986, he found a contract manufacturer who would build twenty units. By 1989, he had built his own factory and was on his way to creating a new segment of the appliance market. From 1990 to 2000, the company grew from virtually nothing to over $200 million in company sales, or roughly $400 million at retail. Like many New Luxury entrepreneurs, he was driven in part by an earlier failure, in his case dropping out of Mississippi State's School of Architecture: "Not fulfilling my dream to finish architecture school at State was a major blow. However, it instilled in me the determination not to let a dream slip away again. I kept this constantly in mind the entire time I struggled to establish Viking Range Corporation. Missing out on one dream enabled me not to miss out on another." Today, Viking Range offers an extensive line of commercial-type appliances, including dishwashers, refrigerators, wine coolers, and cookware for both the indoor and outdoor kitchen.

As Sub-Zero did with its refrigerators, Carl emphasized authenticity, expertise, and technical superiority in everything he did. His stove had four to six high-output burners (traditional high-end ranges generally had none) producing 15,000 BTUs—nearly twice the heat output of other ranges—for restaurant-style searing and browning; grilling surfaces; a 1,500-degree infrared broiler for searing meats; improved insulation and safety features; and the look of an authentic commercial range.

To build his brand, Carl got the endorsements and support of expert chefs, cooking aficionados, and other key influencers, and created a market where none had existed. He created the Viking Culinary Arts Centers (now numbering eleven), worked with prominent chefs to create new recipes and offer cooking advice, cultivated relationships in the designer community, created the Viking Range cooking awards for excellence in culinary media programming, and advertised selectively in upscale magazines like *Architectural Digest*. His marketing created an awareness and aspiration that extended well beyond his base of buyers. As mainstream players followed, the luxury cascade resulted in strong growth in the premium segment.

Sub-Zero and Viking helped create and propel the "kitchen as theater" trend in home goods, but the conventional manufacturers were slow to understand it and see the potential in their own home-goods categories—except, at last, Whirlpool. It showed how a traditional market leader can capitalize on the trading-up phenomenon, with the highly successful launch of the Duet washer and dryer in 2001, priced at $1,299 for the washer and $799 for the companion dryer—more than four times the average price of other Whirlpool washers and dryers. Consumers quickly figured out that the Duet washer and dryer were the best on the market. Retailers sold out of Duets quickly, and Whirlpool has been struggling to meet demand ever since.

To make the breakthrough, Whirlpool had to defy long-held industry beliefs, ignore its own market research, and abandon a number of category practices. "We had convinced ourselves through research that appliances were not an emotional purchase," Joe Foster, marketing director–Whirlpool Brand Fabric Care, told us. "The consumer has lots of ways to spend her disposable income, and there are so many other, more emotional, purchases on the list. We didn't understand how we could turn appliances into an emotional purchase, primarily because our industry had been busy making cost and quality improvements and incremental benefit advances. The typical washer lasts twelve to fourteen years, and we had never given the consumer a reason to trade out sooner than that. We predicted sales using a mathematical formula. How many homes are being built. When was the last big blip in the replacement cycle. We thought we were in a very predictable, mature industry with easily anticipated swings up or down year after year."

In 1997, Maytag launched a premium washer and dryer called Neptune. It offered an updated technology called horizontal access (HA). These HA machines were front-loading washers with large capacity, superior washing properties, and no agitator in the middle of the drum to create wear and tear on clothing. They were popular in Europe, but had never taken root in the United States. Although Maytag's Neptune generated strong initial sales, Whirlpool did not take the threat seriously at first. According to Foster, "We had done research that said the U.S. consumer preferred a top-loading washing machine over a front-loading machine. We did not believe that a front-loading product was going to be successful. A number of in-

dustry experts predicted the front-loading segment would grow to
no more than 5 or 6 percent of the industry." As Maytag was launching Neptune, Whirlpool was finalizing plans for an answer to it—an
innovative, top-loading product called Calypso. Launched in 1998,
Calypso matched many of the functional benefits of the Neptune:
large capacity, no agitator, superior cleaning, gentle on clothes,
energy- and water-efficient. It was strong on technical innovation,
but it looked like a traditional washer, and met with only modest
success.

Duet came about very differently than Calypso. In the late
1990s, Whirlpool had created a global technology organization designed to identify, leverage, and commercialize technologies across
markets. In Germany, the company had over fifty years of experience with horizontal access technology. Engineers tore down and
tested the Calypso and Neptune products and convinced Foster and
his colleagues they could create a technically superior product by
leveraging European technology and design capabilities. Whirlpool
invested a comparatively small amount in engineering capital in a
Europe-based team with the mandate to create a superior front-
loading HA machine designed specifically for the U.S. market—
primarily to hedge its bets, in case Calypso did not succeed. Whirlpool
launched this new platform called Duet in 2001, and it took the
market by storm, quickly outpacing both Calypso and Neptune. Despite all the predictions and the research that showed HA machines
would never gain more than a 6 percent share, Duet helped build HA
share to 10 percent in 2002. "It's a lot bigger than originally pro-
jected," says Foster, "and it continues to grow."

Duet's leap off the industry demand curve was based on breakthrough advantages on all three levels of the consumer benefit ladder.

Technically, the Duet washer has many advantages over a conventional machine: twice the capacity, demonstrably superior cleaning,
gentleness with fabrics (including silk, wool, and fine washables), resource and environmental efficiency (⅔ the water, less energy, reduced need for bleach), higher-revolution spinning (taking out
20 percent more water in the spin cycle), intelligent sensors in the
dryer that vary the heat output over the course of the dry cycle,
and synchronization of the washer and dryer cycles. The European

design is dramatic, sophisticated, and upscale—it stands apart from all other competitors and signals the consumer that this is indeed a radically different and superior appliance. The machines are stackable, or they can be placed side by side on pedestals that make them easier to access, and they contain a drawer for additional storage space as well.

Functionally, these technical advantages allow consumers to get their clothes cleaner, do fewer loads, eliminate the normal downtime between washer and dryer cycles, save precious time, easily wash such big items as comforters, pillows, and pet blankets, take fewer trips to the cleaners, save over $150 per year in energy and resource costs, be more environmentally friendly, protect and take care of clothes, preserve fine washables, and easily handle such big jobs as fabrics covered with pet hair or heavily soiled play clothes. A number of consumers told us that the Duet actually makes doing laundry fun. Imagine that. The major functional advantage, however, is the effect the Duet has on a family's lifestyle. It allows time-pressed, harried families to spend less time doing chores and more time nurturing, Connecting, or Questing. It creates the greatest luxury of all: discretionary time.

Emotionally, as hard as it may be to believe, Duet owners feel emotionally engaged with their machines. We talked with many Duet users and found an emotional connection stronger than we have seen in any other category. We asked several groups of Duet owners to prepare collages about how they feel about their Duet. We have done this exercise in many other categories, but we were surprised by the richness and intensity of the Duet collages. We also asked owners of other types of machines to do the same exercise. The two groups were worlds apart. Duet owners had unbridled energy and enthusiasm.

Duet owners loved their machines as if they were family members. As one said: "I'm a heating and air-conditioning serviceman. I have over one thousand accounts. I'm in people's houses seven or eight times a day, six or seven days a week. If I see somebody with a very old washing machine, I tell them if you're thinking about replacing it, I have the washing machine for you. It takes me a half hour to clean the furnace. We talk about the washing machine for about an hour." Other appliance owners were at best content with their machines and more often held them and the task of doing laundry in contempt.

Through their collages, the Duet owners revealed the multiple layers of their emotional connection with their appliances. They described feeling "happy inside," as if they were living a better life, being a better mom and a better person, free, less stressed, family oriented, proud of their children and the way they looked, loved and appreciated, accomplished and proud, having style, taste, and grace, as if they were taking good care of themselves, smart and intelligent, and environmentally friendly. They said:

"When people ask to see our home, because it's brand-new, I tell them you have to see my pride and joy. They ask me, do you like them? I say, I love them."

"They are our little mechanical buddies. They have personality. It's cool when they are all lit up and you are at the end of the cycle. The washer and dryer are the domestic hub. When they are running efficiently, our lives are running efficiently. They are a part of my family."

"People ask, 'If you ever sell your house, would you leave the washer and dryer?' I say, 'No, I would never leave them.' I teasingly say, 'I would rather leave my husband than my washer and dryer.'"

Many of the consumers told us that the Duet pair had allowed them to think differently about the concept of the laundry room. Laundry rooms are moving from the basement to the first floor, as part of a utility or workroom off the garage, mudroom, or kitchen. Or laundry appliances are staying in the basement but as part of a larger, better-equipped multipurpose room. The average size of the room that contains the laundry appliances has doubled over the past five years. A builder of new homes says the laundry room used to contain little more than the appliances, some wire shelving, and a fiberglass exhaust hose. "Now it's wall cabinets, undermount sinks,

Corian countertops, computer workstations, and space for potting plants or sewing. They don't even look like laundry rooms anymore. They look like kitchens." Laundry rooms—unexpectedly—have become a source of pride and a badge of style and sophistication.

While Whirlpool is aggressively developing the next generation of products to capitalize on the "laundry room as family hub" movement, other large manufacturers are missing the point. They are falling into what we call the average-customer trap: characterizing consumers in a uniform and overly simplistic way, neglecting segments that have the potential to trade up. In a typical comment, a Maytag Corporation executive said: "Our research does not indicate that people are spending more time in their laundry rooms, nor that they have a desire to."

By falling into the average-customer trap, companies can miss opportunities. It is true that a significant percentage of consumers do not care much about laundry appliances, nor are they likely to trade up in the future. And since the category is unimportant to them, they will trade down. That is why the low end of the appliance market is growing. For many others, however, the new generation of appliances fulfills a compelling emotional need, and they will trade up to it. The result is the market polarization we have seen in every product category in which a New Luxury product has had success— growth at the extremes of the market and a declining middle segment. From 1997 to 2001 the market polarized, as the midprice segment of washing machines ($400 to $600) went from 49 percent to 34 percent of the units sold, while the over $600 premium segment grew from 10 percent to 19 percent of units, and the under $400 economy segment grew from 41 percent to 53 percent unit share.

The Winning Practices of New Luxury Home Players

1. Never underestimate the customer. Targeting the "average customer" and testing against the "general population" are common pitfalls of traditional market research. Researchers have killed many new ideas with such ill-advised techniques, because no New Luxury products are aimed at an "average" consumer or "general" anything—they are meant for well-defined groups of core consumers with strong needs and interests. In the home goods category,

Martha Stewart knew this and broke the compromise between budget and taste by offering her premium home goods through the mass channel. Her $1.5 billion Martha Stewart Everyday line was based on the belief that even consumers on tight budgets would trade up within their means to products that offered better quality and more appealing aesthetics.

Target has improved on the execution of this concept, enlisting the help of world-renowned designers such as Michael Graves, Philippe Starck, Todd Oldham, and Cynthia Rowley to bring high-end, designer housewares to its very large middle-market audience. The retailer's home division represents an estimated $6 billion in sales and is one of the company's top-performing divisions, thanks in part to bestsellers like the $11 toilet brush by Michael Graves and a colorful food-storage set by Philippe Starck that sells for $13. Target increasingly appears on the wedding registries of middle-market couples alongside the specialty retailers such as Williams-Sonoma and the traditional department stores.

2. *Shatter the price-volume demand curve.* Whirlpool Duet is disproving the conventional wisdom that there is limited volume in premium-priced household durables.

3. *Create a ladder of genuine benefits.* In comparison to conventional washers, Duet has genuine technical differences that translate into functional benefits that lead to unprecedented emotional engagement for consumers. How often have you heard a consumer say that she "loves" her washing machine?

4. *Escalate innovation, elevate quality, deliver a flawless experience.* Crate and Barrel and Williams-Sonoma are masters at delivering an emotionally engaging brand experience. They offer unique, high-quality products by scouring the world for new and interesting items. They tell product stories that appeal to consumers' emotions and provide inspiration and guidance for product use. Williams-Sonoma Grand Cuisine stores offer customers cooking demonstrations and product tastings. At all these stores, shopping becomes a Questing activity, and the products offer a way to express Individual Style.

5. *Extend the price range and positioning of the brand.* Over the past three decades, Williams-Sonoma has extended its positioning from a brand focused on high-end kitchenware to cooking aficionados

(Williams-Sonoma) to an all-encompassing lifestyle brand with mass-market appeal (Pottery Barn, Pottery Barn Kids, Pottery Barn Bed & Bath). The company is now attempting to extend its price range and demographic appeal through its newest concept, West Elm—a younger, slightly less expensive alternative to Pottery Barn with a more urban-design aesthetic.

6. *Customize your value chain to deliver on the benefit ladder.* Crate and Barrel's Gordon Segal had a vision to bring high-quality European-style housewares to American consumers at a reasonable price. To do so, he recognized the need to bypass the established wholesaler-importer-retailer value chain. Working directly with smaller suppliers abroad enabled him to realize all aspects of his vision. He was able to identify distinctive products at the quality level he demanded rather than select from the same limited offering of existing wholesalers. And he could bring these distinctive products to market profitably without charging prices that the middle-market consumer could not afford.

7. *Use influence marketing—seed your success through brand apostles.* A combination of strategy and serendipity enabled Chuck Williams to leverage the popularity of Julia Child and other prominent foodies in the early 1960s to seed the success of his new store. Child became a regular at Williams-Sonoma, using its equipment on her show, *The French Chef.* Williams recalls that "The timing was perfect. Julia Child's cooking show was finding an audience. She would show how to make a soufflé one night, and the next day people would come in asking about soufflé dishes. James Beard had also started coming by the store, and we became good friends." By 1972, Williams's store had more than doubled in size, and his growing catalog business was laying the foundation for national expansion.

8. *Continually attack the category like an outsider.* Lowe's has carved out its success in the shadow of fellow big-box discounter Home Depot. Now, with its "Up the Continuum" strategy, the company is attempting to build an expanded premium-priced offering. By offering premium products in a discount format, Lowe's is both one-upping rival Home Depot (whose strategy of offering high-end product in a separate, upscale concept called "Expo" seems not to be gaining traction in the marketplace) and staving off potential threats from smaller specialty players.

Nine

Awakening the American Palate to Wine

The wine industry grew and developed in Europe over a period of centuries; it took American winemakers less than three decades to adapt and Americanize the European model, improve technical aspects of the process, create a new American taste, and trade up the middle-market consumer to a new level of wine appreciation and discernment. During the last thirty years, we have experienced a revolution—still under way—in the way Americans produce and consume wine.

Today American vintners, along with a number of influential wine critics, contend that the best American wines stand side by side in quality with the best from Bordeaux and Burgundy. While that claim may be enmeshed in a chauvinistic dispute, one thing is clear: wines of better quality and consistency have become available to the middle market at a rapid and accelerating rate, and the American wine consumer now has more wines to choose from than ever before—and with better value for the money.

Not long ago, the palate of the typical American consumer was considered crude and unsophisticated, especially in comparison to the European palate; but the new American taste in wines has had a major influence on the flavor profiles of wineries around the world. The richness and intensity of the fruit itself was first celebrated by Robert Mondavi, further commercialized by Jess Jackson, and evangelized by wine critic Robert Parker. As Italian winemaker Tina Cola writes: "To some extent, the American palate is becoming the international palate. Most people everywhere now want richer, fresher, fruitier wines." This trend, of course, has been criticized, even reviled, by many in the wine world—including winemakers, retailers, critics, and consumers—because they believe it has led to a homogenization of wine worldwide and caused consumers to be less appreciative of local tastes and differences. For American middle-market consumers, however, the trend has meant a great awakening to the pleasures and complexities of wine.

When Prohibition ended in 1933, there was virtually no American wine industry. The subsequent three decades marked the industry's darkest days, when American wine was largely a cheap, "fortified" (high-alcohol) intoxicant, associated more with skid row than taste and sophistication. The American wine awakening did not begin until the mid-1960s, when American visionaries and entrepreneurs began to build a world-class industry.

But since 1965, the wine industry in America has grown and changed significantly. Wine sales in the United States have grown on average at 8 percent annually. While consumption has shown some variability over the decades, rising and falling with various alcohol-consumption trends, per capita consumption has doubled, from about one gallon in 1966 to over two gallons in 2001. (That is still far below the per capita consumption in Europe.) In 1980, wine consumption in the United States overtook the consumption of spirits for the first time, and it now outpaces hard liquor by almost 50 percent. In the last five years, the robust growth and vitality of the trading-up phenomenon have led to the largest increase in both volume and price in the last twenty-five years. Even in the down market of 2001, sales of premium and superpremium wine grew more than 10 percent.

More striking than sales growth, however, has been the dramatic shift in the composition of wine consumption. Table wines (cork-finished 750-milliliter bottles) accounted for less than half of total U.S. consumption in the mid-1960s, with jug and bulk wine representing the dominant share. Today table wine holds an 85 percent share. Similarly, the share of better "varietal" wines—named after grape types such as Chardonnay, Cabernet Sauvignon, Merlot, and Pinot Noir and corresponding to such French wine types as white Burgundy, Bordeaux, and red Burgundy—overtook cheaper, less sophisticated blends at a remarkable rate. Varietals represented less than 10 percent of California table-wine consumption in the mid-1960s. By 2000, varietals commanded almost three-quarters of the California table-wine market in the United States. In the past decade alone, cases of California varietals consumed more than doubled.

From a consumer's perspective, the trading-up phenomenon in wine has been driven by all four of the emotional needs. The first has to do with Taking Care of Me—the simple pleasure and emotional release that comes from drinking wine. The consumer feels a sense of calm and warmth, along with a momentary escape from the pressures of the day. In our survey, respondents said drinking wine makes them feel "comforted," "pampered," and "less stressed out." Second, those who trade up in wine view it as a means of Connecting and making affiliations with others. Wine is also a way for consumers to express Individual Style—signaling that they are individuals of taste, sophistication, experience, and intelligence. "Stylish" and "worldly," said our survey respondents. Many wine consumers are also engaging in Questing—fulfilling their need for learning, discovery, adventure, and experience. Survey respondents agreed that drinking wine makes them feel "adventurous," "knowledgeable," and as if they're "living their best life."

The conditions and forces behind the trading-up phenomenon in wine are strikingly similar to those that have transformed many other consumer categories. Typically, the category has been neglected for years. The major players in the category have generally favored volume over quality, pursued incremental improvements in technical features and functional performance, and ignored the emotional aspects of their products and brands—seeking above all to maximize profit and minimize cost. As a result, the category became exhausted, devoid of interest, and ready for a countermovement. Along comes an entrepreneur with a vision for a new kind of product in the category, a better understanding of the emotional needs of the consumer, and an unshakable faith that consumers will trade up if given a product with genuine differences and emotional engagement. He or she is usually an outsider, often an iconoclast, who attacks the category with a stream of innovations, applies science and technology to what has long been a craft business, and aligns the product with new consumer attitudes and needs caused by social shifts and changes in demographics. Often, the new business is aided by a concomitant shift in retailing—in this case it was the restaurateurs who realized they could double their margin per meal by offering premium wines—and the stage is set for category transformation.

The Post-Prohibition Era: "What's the Word? Thunderbird"

In *American Vintage: The Rise of American Wine*, Paul Lukacs describes the dark days of winemaking in America:

> The story of American wine in the first two-thirds of the twentieth century, the years of Prohibition and its legacy, is the story of its gradual but steady cheapening—not so much in terms of price or even overall quality, as in terms of reputation and renown. . . . Wine increasingly became associated in the public eye with drunkenness, while spirit-based cocktails acquired a chic and sophisticated reputation.

Prohibition—which came about with the adoption of the Eighteenth Amendment to the Constitution and prohibited the business activities of all brewers, distillers, vintners, and retailers of alcoholic beverages—nearly destroyed the U.S. wine industry. During the thirteen years Prohibition was in effect, from 1920 to 1933, the number of commercial wineries in America shrank from 1,000 to just 150, most of which were producing medicinal, wine-based products with government certification. Even after repeal of the Eighteenth Amendment, the wine industry had a difficult time regenerating itself during the difficult times that followed—starting with the Great Depression and then World War II. There was also a wide variation in state regulations concerning alcohol production and consumption—nineteen states chose to remain "dry" after Prohibition.

Into this vacuum stepped Ernest and Julio Gallo, who founded their company in 1933 with the ambition of becoming the "Campbell Soup Company of the wine industry" by marketing cheap wines to the mass market. Gallo's success was built on fortified wines targeted at what critics called the "misery market"—consumers down on their luck, out of work, poor, sometimes living in the streets. (Fortified wines have spirits added to boost alcohol content from the 10 to 12 percent typical of wines, up to 17 to 21 percent.) By the 1950s, E.&J. Gallo was the third largest volume producer in the United States. The focus was volume, volume, volume, in the ambition to become the largest winery in the country.

In 1957, Gallo launched a new type of wine called Thunderbird—a high-alcohol port mixed with concentrated lemon juice—and it offered a cheap route to inebriation. Thunderbird quickly became America's best-selling wine, with heaviest sales in the impoverished inner city and on skid rows throughout the land. The radio jingle for Thunderbird was vivid and memorable:

What's the word? Thunderbird.
How's it sold? Good and cold.
What's the jive? Bird's alive.
What's the price? Thirty twice. [That is: $.60.]

The story is told that Ernest Gallo liked to drive through depressed inner-city neighborhoods and, when he saw a group of likely drinkers on the street, roll down his car window and call out, "What's the word?" He delighted in the universal response: "Thunderbird."

By 1957, 70 percent of American "wine" consumption was of such fortified wines. They were cheap and easy to make. The additives gave the product stability, compensated for imperfections in the fruit, and disguised the lack of consistency. Gallo gained share rapidly—although competitors responded to Thunderbird with their own fortified wine products—and by the mid-1960s had become America's largest winemaker, just as it had intended. Gallo's was a strategy of trading down: selling low-quality wine in high volumes at low prices to consumers with no interest in the taste or provenance of what they were guzzling.

The American Awakening

In the early 1960s better wines began to appear, and Americans began to show greater appreciation for wines in general. As with other New Luxury categories, a number of factors came together to spawn this new movement. As we have discussed in earlier chapters, these factors include the rising incomes of the middle class, an appreciation of European cuisine—especially the French cooking made popular by Julia Child and her television program *The French Chef*—and the increase in European travel made possible by falling airfares. There were also advances made in the science of winemaking, particularly by experts at the University of California, Davis (and other universities throughout the world), that helped make possible new approaches to winemaking and viticulture. The one missing element was a visionary leader to break the industry out of the strictures of history and convention.

In 1965, the leader emerged: Robert Mondavi. Following their father's death in 1959, brothers Robert and Peter Mondavi had been jointly running the Charles Krug Winery, just north of St. Helena in the Napa Valley. Their father had purchased the winery in 1943, and mother Rosa Mondavi was the matriarch who had controlled the family business since her husband's death. Robert had a bold vision for where he wanted to take the business—he wanted to make the best wines in the world, and to do so he wanted to invest aggressively in new equipment, better vines, and new methods. Peter was more content with what the family had achieved at Charles Krug and with a slower pace of incremental change and improvement. The tension between their divergent philosophies came to a head at a family gathering in 1965—tempers boiled, fists flew, and the family was irreconcilably divided. Mother Rosa sided with Peter. Robert was out.

Instantaneously, an outsider was created. Although not an industry outsider, Robert began to feel and think like one. He had a vision for a far better product, was determined to make his mark on the world, and felt emancipated from the constraints of the current business. A desire for revenge added to his drive and ambition. "Out of our terrible fight . . . came my liberation. . . . I was forced to re-

think my entire direction in life," he wrote in *Harvest of Joy*. "In
1965, at the age of fifty-two, I was at a decisive crossroads and I
knew it. If I was ever going to make a dramatic change in my life, if
I was every going to summon the courage to follow my own star,
now was the time to do it."

In 1966, less than a year later, Robert Mondavi broke ground on
a major new winery in Napa Valley.

> Everyone thought I was crazy, of course. As soon as word
> spread of my plan to build my own winery—the first new
> winery in Napa Valley since the late 1930s—I began to get
> skeptical looks and comments. Start a new winery? Make
> wine that would stand beside the greatest wines in the
> world? Set out to transform the eating and drinking habits
> of an entire nation? What arrogance! What folly! Bob Mon-
> davi has a screw loose. . . . I could hear the guffaws up and
> down the Napa Valley.

Mondavi pushed forward anyway, understanding the long odds
of success and aware of the formidable obstacles that lay ahead, not
the least of which was the lack of a proven market. He had no market research or consumer studies to validate his concept. Besides, as
we've learned, it is doubtful that any kind of research could have
predicted that consumers would be willing to embrace what Mondavi intended to create:

> There was simply no significant market in America for fine
> wine at that time. While Italian families like ours ate and
> drank as our parents and ancestors had for centuries, we
> were the exception. For the vast majority, America was still
> a steak, potatoes, and beer kind of country. To millions of
> consumers, cheese meant Velveeta and bread meant Won-
> der or Roman Meal. . . . As a result, the prevailing wisdom
> in Napa Valley back in 1966 was that if you wanted to make
> truly fine wines to compete with the French and Italians in
> that very narrow niche, good luck.

During his first year in business, Mondavi tapped deeply into his ambition, passion, and energy. Even before his winery's roof was complete, he stunned the winemakers in the valley by introducing a wine for which he coined a name, "fumé blanc." Made with the Sauvignon Blanc grape, the wine had a smoky quality that he thought was captured in the word *fumé*, from the French verb *fumer*, meaning "to smoke." The wine was widely praised.

From the beginning, Mondavi had a clear vision, similar in many respects to the visions of other New Luxury entrepreneurs:

> I decided to create a winery with several interlocking layers of ambition. One, to make great world-class wines. Two, to combine European craft and tradition with the latest in American technology and management and marketing know-how. Three, I wanted the winery to be stunningly beautiful, so that it would become a magnet for tourists and wine lovers from all over the globe. Four, every day we would invite visitors in to taste our wines, and via tours and educational events, we would help them learn how to appreciate fine food and wine. Maybe there was no market yet for fine wine in America, but so what? I was determined to create the market we needed, even if we had to do it one visitor at a time! I knew that if we made an outstanding wine, the market would follow.

Like Howard Schultz of Starbucks and Chuck Williams of Williams-Sonoma, Robert Mondavi had a vision that largely resulted from a trip to Europe, his first, which he took in 1962, at the age of forty-eight—an experience he called seminal and life-changing. While there, he carefully studied the growing and winemaking methods of the great châteaux. He realized that while American wine producers had only two basic approaches—one for white and one for red—the European producers followed a unique process for each type of wine. He noted fundamental differences in growing and production methods. He observed that the best châteaux aged their wines in French oak barrels, which gave the wine what he called "gentleness, subtlety, and complex layers of flavor." Americans, by contrast, made their wines in bulk, aging it in large casks and redwood tanks. He would later call the French oak barrel "the cornerstone of our efforts to revolutionize American winemaking."

Although in awe of the legendary châteaux, Mondavi also noticed great extremes in winemaking across Europe. He found that many wineries with famous and elite names often produced wines that were inconsistent and off character from year to year. A major cause, in his view, was that these wineries followed a traditional practice of reusing their wine barrels for aging. In addition, many small wineries were benefiting from the legacy of a famous place-name—there were dozens of Pommard wines made in Burgundy, for example—but not all were worthy of the great name. Also, many winemakers took a traditional, nonscientific, eyes-closed approach to their winemaking process. Mondavi wanted to learn which of the traditional elements of the process were critical to product quality, which could get in the way, and which were followed simply because that's the way they had always done things. The reuse of barrels, for example, could mar the flavor profile of the wine, as well as create bacterial defects that led to spoilage and "spent" flavors. The European winemakers, Mondavi wrote, seemed to be "asleep at the switch." He saw an opportunity to broaden the base of great winemaking—to bring the best methods to a larger scale, with greater consistency and quality.

Mondavi chose to pattern his winery after only the finest winemakers, and he embraced not only their methods, but their philosophies as well. He lamented that Americans treated wine "as a business" while the great European châteaux thought of wine as "high art." He came to understand and appreciate the French concept of *terroir*—that every vineyard has a unique sense of place, a character defined by environmental factors such as soil, climate, drainage, vegetation, and terrain. Like a chef's bringing out the subtle flavors from fresh local ingredients, the winemaker's art involved maximizing the unique subtleties and nuances of the vineyard's *terroir*. In adopting this idea, Mondavi realized that his wines would have to have their own distinctive and unique flavors: "I had no intention of trying to copy or imitate the great wines. . . . No, I felt strongly that our California wines should have their own style and character; they should reflect our climate, our soil, our grapes, and—yes—our own unique American character and spirit."

Mondavi's vision was not about just wine. His trip to Europe had unlocked a deeper passion, a more profound philosophy. It was *taste*. The taste not just of great wine, but of great wine interacting with wonderful food, as well as connecting with culture, music, and art. After an "absolutely unbelievable" meal at the famous French restaurant La Pyramide, Mondavi was "dazzled": "I'd go so far as to say that the food and the wine transported us into a world of gentleness and balance, of grace and artistry. La Pyramide to me epitomized the artistry and aesthetics we had been discovering all across Europe."

From this inspiration came Mondavi's broader aspiration. He didn't call it trading up, but that was the essence of his vision: to bring Americans to new levels of quality and taste—in wine, in cuisine, and in culture as well. As much as Mondavi lamented the state of winemaking in the United States, he equally lamented the lack of fine cuisine, complaining that there was not a single world-class restaurant in the Napa Valley. He imagined a winery that would become a cultural and educational center—a tourist destination where Americans could learn about wine, food, and the arts. In 1969, he began holding summer music festivals at the winery, featuring big names in jazz, rhythm and blues, and pop. He launched a "Great Chefs" program in 1976, with the best chefs from France conducting courses and tastings in wine and fine cuisine at the winery. Mondavi aspired to nothing less than bringing about a revolution in American taste—beyond wine, and into food, culture, art, design, and crafts. He understood how deeply wine can and should connect with fundamental emotional needs—that it is about Connecting, expressing Individual Style, and Questing for knowledge and experience.

With the groundbreaking for the Robert Mondavi Winery in 1966, the American wine awakening began in earnest. The decade that followed was one of remarkable transition for California winemaking. Vineyards were steadily upgraded with better-quality vines—"everywhere you looked, old vines were being ripped out and being replanted with high-quality varietals." World-class winemaking talent and know-how flowed into the Napa Valley. In 1971,

Bernard Portet, a French winemaker from Bordeaux, founded Clos du Val. In 1972, two of Mondavi's protégés took leadership positions at Napa wineries and set out to produce world-class wine. The first was Warren Winiarski, who built the Stag's Leap Wine Cellars in 1972. The second, Miljenko "Mike" Grgich, took over winemaking at Chateau Montelena. These leaders, along with Mondavi and others, would shortly put the United States on the world map of great winemaking.

In 1976, a critical year for the Napa Valley, a tasting was organized in which several leading Napa Valley wines were matched against several of the best and most famous French wines from Burgundy and Bordeaux. The tasting was blind—meaning that the identities of the wines would not be revealed until after the judging was complete—and the nine judges were elite members of France's wine establishment. The results shocked the world. In the white category, which pitted Napa's best Chardonnays against the elite white Burgundies, American wines took three of the four top spots. Grgich's 1973 Chateau Montelena Chardonnay took first place over a famous Meursault-Charmes. The results in the red category were just as dramatic. Warren Winiarski's 1973 Cabernet Sauvignon from Stag's Leap took top honors, beating a 1970 Château Mouton-Rothschild, a 1970 Château Haut-Brion, a 1970 Château Montrose, and a 1971 Château Leoville-Las-Cases. The French wines had been picked as the very best France could offer, from vintages that Robert Parker, the noted American wine critic, calls the best years between 1961 and 1982. "The judges mistook the best wines for French wines," according to Winiarski. "They thought the most complete wines were French wines. They were mistaken." *Time* magazine covered the event in an article called "The Judgment of Paris." The organizer of the event, Steven Spurrier, was threatened, the judges were hanged in effigy in Paris, and government officials were fired.

Ten years after Mondavi broke ground for his winery, the Napa Valley had made breathtaking progress. Elite wines from the United States could in fact stand side by side with elite wines from Europe. But the revolution was far from complete. These wines represented only a tiny fraction of the market and were largely unavailable to most Americans. Progress had its own irony: what Mondavi called the "great extremes" in winemaking now existed in the United States as well in France. Better wine had yet to cascade to the mass market in any meaningful way. But the second wave of the revolution—the rise of accessible, high-quality wine—was about to break.

Jess Jackson and the "Fighting Varietal"

More than any other figure in the Napa Valley, Jess Jackson was responsible for catalyzing the second part of the revolution of American winemaking: the democratization of better wine, the closing of the "great extremes" of superpremium Old Luxury wines and the cheap wines that had prevailed in the United States for years. While Mondavi was an outsider by virtue of being forced out of the family business, Jackson was a true outsider—a successful San Francisco attorney with no real experience in winemaking until the early 1980s. He was a maverick in the Mondavi mold, and he had a tremendous impact on the commercialization of a style and class of wine that we define as New Luxury.

Unencumbered by history and convention, Jess Jackson took a radically different approach to winemaking than others in the wine establishment of the Napa Valley. In less than two decades, he built the most commercially successful winery in California, profoundly changing both the production and consumption of high-quality wine in the United States. Today, Kendall-Jackson is the number one brand of table wine in the United States with more than $600 million in retail sales. Kendall-Jackson Wine Estates, the mid-price label, has won more awards than any other winery in the last decade—although that may be a function of a much higher number of entries than of absolute overall superiority.

In the early 1970s, Jess Jackson purchased an eighty-acre pear-and-walnut orchard just north of the Napa Valley as a country retreat. Seeing the increasing demand for high-quality grapes in the valley, he converted his property to grow premium Chardonnay and other varietals, which he sold to local wineries. In 1981, the bottom fell out of the market. Grapes were in surplus and prices were falling, and Jackson could not find buyers for his harvest. He decided to convert the grapes into wine himself. But he resisted the

Jess Jackson, founder of Kendall-Jackson, in the early years of his business.
Photo courtesy of Kendall-Jackson Wine Estates, Ltd.

temptation to follow the down market, which would mean producing mediocre, midprice wines. Instead, Jackson studied the industry
and realized "there was a hole in the market I could drive a truck
through . . . really good wines that the average person could afford."
The gap between elite and economy was about to be closed.

From the beginning, Jackson relentlessly focused on creating affordable wines with superior quality and distinctive taste profiles.
But, rather than make wines primarily identified by the geographic
location of the vineyard, he started by defining the unique taste profile and character for the wine that he wanted to produce—profiles
that were as complex, rich, subtle, and balanced as the elite artisanal
wines in the valley. He would then select the high-quality grapes
from the better vineyards in a seven-county area he would later de-

fine as the True Coast region of Northern California. Recognizing that each vineyard had it own unique flavor "domaine" (as he spells it), Jackson used a combination of art and science to blend the wines to match the defined flavor profile. He used only French oak barrels for aging.

Jackson's approach represented a fundamental departure for premium winemaking. At the time, blending wine according to a formula was a practice found mostly in the economy segment, notably in jug wines. Jackson and his winemaker, Jed Steele, used the principles of enology developed at the University of California, Davis, to take the practice of blending to a new level—an art unto itself. Jackson was betting on a breakthrough in the technical layer of the benefit ladder: that consumers would care more about the taste of the wine than the vineyard from which it was made. A key element of Jackson's proprietary method was a blending formula that produced a balance of residual fructose and tartness—a wine just slightly sweeter than European wines and more pleasing to the middle-market palate. With this scientific approach to winemaking, Jackson was able to break the trade-off between quality and affordability, producing premium wine on a much larger scale than had been achieved before, and with less variation. (Jackson would later successfully sue Steele, enjoining him from taking these proprietary methods of scientific winemaking to other vintners.)

Jackson's first wine, a 1982 Kendall-Jackson Vintner's Reserve Chardonnay, was a blockbuster success. He priced it in the sweet spot of the market—$5 a bottle, well below the $10 and up pricing of the boutique wines but above the $2 price point of the economy wines. Because he used premium grapes from several coastal counties, he had to use the less prestigious "California" appellation, rather than the name of a specific region or vineyard, but neither consumers nor wine aficionados seemed to care. This first release was named the "Best American Chardonnay" in the American Wine Competition, and the entire bottling sold out in six months. The overwhelming response validated what Jackson deeply believed— that quality and taste were what mattered most. "I created a new category," he said, and he called it the "fighting varietal." Masstige had come to wine. Over the next twenty years, Jess Jackson adapted and extended his winning model—first to the red varietals Cabernet and Merlot, then to new premium tiers above the Kendall-Jackson label, and ultimately to wines from emerging wine-producing countries, including Chile and Australia. Jackson never rested on the laurels of his success. "Fear," he says, "is what drove me." He saw the cycle time of innovation in wine collapsing and competitors inexorably closing in, so he moved quickly and systematically to build out his model, aggressively acquiring land and wineries that would fit in his system while maintaining the element that mattered most to him: control and continuous improvement of the winemaking process. And he continued to accelerate the rate of innovation, from viticulture to enology to advancements in process technology.

By 2002, Jackson owned or controlled over thirteen thousand acres of prime wine-growing territory and fifteen wineries. Unlike Robert Mondavi and other vintners, who have extended their brands down to lower price points, Jackson ignored (until recently) the segment below the masstige price point. Instead, he kept his focus on trading up. The future, he believed, was in a rising standard of quality and taste. He always wanted to be ahead of the market, at the forefront of the quality movement. When the price of premium varietals soared in the early 1990s, he resisted the temptation to blend with less expensive grapes. He maintained his focus on premium quality and raised the price of Kendall-Jackson Vintner's Reserve to over $10 a bottle. From there, he systematically expanded his portfolio of wines to cover the upper segments of the wine market, giving him the ability to manage the quality cascade for himself. Today, the expansive portfolio of wines under the Kendall-Jackson Wine Estates umbrella reflects that philosophy. Each label has a clear positioning, from Vintner's Reserve at the low end to the Stature label at $70 plus per bottle.

"We've taken the *grand cru* approach," Jackson explains. "We have three tiers of quality. At the very top, we have our micro-crus, our equivalent of a *grand cru*. These are wonderful, limited-production wines made with the best grapes in California. This tier includes labels like Stature and some boutique wines from our Great Estates portfolio. The second tier is more like superpremium. Incredible quality, but more like $30 a bottle, rather than $100 a bottle. Then we have our premium offer, which is Kendall-Jackson Vintner's Reserve. You have to be positioned to select down from the very best and define your own standard of quality at each level. I believe that at every price level, our wines have better taste and quality than most of their counterparts in the market."

⌐ We visited Jess Jackson in the fall of 2002, almost twenty years after he first changed the course of American winemaking, to get additional insight into this outsider's remarkable success. We were greeted by Barbara Banke, the current CEO, and taken by helicopter on an aerial tour of the prime vineyards of the Kendall-Jackson Wine Estates. As we would shortly learn, the choice of transportation itself offered an important insight into the company's strategy and unique position in the market. When we landed, we met Jess Jackson on a carefully chosen mountaintop overlooking his ranch estate and the Alexander Valley. He was gracious, warmly approachable, and completely open about his business.

"To understand and appreciate what we have done," he told us, "you have to see it from this perspective." Of the nearly thirteen thousand acres of prime True Coast vineyards under control of the Kendall-Jackson portfolio, nearly ten thousand of those acres are mountainside or hillside vineyards, which makes it difficult to appreciate or even cover the properties by car. Jackson's strategy, quite literally, is to hold the high ground on taste and quality. "Grapes grown on mountainsides or hillsides have a very different character," he explains. "Water runs off this terrain, so less moisture gets trapped inside the grape. As a result, the berries are smaller and have a much more intense, rich flavor profile. These vineyards make much more interesting, more complex wine."

"I really like the French concept of *terroir*," Jackson says. "It means that every microenvironment has its own unique flavor and character by virtue of its soil, climate, terrain, vegetation, irrigation, et cetera." A microenvironment for Jackson could be as small as an acre or the particular slope of a hillside. His staff knows the taste nuance and chemical profile of every microenvironment. His vineyard positions are strategic—acquired to ensure access to *terroir* with the most intense, unique flavor profiles. But Jackson's application of *terroir* was quite different from other vintners'—it was less about expressing a sense of place than ensuring access to grapes with the right taste profiles and "layers" to blend in superior tasting wines.

Barbara Banke describes Kendall-Jackson as a "mass boutique," and Jackson agrees. "I am a populist. I saw the opportunity to create great-tasting wine for the average person. I took the French model and anglicized it. I gave it my own adaptations, but the principles are the same. Technology has allowed us to handcraft wines on a larger scale using grapes from different vineyards."

Reflecting on his success, Jackson echoes the outsider theme. "We were outsiders to the industry. When we started, we didn't own very much land. We had no choice but to do things differently. We had to be inventive. We also had a certain freedom—freedom from doing things the traditional way. I believe a lot of our innovation came exactly because we were outsiders."

As a new entrant to the category, Jackson rearranged the sequence of steps that wineries had traditionally taken to build their brands. The conventional model was sequential and logical: acquire the land, plant and develop the vines, define (and refine) the winemaking process, distribute the product, brand it. The trouble, of course, is that it takes time and resources to acquire the land, at least three to five years for the vines to mature, and years to acquire the taste and skill of winemaking. Jackson saw a way to reconfigure the value chain, cutting his time to market and lowering his initial investment. He describes his sequence as: (1) controlling the process of winemaking, (2) building the brand, and (3) getting the land.

In the early days, Jackson's production model was one of open sourcing. He grew few of his own grapes; instead, he would define his Flavor Domaines and negotiate buying agreements with the vineyards that could produce grapes to his flavor specifications. Jackson and his winemakers would then assess each crop, using the scientific methods adapted from the university experts, to ensure that the quality was high and the flavor profile was right. Next he would work on the blending process, iterating the mixing formula until he got the taste exactly right. And, starting with Jed Steele, he hired the best possible winemakers to make sure he was getting the very best wine. "Control," he said, "is everything. You have to control every element of the production process."

The next step was going to market. As a small winery, Kendall-Jackson did not have as much distribution and marketing clout as the big producers had, so he was again forced to invent a new approach—and he proved to be a clever marketer and brand builder. "Every wine has a story to be told," he said. "You have to create the excitement with the consumer." Jackson focused his attention first on winning prestigious awards from the various wine competitions in California. He wanted outside validation of his quality and taste claims; he wanted to create a buzz for every wine. From his first Chardonnay, he proved more skillful at winning tasting awards than any other vintner. He then used these awards to create excitement with both the trade and the consumer. Frustrated with the three-tier distribution system, he also built a disproportionately large retail-sales team to supplement the wholesale-and-broker channel and ensure that his wines got the right account authorization, placement, and sell-through at retail. Finally, he created compelling, consumer-friendly vignettes to express the uniqueness of his labels, trademarking his invented appellations, such as True Coast and Flavor Domaine.

As his business grew, Jackson gradually purchased more vineyards. His priority was to acquire unique properties that would ensure his supply of the highest-quality varietals; hence the focus on hillside or mountain vineyards. He also wanted to raise the quality of the vineyards he acquired to maximize the richness of the *terroir*. He recruited the best talent in viticulture and charged them with delivering constant, state-of-the-art innovation in the process of growing and harvesting grapes. This would complete, in Jackson's view, the "tripod of quality": varietal selection, viticulture (grape growing), and enology (winemaking).

A "New World" Order

The American revolution has catalyzed a global wine revolution. The United States, Australia, Chile, and South Africa are constantly innovating, raising quality at all price points, gaining market share, and making the American "big" taste dominant worldwide. In addition to innovations in blending, many advances have been made in vineyard practices, especially trellising and canopy management—

producers have learned how to maximize the photosynthetic input to each plant and thereby raise the yields without diluting quality.

Meanwhile, producers in the old-world wine-producing countries are, in many cases, losing ground—suffering from excess capacity, falling share in foreign markets, domestic insulation, stifling regulations, and blinding adherence to tradition. But, as we have seen in every category transformed by a New Luxury brand, new producers have entered the market in America and elsewhere, seeking to capitalize on the traded-up tastes of its consumers—and many of them offer little more than lower prices and knockoff styles. One result is polarization of the market, with many choices at the low end, a proliferation of high-end boutiques, and pressure on the wineries that offer midprice labels to maintain their brand distinction.

European producers once controlled 90 percent of all wine imports to the United States. Today, their share is 60 percent and still falling, leading to a wine glut in the major European countries. In the last ten years, global share of the old-world (western European) producers has dropped from 79 percent to 67 percent. The outsiders are winning because they have lower costs, a greater investment in advanced technology, and more sophisticated marketing methods and pricing strategies.

The Australian wine industry, in particular, has experienced tremendous growth over the past decade. From 1988 to 1998, the acreage under vines doubled. Export volume share in the world market has increased from 1 percent to 5 percent in the last decade, with export sales growing at 45 percent annually. The mix has shifted dramatically to premium and superpremium wines, driving an 8 percent annual growth in price per liter for the last seven years. Australia's share of the bellwether U.K. market surpassed that of France for the first time in 2002. Australian wines are not dependent on weather for great vintages; the latest-generation irrigation systems ensure a reduction in the differences in grape quality from year to year. France's wine-growing regions, by contrast, are far more affected by the weather—they may have a string of good years followed by a series of weaker vintages.

Australia's success has been driven primarily by three factors: the richness and availability of land, advancements in science and technology, and the speed with which industry leaders have reacted to the trading-up phenomenon. For Australian wines, the total cost of the land involved in producing a $14 bottle of wine accounts for about 3 percent of the retail price, compared with roughly 7.5 percent for a similar American wine. More important are the innovations the Australians have made in the science of wine. Although Australia produces only 3 percent of the world's wine volume, Australians have contributed a disproportionate number of the world's scientific papers on viticulture and enology. As one industry expert observed: "The development and implementation of technology is the real secret of Australia's success. Unlike many European vineyards, the head winemaker is rarely the son of the owner. Rather, it is someone who has completed a university degree and furthered his education by traveling and working in the vineyards of the world." This has led to the rise of the "flying winemaker"—the expert who consults to several wineries in his own home country during its wine-producing season and then travels to the other hemisphere for its seasons, thereby doubling his rate of learning. This willingness to explore, combined with a tendency to be critical of established practices and to accumulate learning faster, has produced a winemaking culture whose members have a remarkable ability to understand, adapt, and improve on the winemaking techniques of other countries and cultures.

The Master Blender's New Luxury Practices

The story of trading up in wine reinforces the eight key practices of New Luxury leaders:

1. Robert Mondavi and Jess Jackson *never underestimated the customer.* They believed they could trade up the middle market to high levels of quality, taste, and aspiration even if there was not a proven model to follow. It became their mission and guiding ethos.

2. Jackson, in particular, sought to *shatter the price-volume demand curve and then redraw it,* not move along it. He saw the potential to create a new segment in the market with both higher prices and higher volume. Today, his major brands continue to occupy a position off the demand curve for the industry as a whole.

3. Consumers traded up based on the *ladder of genuine benefits.* The big breakthrough was in taste and affordability, but the category overall played to an emotional need for pleasure, social connection, affinity, self expression, and discovery. Attaining knowledge of wine became a way for consumers to make affiliation and connection with other wine enthusiasts.

4. Jackson and other leaders continued to *escalate innovation, elevate quality, and deliver a flawless experience,* knowing that the competitors were not far behind. In the last five years, vintners have reduced yield per acre in the prime Napa and Sonoma vineyards by 10 percent in order to increase the quality and flavor intensity of their harvests.

5. Both Mondavi and Jackson *extended the price range and positioning of the brand,* with a seven-to-ten-times range from low to high. They built their brands on the premise of creating the best possible quality and taste at any given price point.

6. Jackson *customized his value chain to deliver on the benefit ladder.* He used an open-sourcing model to overcome structural barriers. He put the emphasis on control, not necessarily ownership, of the value chain. And he proved to be the master of orchestrating the value chain from end to end.

7. Jackson and Mondavi *used influence marketing and seeded their success through brand apostles.* Mondavi put the emphasis on the good life, surrounding wine with fine cuisine, culture, and the arts. He invented the concept of the winery as a tourist destination and made his winery an enticing, multisensory consumer experience. Jackson used key influencers and competitions to create a buzz for his wines, created compelling stories around his labels, and developed an innovative field sales force to manage his product placement and channel of distribution.

A key to the development of the category was the idea of *marketing as education,* encouraging consumer involvement and connoisseurship in the category. The rise of consumer-oriented educational periodicals such as *Wine Spectator* and Robert Parker's *Wine Advocate* was a significant development. In these publications, whose circulation rose dramatically between 1985 and 2000, wine reviews are written not in the obscure poetic phrasing favored by junket-happy (and sometimes tipsy) journalists. The wines are graded, objectively, on a numerical scale—tasted blind, "price and label be damned," demystifying the old-world complexity and stuffiness of the category. These magazines, combined with the heavy investment of leading California wineries in on-site promotion and consumer education, have empowered a new generation of wine consumers to develop the interest and knowledge necessary to trade up with confidence.

8. Mondavi and Jackson both *attacked the category as outsiders*, unencumbered by and often in opposition to the rules of convention. Jackson in particular seems to have applied this to his next generation of labels, which have come from all over the world, including Australia, Chile, and Italy. He has recognized that the inspiration and innovation will increasingly come from wine countries of the New World.

The Trading-Up Pattern in Wine

We expect that the pattern of trading up in wine will continue. Driven by intense competitive pressure and advancements in science, the quality and consistency of wine at all price points will improve still further. Production surplus likely will outstrip growth in consumer demand. In California, for example, nearly 20 percent of acreage under vines is too young to have yet produced a winemaking crop. Quality will continue to improve, creating excess supply at the low end. Those with significant sales in the economy and near-premium segments will either be forced out of business or suffer sustained operating losses. Growth and profitability will be at the higher price points. The Australians will quickly grow share in the United States, and many old-world producers will continue their global decline. However, many other European producers have jumped onto the trading-up bandwagon and are producing wines to higher aspirations of quality and emotional engagement, and many have even adopted the international "big taste" style. Still other European producers—iconoclasts and mavericks—are seeking to create new brands not in the international style, but with more local variation, difference, and balance. The next New Luxury producers to challenge the New World's leaders could emerge from the Old World.

For an agrarian industry with artisanal roots, the rate of change over the past thirty years has been unprecedented. As Jess Jackson says, "It used to be that a major advance in winemaking came every fifty years or so. Then that fell to every twenty. Now it's every three to four years. The rate of innovation and improvement is astonishing. Beliefs about winemaking seem to become obsolete about every ten years. This creates an enormous challenge for us. We have to keep reinventing ourselves."

This admonition applies to all the established players in the U.S. wine trade. They face two potential threats. The old-world producers have a tremendous amount of wine expertise and commitment to their craft and industry; they could develop new offerings that deliver new and appealing taste profiles that take advantage of the emotional connection with old-world vineyard, grape, and country names. Also, there are other countries, such as Romania and the Czech Republic, that are capable of producing high-quality, low-priced wines that could transform the market once again.

American wines and American producers have changed the world's taste in wine, but taste is akin to fashion—the new one is always the most delicious.

Ten

The Old World in New Luxury Bottles

Can New Luxury brands be created even in a declining category? In the case of vodka and other premium spirits, as well as beer, the answer is a resounding yes. New Luxury is about birth and regeneration, about creating demand, even when the tide seems to be moving inexorably the other way. Millennium Import LLC proved this to be true with Belvedere vodka, as did The Boston Beer Company with its Samuel Adams Boston Lager.

Belvedere: Reinventing Vodka

Vodka is one of those categories in which, on first inspection, trading up seems to be an unlikely prospect. In sharp contrast to wine, per capita consumption of spirits in the United States has been flat or declining for more than three decades. In 1975, Americans consumed two gallons per capita of hard liquor every year. By 1995, that figure had fallen to 1.2 gallons, just over half its previous level. Wine consumption, which overtook spirits in 1980 for the first time, now outpaces hard liquor by more than 50 percent. Traditional whiskey consumption fell from forty-three million cases in 1985 to thirty million cases in 1990, a sustained volume decline of 3.6 percent per year. Other spirits also declined over the same period: gin fell 2.3 percent annually, bourbon 2.7 percent, and scotch blends 5.2 per-

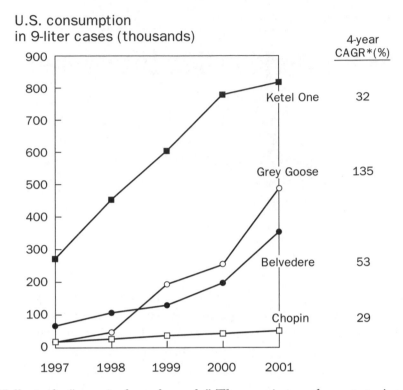

Vodka is the "new single-malt scotch." The premium and superpremium vodka brands are the fastest-growing segment of the vodka market.

Compound annual growth rate.

cent. During the 1970s and early 1980s, the industry consolidated, share positions stabilized, and the large players were content to milk long-established brands for profitability.

Against this trend, however, a countermovement began in the early 1980s, as small premium innovative spirits makers started to challenge established incumbents with New Luxury brands. Since 1995, these premium brands have created a renaissance in the spirits category, growing the premium segment by 40 percent in volume from 1995 to 2001, while the nonpremium segment declined 5 percent.

Nowhere is this renaissance more striking than in vodka. Michael Roux, the creator of Absolut vodka, puts it in perspective: "Twenty-five to thirty years ago, the imagery for vodka was that it had no flavor and no smell. Today, vodka is almost like wine. One is different from the other like Bordeaux is different from Burgundy." Roux was the first to seize the opportunity to break away from the pack of tired, relatively undifferentiated, emotionally bereft brands. Absolut was priced 75 percent above the industry leader, Smirnoff, and experienced explosive growth during the 1980s. From 1985 to 2000, consumption of Absolut grew from fewer than one million cases to almost five million worldwide, a compound annual growth rate in volume of 13 percent. Segment leader Smirnoff, meanwhile, declined from 7.5 million cases to 6.5 million cases. In dollar sales, the upstart overtook the category leader within about ten years.

Then it happened again. Just as Absolut became the clear segment leader, a new set of upstarts entered the market with luxury vodkas priced at 75 percent premium (or more) to Absolut; Belvedere and Grey Goose were the most prominent. In a period of five years, from 1996 to 2001, these new superpremiums had matched Absolut's dollar share of the vodka category. Revolution happened twice in two decades. And by 2001, the premium and superpremium segments combined for a total of 30 percent of the category volume, 50 percent of the category dollar sales, and an astounding 70 percent of the category profits. As in other categories, these back-to-back revolutions came about as a result of a fundamental realignment of consumer needs and business breakthroughs.

On the consumer side, New Luxury vodkas operate in three of the four emotional spaces. First and foremost, luxury vodka plays to the signaling aspect of Individual Style. Consumers distinguish themselves and make a statement about their sophistication, taste, and hipness by the drink they call for at the bar. It's fashion. Calling for a Belvedere martini is sophisticated and hip; calling for Absolut is, one consumer told us, "so last century." And for those who rocket, paying $15 for a Belvedere martini is an attainable bit of exclusivity.

The bellwether of success in this emotional space is a high ratio of on-premise (bars and restaurants) versus retail (liquor stores) sales. When the ratio falls, a brand is typically losing its ability to be the called drink, to be a badge of distinction.

The second emotional space is Questing. For a significant sub-

segment of New Luxury consumers, part of the luxury vodka experience is about developing a sophisticated palate, learning to discern
the differences in flavor profiles, and understanding the heritage
and product stories of the different vodka brands. For these consumers, it's at least as much about becoming a connoisseur and mastering a new skill as it is about being in fashion. Finally, luxe vodkas
play to the Connecting emotion. Drinking is, after all, fundamentally a social activity.

Ellen, a fifty-four-year-old widow who owns a vineyard, demonstrates the linkage between the benefit layers in vodka that exist in
the mind of a vodka connoisseur. She enjoys a martini with dinner
out, but only if it's made with Ketel One, Voxx, or Grey Goose
vodka. "If I cannot get one of those three, maybe I'll do Absolut, but
I won't go below that. I will not drink Stoli because there are too
many good vodkas out there and I won't settle for less." To Ellen,
vodka is more about Questing than signaling. She doesn't like to go
out to drink at trendy bars; her preference is instead rooted in a set
of technical and functional benefits that she is able to articulate. "If
I have a martini it has to be a good martini or I am not going to have
it in the first place. The main difference is the smoothness. I am very
selective."

Other vodka drinkers we interviewed were similarly able to discuss the fine technical and functional attributes of their preferred
brand. An Absolut vodka gimlet, straight up, is the drink of choice
for Craig, a thirty-five-year-old single from Los Angeles. "Absolut
is filtered really well so it's pretty pure and doesn't give you a hangover." And while he admits he may not be able to actually taste
the difference between an Absolut gimlet and one made with
another brand, "I'd be able to tell the difference the next morning."
Nadyenka, too, can articulate the functional differences (taste,
hangovers) of Belvedere, her vodka of choice. But to her, calling for
Belvedere is as much about signaling as it is about flavor—adding
glamour by the glassful in "a dull place like Michigan," where she is
working toward an MBA. She told us that "Belvedere is very fashionable. My standard used to be an Absolut martini and a couple of
olives. Now, it's a Belvedere martini and a couple of olives. I saw a
friend a couple of months ago whom I hadn't seen in five years. She

drinks Belvedere, and in my eyes she is a very fashionable, very cutting-edge girl. She lives in New York and knows about the latest trends—what is in and what is out—and she is quite popular. That kind of image goes hand in hand with drinking Belvedere."

The vodka story follows the familiar pattern seen across many of the New Luxury categories: revolution brought on by a category newcomer who is unencumbered by conventional beliefs and possesses a clear vision of how to create a superior brand on all three rungs of the ladder of genuine differences.

Belvedere—the brand as we know it today—was created by Edward Phillips, CEO of Millennium Import LLC. It was launched in 1996 in the United States and has achieved $1 billion in retail sales to date. Belvedere—and Phillips—created the luxury vodka segment. Like leaders in other categories, Phillips developed his vision for this category by patterning, creating a clear brand concept, and then delivering the right combination of technical, functional, and emotional benefits to the consumer.

With years of experience in the spirits category, Phillips watched with interest as Absolut built the lead position in vodka. "They had the very best marketing and certainly the best advertising of any brand I have seen in the distilled-spirits category," he told us. But through his own patterning, he also saw a void in the market. "There simply was not a real luxury offering in what was then the largest segment of distilled spirits: vodka. Every other category, including scotch, tequila, and gin, had a luxury offering. We learned as we traveled extensively through Poland that the old paradigm—that all vodkas are the same—was fallacious. We realized not only that there are differences between vodkas but also that there are segments and a history in Poland quite analogous to some of the finest wine-growing regions in the world. Poland has a rich history of vodka distillation as a regional industry. At the time there were thirty different regions, each one unique in terms of its indigenous crops. As I was learning as much as possible about Poland and its brands and history and future, quite by chance I bumped into a bottle of Belvedere at the duty-free shop. And there was an epiphany at that moment, a vision for a luxury vodka."

To bring his vision to life, Phillips went through four major phases: (1) developing a truly superior, highly differentiated product; (2) creating the signaling cues of authenticity and specialness; (3) launching the new brand; and (4) building brand equity.

In developing Belvedere vodka, Phillips and his team started with the essential core of old-world vodka making, using premium Dankowski rye from the Mazovia region of Poland and master distillation methods developed over a period of some six hundred years. According to Phillips, the soil in the Mazovia region is unique, producing a rye higher in starch content than other ryes. The Dankowski golden rye, which grows only in Mazovia, produces a flavor profile that has a "semisweet, vanilla kind of aftertaste and a vanilla nose."

Phillips and his team went through a rigorous process of product refinement to get the taste profile of Belvedere exactly right. Research and development required more than two years of intensive work. He used customers not to give him feedback on the abstract concept of luxury vodka, but to help improve the product in an exacting, tangible way. He recruited a combination of vodka consumer experts and 350 professional bartenders to serve as experts on tasting panels. Using these panels in a systematic process of trial and refinement, the product development team created a production process that involved four distillations. The tasting panels concluded that four distillations delivered the optimum taste profile for Belvedere. Five distillations (or more) yielded diminishing returns and removed some of the most compelling elements of Belvedere's taste. This process with expert consumers and bartenders not only created a smooth, subtle, and complex taste, it also removed hangover producing "cogeners"—bits of amyl, propyl, and isopropyl alcohol (and other impurities). Vodka, already the most "hangover free" of the major spirits, became even more drinker-friendly.

Phillips and his team began, in essence, by creating a platform of consumer driven technical and functional benefits. Technically, Belvedere would claim a four times distillation process, charcoal filtering, six hundred years of master distilling expertise, and a unique source of ingredients. Functionally, the brand would deliver an ultra-smooth taste, superior drinkability, and a unique taste profile— "an aromatic nose and a creamy, semisweet lingering finish."

Having developed a clearly superior vodka, Phillips then turned his attention to creating a brand story that romanced the origins, authenticity, and heritage of his product: "Authenticity and heritage and its Polish roots are extremely important to the essence of the brand. We are a six-hundred-year-old brand in terms of origins. The name itself represents the historical residency of Poland's presidents and royalty, dating back to the 1700s. It is currently one of the most beautiful buildings in Warsaw in one of the most picturesque parks." Phillips created a beautiful, distinctive package to signal the quality and sophistication of the product. The bottle was cork finished, the first of its kind in vodka, and prominently featured the Belvedere Palace. Back labeling clearly communicated the product's origins and point of difference, giving brand apostles a way to retell the brand story and signal their knowledge, intelligence, and sophistication.

Launching the luxury brand was the next step. Phillips and his team pioneered a brand-building model called "discovery marketing." Discovery marketing focuses on identifying and converting brand apostles, early adopters who are influential in creating trends in a category. The idea is to allow these best consumers to discover the next great thing—to be "in the know" and, as a result, influential with other people in the target consumer group. "We call it information one-upmanship," said Phillips. Prior to launch, Belvedere ran small teaser ads in the "Tiffany corner" (the upper right corner of page three) of *The Wall Street Journal*. "We didn't want to hit people over the head with advertising for our brand. When they came across the ad, they had the sense that they had been smart enough to discover something special, as opposed to having a new brand forced on them."

Phillips focused on three sets of influencers to create a buzz for the brand and drive early sales. First, he developed a list of prominent celebrities and leaders—including Robert Redford, Jack Smith (then CEO of General Motors), Bill Clinton, Barbra Streisand, Robert De Niro, and many others—and sent them a beautifully packaged bottle of Belvedere, along with a personal note. Second, he worked to convert influential bartenders and started by involving more than three hundred of them in product development. "When Belvedere came out, they thought of it as *their* brand," said Phillips.

"They felt they had helped to create it." In addition, the Millennium team held a series of events for bartenders around the country, to teach them the fine points of Belvedere luxury vodka and to build their loyalty. Finally, Phillips and his team focused on the finest white tablecloth restaurants in the country. They taught the staff the technical tasting points of luxury vodka, and explained to the management the attractive economics of trading up their customers to a $15 Belvedere martini. Phillips and his team worked market by market, establishment by establishment, to ensure their placement in these influential venues. One of the metrics for the brand is its penetration share on the drink menus of the best bars and restaurants. The result is high on-premise sales of 55 to 60 percent of volume, a vital indictor of the strength of the brand.

Having created the first significant luxury vodka brand, Phillips worked hard to protect it. He was vigilant about managing brand equity—not growing too quickly, always staying true to the heritage of the brand, and avoiding brand dilution. He and his team defined their "Principles of Luxury Marketing" to guide the company, and they are displayed on Phillips's office wall:

1. Luxury brands are held to a higher standard

2. Brand equity is the metric

3. Less is often more

4. Preserve brand equity by controlling unit sales

5. Any subluxury association with the brand spends brand equity

6. If it has been done before, redefine it or do not do it

7. Align goals and rewards to luxury principles

8. Luxury brands create luxury profits

Belvedere, an accessible superpremium New Luxury product, has been a major success and helped to reenergize the entire spirits category. A $12 Belvedere martini is within reach of any consumer who wants to make a statement about his or her taste and sophistication. However, the share positions of superpremium brands are unstable and first-mover advantage does not guarantee the lead position. Grey Goose was the third superpremium vodka to enter the market, after Belvedere and Chopin, but it is now the larger player in the segment. The newcomer overtook Belvedere largely on the strength of a different method of influence than the bartender endorsements used by Belvedere—Grey Goose won an important taste test, conducted by the Chicago Beverage Tasting Institute, and promoted the results heavily. For consumers, the rating provided validation of their choice and gave them "talking points" they could incorporate into their conversations about vodka—much as wine consumers do with influential wine ratings. Phillips and his team refute the Chicago Beverage Tasting Institute's methodology and point out that in subsequent tastings Belvedere and Grey Goose ended in a statistical dead heat. However, just as Jess Jackson built the success of his winery on the strength of an early tasting win, Grey Goose used its prize effectively in the game of one-upmanship.

But luxury vodka is about fashion, and today's leader may be tomorrow's laggard. The battle for influence will continue.

Samuel Adams: Brewing the Best Beer in America

The production process, as with vodka, was also central to the development of a new beer with an old-world character, Samuel Adams Boston Lager.

Beer was one of the first American industries revolutionized by low-cost, high-speed, high-throughput methods of manufacture and distribution in the late nineteenth century. After Prohibition, the surviving brewers invested in the industrialization of beer, lightening it to reduce the cost of raw materials, shortening the brewing time, increasing batch size, adding high-speed packaging equipment, and achieving cost reductions in distribution. In addition, the brewers discovered image advertising and mass promotion that squeezed the weaker producers out of market. As a result, tremendous consolidation has taken place in the industry. Over the past one hundred years, a business with two thousand independent local producers has been consolidated to three national brewers who have a combined 80 percent share. Today, market leader Anheuser-Busch is a $13 billion company earning 21 percent operating profit and investing $1 billion per year in capital improvements. The company has just over 49 percent of industry volume but 72 percent of industry profit. It is perhaps the toughest, most street-smart competitor in the world. Its competitive intensity, along with that of Miller Brewing Company and Coors Brewing Company, has driven the smaller brewers out of the market.

Over the years, the big players have perfected the game of producing huge quantities of product, with consistent quality, at low cost. The economies of scale are remarkable. When beer is brewed in a ten-million-barrel brewery, the cost can be as much as 20 percent lower than when it is brewed in a five hundred thousand-barrel brewery. The only "problem" with this business model is the product. It is consistent, fresh, and cheap but lacking in flavor and "craft" appeal, and it has a decidedly down-market image. Taste, ingredients, and aroma are secondary benefits held aside by the major producers. But the industry stagnated with few product innovations, and was relying on making an emotional connection with its core audience. Midprice beer is marketed by "bimbos in bikinis"—targeted to twenty-one- to twenty-five-year-old males by scantily clad women. As a result, the average real beer price has been in a fifty-year decline, putting pressure on brewers to drive even more operational improvements.

Then, in 1984, along came Jim Koch. At that time, Koch was a project manager, the equivalent of a junior partner at The Boston Consulting Group (BCG). He was on his way to becoming a full partner when the entrepreneurial itch hit him. "I am the first son of a man who was a fifth-generation brew master. My great-great-great-grandfather left Germany in the 1840s and went to St. Louis, where his son started the Louis Koch brewery. His brewery became part of the beer cartel. My grandfather worked for Anheuser-Busch. My father worked in many different breweries. So beer is in my blood." Koch hung up his calculator and raised $240,000—$100,000 of it, his own money—to start The Boston Beer Company. "My mission was and is to brew the best beer in America and to educate people to appreciate what makes great beer," he says.

By joining BCG, Koch had intended to break the generational

Jim Koch is the founder of The Boston Beer Company.
Photo courtesy of The Boston Beer Company.

cycle and end the lineage of continuous beer makers. "But I saw a beer market in which domestic beers were low cost but only moderate in quality, while imports were high priced, but even worse tasting than domestic beer. I said, 'If I can use the best ingredients to make a fresh, quality product, I can change the market.' I had my great-great-grandfather's recipe and the advice and counsel of my father."

Koch believed that the beer market was ripe for segmentation because the sales of imports were growing in the major East Coast cities. "But the beer itself was skunky," says Koch. "It was bad tasting and had bad aroma—it was at least ninety days old when it arrived at the retailers and had often suffered extreme fluctuations in temperature during shipping. I told my dad, 'The market is ripe for really good beer. I think I can start a brewery.'"

Koch prepared a business plan. "I laid out the price-volume demand curve for the U.S. beer market on log paper. I figured we could sell eight thousand barrels a year by the end of five years. But it turned out that our beer was off the curve. Little did I know that higher quality would translate into higher volume. I believed there were people who wanted something better than Michelob. We reached our eight thousand-barrel goal in just five months. And, at 1.3 million barrels today, we have exceeded my wildest dreams."

Like many other New Luxury start-ups, The Boston Beer Company started very small. At first, there were only two employees: Jim and his former secretary from BCG, Rhonda Kallman, who became the sales manager. They had no office for the first six months of operation. Everything was done with an answering service and pay phones. Meetings were held in bars. Bills were written and stamped "paid" by hand. New-product development was done in Jim's kitchen. "In the beginning, it was Rhonda and me," says Koch. "She knew the bars, related to the customers, had the interpersonal skills. We started in Boston. Rhonda and I sold. I delivered. In the second year, we got some distribution in Washington and New York. I commuted three days a week."

Among the first hires was one of America's most distinguished brew masters, Dr. Joe Owades, the inventor of light beer for Gablinger's, the first light beer in the United States. Dr. Owades helped Koch standardize the brewing process so it could be replicated and scaled up, using the small-scale brewing chambers characteristic of nineteenth-century brewing equipment, combined with the twentieth-century methods of quality control—including mild pasteurization, stainless-steel equipment, automated temperature control, fast temperature reduction as needed, and computerized record keeping.

"Although we struggled in the early days, we knew we had a better glass of beer." Accordingly, Koch priced his beer at a 50 percent premium to Heineken and a 100 percent premium to Budweiser. "We didn't have a choice," he says. "Our costs were higher. We needed the price. When the customer tried it, we won." Within six weeks of its first shipments, Samuel Adams Boston Lager was named "Best Beer in America" by five thousand judges at the largest beer festival in the United States. Since that first honor, Koch's brewery has won more than seventy international awards from world beer competitions in Australia, Belgium, England, Sweden, and the Great American Beer Festival—where The Boston Beer Company is the only craft brewer to have won top awards every year for fifteen consecutive years. Samuel Adams Boston Lager was voted "Best Beer in America" in the critical start-up years from 1985 through 1989. *Time* rated it the best beer of the decade.

Today, Boston Beer is the largest specialty brewer, with sales of $250 million in 2002—at price premiums of roughly 100 percent over Budweiser, Miller Lite, and Coors—and a market capitalization of $250 million.

How do you create a beer company from scratch, with only $240,000 in capital? You start by identifying and controlling the most important elements of the value chain. Boston Beer is a "layer" player—the company controls some parts of the beer production process directly but contracts out many elements of the value chain. Although the company owns breweries in Boston and Cincinnati, half of the beer is still brewed under contract. Koch works with selected brewers, who must use the highest-quality "noble" hops (imported from the Czech Republic and Germany) and malted barley specified in his great-grandfather's recipe. Unlike the mass marketers, Koch does not use corn, rice, syrup, sugar, or stabilizers in the recipe, and there is "no water dilution" in the final processing steps. As a result, Samuel Adams Boston Lager was the first American beer accepted for import into Germany, where strict "purity" regulations stopped Budweiser and Heineken at the border.

In addition to controlling the selection of ingredients and the recipe, Koch also controls labeling, packaging, and distribution. According to Koch, beer tastes best immediately after production. So the product is marked with a "freshness date"—the first in the industry—a sell-by date on each bottle that the consumer can read and understand. In other food businesses, such code dates are unreadable without a codebook. "Selling quality means selling fresh-

ness. We beat the imports hands down on freshness. A bottle of imported beer sold at a bar can be six months or more from production. We try to manage consumption of our beer within one month
for peak-flavor release."

Next you identify the core consumer. "I never did marketing at
BCG," says Koch. "I had hunches. We went after them. Our ideal
drinker was a twenty-six-year-old male stockbroker. We went to the
upscale bars that they went to after work. Why stockbrokers? They
talk to everybody. Make one stockbroker happy and you get one
hundred recommendations a day. It was a radically different approach—no advertising, lots of PR." It worked: the business grew
sales at 40 percent per year from 1984 to 1996. The Boston Beer
Company went public in 1995, and the original investors realized a
return of six hundred to one.

But, as generally happens with the success of a New Luxury entry, the emergence of the Sam Adams brand provoked a dramatic
competitive response. Anheuser-Busch made investments in micro-
brewers, relaunched its premium Michelob brand, and pushed its
distributors to handle their brands exclusively. Hundreds of competitors in the craft-brewing segment started up, including Pete's
Brewing, Sierra Nevada Brewing, Hart Brewing, and Mendocino
Brewing. As a result, the steady increase in sales of Sam Adams
slowed; but Boston Beer remained dominant in the craft segment,
with sales about equal to the combined volume of the next five
largest craft brewers.

Despite the extraordinary success of Sam Adams, Jim Koch has
realistic expectations about the brand's potential. Today, New Luxury beer drinkers consume a variety of brands. In the industry, it is
known as a "circle of brands." Each is consumed for a different oc-
casion—at home either alone or with friends, or on premises at a
bar. Consumers change favorite beers frequently, in response to recommendations from their peers or because they try a new beer and
like it. Drinking a superpremium brand is a statement of prestige,
affluence, and sophistication. Koch does not expect, however, that
the beer drinker will switch all his consumption from Budweiser,
Coors, or Miller to Sam Adams. Koch's target consumer will use
Sam Adams for high visibility when drinking on premises, and at

home when he wants the highest-quality product. In the words of Jake, the golfer with Callaway clubs, "Bud is a great everyday product but no one is going to be impressed when you call out for a Bud Light. When I'm on a date, if I say 'Give me a Sam Adams,' I know she knows I'm special and have some taste."

For New Luxury beer makers, the U.S. market is a tough place to succeed. Most product goes to market through a three-tier distribution system—factory to distributor to retailer. Over the past five years, the distributors have moved rapidly to "exclusivity" with a single major manufacturer. The cost of distribution is affected by the "drop size"—the amount of beer delivered to each retail outlet. The bigger the market share of the brand, the bigger the average drop size. Anheuser-Busch's share in the U.S. market is approaching 50 percent, which gives the company crushing control of the on-premises channel, including pubs and bars. The company has forced the distributor to put time and activity into serving the most prominent retailers, put extra effort into creating Anheuser-Busch displays and facings, and devote more shelf space to its products. For distributors, the benefits of exclusivity are real. They receive extra money per case and better credit terms, and often they receive capital to buy equipment and systems. So by 2002, some 34 percent of distributors were handling only Anheuser-Busch brands. The company's get-tough distribution policies have been successful in delivering a gain of a share point each year.

The premium beer segment is now crowded with me-too competitors. Import brands have been aggressive in marketing and promotion. The major domestics have countered with niche brands and partial shares of craft brewers—both Anheuser-Busch and Miller have bought microbreweries and launched high-end products produced under labels distinct from their parents. In 2002, Boston Beer countered with the successful introduction of Sam Adams Light, bringing new growth into the business and accounting for up to 25 percent of its total beer sales.

Jim Koch is an archetypal New Luxury competitor. He entered the industry as an outsider, an industrial consultant; he ignored all the rules of competition. He went for class, not mass. He held true to standards of quality and detail not seen in the industry. And he fearlessly went against one of the world's toughest competitors, Anheuser-Busch, and operated outside the view of its radar screen until his brand and product following were strong enough and big enough to take a pummeling attack. He priced his product 50 percent higher than the segment leader, didn't advertise for the first decade of the company's existence, and picked his points of distribution selectively, selling only to accounts that would give him high profile and promotion.

"We make beer for people who love great-tasting, full-bodied beer. People who want authenticity and quality and freshness. Our product is demonstrably better than the competition. It has better color, aroma, balance, mouth feel, and consistency. The taste lingers nicely. It's not bitter. It's balanced. The ingredients are more expensive, but it's worth it. Now we've done it again for light beer." This is a man who loves his product.

Now The Boston Beer Company is doing what every New Luxury company must do: seeking new ways to reach the core consumer, without compromising the quality, performance, and emotional connection of the product. If you arrive at Atlanta's airport around midnight, the airport shops are closed except for one: the Sam Adams Brewhouse—a beer and food emporium that exclusively features Boston Beer Company products. It's a joint venture with Host Marriott and serves as a "beer education center." It is usually packed with travelers enjoying and learning about America's better beers. Koch calls it a sampling station—visible, high-profile, expensive real estate that will provide the next generation of Sam Adams growth.

Eleven

Demonstrably Superior and Pleasingly Different

Ely Callaway was a man who had four careers; the final two involved the founding and leadership of two iconic New Luxury companies: Callaway Vineyard & Winery and Callaway Golf. He is a model for the New Luxury entrepreneur—a relentless innovator, an outsider unafraid to attack a stagnating market, and an entrepreneur closely in touch with the emotional needs of his consumers.

Born in 1919, Callaway attended Emory University to get a liberal arts education and also to avoid the family business, a textile concern called Callaway Mills. In 1941, after graduating, he joined the Army Quartermaster Corps. When the Army learned of his family's background, he was assigned to the centralized procurement facility for all textiles and apparel. After the Japanese attack on Pearl Harbor, his job took on startling dimensions. "All of a sudden we were buying hundreds of millions of items of apparel and all of the fabrics," he told *Emory* magazine. At the end of the war, Callaway, by then the youngest-ever major in the Army Quartermaster Corps, "had twenty-five thousand people working there, administering contracts all over the United States. I was spending at the rate of something like $700 million a year under just my jurisdiction, with my name on every contract. So you learn business real quick."

After discharge, Callaway received several job offers, many from the companies from whom he had been procuring cotton and wool.

He joined Deering Milliken Company and began a career in the textile industry that spanned nearly thirty years. He spent the last seventeen of those years at Burlington Industries, the last five of those as president. During that time, he proved himself to be a relentless innovator—especially in developing blended fabrics, using such components as Dacron and wool. But when the chairmanship position became open, Callaway was not offered the job, and he retired, at the age of fifty-four, to the vineyard in Temecula, California, he had bought some years earlier. He turned his attention to Callaway Vineyard & Winery (career number three) and began producing wines whose quality far exceeded the expectations of rivals, critics, and consumers. In 1981, he sold his company to spirits giant Hiram Walker for $14 million, realizing a profit of nearly $9 million. The next year, Callaway was playing golf, and he tried a club unfamiliar to him—a putter based on a traditional design, featuring a shaft made of steel encased in hickory wood. Within two weeks, he bought half of the company that made it, Hickory Stick, USA; over the next twenty years, he built it into the largest and most successful supplier of golf equipment in the world.

Callaway Golf grew from one of the smallest golf companies in the world, with revenues of $364,000 in 1982, to the number one player in golf equipment globally in just a decade, with peak market share as high as 40 percent. Most remarkably, the company made a huge leap in just three years. In 1989, Callaway had sales of $10 million and did not appear on the list of the top ten golf-club manufacturers. By 1992, Callaway sales had leaped to $100 million and it was at the top of the list.

Along the way, Callaway set a clear model for New Luxury entrepreneurs: he looked for, and found, openings in markets where the existing competitors had stopped listening (if they ever had listened) to their customers. He employed technology to create genuine technical differences and meaningful performance benefits in his products. He marketed his products relentlessly, committing his own resources and influence, reaching out to important authorities and modelers, and creating apostles for the brand. He did not fear asking a premium price for his goods, because he believed that his products were better and that consumers would pay for quality, innovation, improved performance, and emotional engagement. He expected that consumers would be loyal to—even worship—providers that could deliver such products. He followed the model once, and then he did it again and again.

Callaway also left a legacy for the company that continues under his name. Employees at "his" golf company use his words today to mark and guide their work. "He set us on a path to always be the leader—innovative, built on connection to the recreational golfer, appealing to his emotions and needs," Callaway's head of marketing told us. "We set out each year to bring the market real innovation. We need to use our research and development to deliver break-throughs to the game of golf." A year after his death, employees were still mourning him. They think of him as "sunshine and pep," "imagination and dreams," and "fun and ideas."

To the would-be New Luxury innovator, Callaway's ideas, careers, and products offer both encouragement and insight.

Ely's Vision: To Popularize the Game of the Rich, Famous, and Skilled

If you play golf, you know that as you step up to the first tee, all eyes of the others in your foursome—and, most likely, those of the foursome teeing up after you—are watching. As you stand in front of the ball, a small voice in your mind whispers your latest swing-related mantra. "Swing easy," says the voice, and "follow through." Or, "One on the take-away, two on the turn." Or, "Finish the swing." There are many such mantras, but not many good tee shots. The average weekend player, more often than not, ends up hitting the ball "fat" (stabbing the ground before hitting the ball) or "thin" (hitting it too near the top), "hooking it" (soaring to the left of a right-handed player) or "slicing it" (going to the right for a righty). An eighteen-hole course typically has a par of seventy-one or seventy-two, but more than 80 percent of all rounds played end in scores over one hundred. Fewer than 2 percent of America's twenty-six million golfers have earned a single-digit handicap—meaning hardly anyone regularly scores lower than eighty.

As a result, many golfers suffer from feelings of "golf inadequacy"—especially when they tee up next to more skilled golfers.

The feeling becomes particularly acute when the golfer is playing a new course with an experienced partner or finds himself in a match with strangers. The feelings of inadequacy become all the more acute when bets are laid on the game, as they very often are. The stakes are usually modest—a "Nassau" bet, a wager on who will win the front nine holes, the back nine, and the eighteenth, is seldom more than $20. But ego and pride are really what's at stake, and the players become so intense, earnest, and nervous that they might as well be playing at the U.S. Open. Golf is a game of practiced frustration, which may be why three million golfers give up the sport each year. It's also a game of hope and challenge, which is why another three million take it up each year. "I hate the game, and I love the game," one golfer told us. "I'm out here every Saturday and every Sunday. I get fresh air, time with my friends, and the agony of always knowing on every shot that I can do better. Sometimes I hit the ball badly and take a mulligan. My next shot is perfect. I ask myself, Who was that other guy who hit so poorly?"

Golf is primarily a man's game—75 percent of golfers are male—and, historically, a game for rich and famous men. Every president in the twentieth century, except for Franklin Delano Roosevelt, has played golf. Presidents George H. W. Bush and George W. Bush meet at their summer place in Kennebunkport, Maine, to play golf together. On Ely Callaway's seventy-fifth birthday, he received a video from President Bill Clinton, who said, "I wish that you'd find a way to make my game as good as my clubs." Clinton played, of course, with Callaway clubs.

And so, combined with their feelings of inadequacy, golfers have delusions of grandeur and alignment with the great players, both pros and amateurs. "In the art of self-delusion, the golfer has few peers among sportsmen," says the *Economist*. "This aptitude is especially impressive when he enters the professional's shop, with its glittering array of clubs, balls, and training aids that promise a miraculous cure for human frailty. Around the world, golfers spend $5 billion a year on the means of pursuing their passion, as much as the GNP of Lithuania."

Ely Callaway, as an experienced golfer who had many golfing friends, knew firsthand about the emotions of the average golfer.

There was golf in the family—the great golfer Bobby Jones, the first golfer to win the four major tournaments of the time in a single year, was a distant cousin. Ely grew up in LaGrange, Georgia, and was club champion at his local course as a young man. Throughout his life, he loved to play and talk golf. He understood the golfer's complaints and misgivings.

Callaway wanted to ease the feelings of inadequacy for the average player who could never match the skill, put in as much practice, or achieve the intensity of a pro. But he also wanted to enable every golfer to feel like a pro, at least now and again—hitting a sweet, thundering drive, tapping in a forty-foot putt, making a shot he could play back in his mind, over and over. Callaway believed that better clubs could make the difference between a game that is mostly frustration and pain and one with flashes of pride and pleasure.

Golf is about physics as well as emotions. To make the head of a golf club connect with a golf ball in such a way that the ball travels in a specific direction for a desired distance requires a complex combination of muscle control, hand-eye coordination, and strength. Traditional golf clubs are designed for experienced, avid golfers and golf pros. With a "pro" club, the rotation of the golfer's body and the angle of the head need to be just right in order for the golfer to hit the ball precisely. To the duffer a pro club is virtually untamable. If the average player hits a ball .039 inches off the center of the club, the ball will travel 5 percent less distance than if it had been smacked dead center—that's a "distance penalty" of 12.5 yards on a typical 250-yard drive. But most weekend golfers would be thrilled to hit the ball as little as .039 inches off the center of the club. More often, they hit it far enough off-center that it misses the fairway altogether, lands in the rough, or drops in a pond. The average golfer buys more than one hundred balls to play a dozen rounds of golf each year. That means he loses an average of eight balls per round. Beginners lose many more.

When Callaway entered the industry, golf clubs looked much as they had for decades. There had been a few innovations along the way—cavity back irons, graphite shafts, metal heads to replace the traditional persimmon wood—but golfers were still struggling to master the club as much as the game itself.

At first, Callaway concentrated on promoting the existing line of hickory shaft putters and wedges, doing little more than changing the name of his newly acquired company to Callaway Hickory Stick USA. *Sports Illustrated* reports that he offered famed golfer Chi Chi Rodriguez $250,000 to play with Callaway Hickory Stick wedges on the Senior PGA Championship. "I told him I wouldn't play with them for $1 million," Rodriguez is reported as replying. The clubs were too heavy and unforgiving for most golfers.

Callaway realized that in order to realize his ambition, he needed to innovate and create a different kind of golf club. To do so, he needed first-rate talent, and he found it in Richard C. Helmstetter, who had long experience in the sporting goods industry. Helmstetter had lived and worked for some twenty years in Japan, a major golf market. "Dick-san," as he is known at Callaway, joined the company in 1986 as head of research and development.

Callaway also needed money to fund his innovations. He had invested $400,000 of his own money to buy Hickory Stick in 1982, and he had convinced two small investment firms to commit some $500,000 for equipment and working capital. In 1988, he convinced the General Electric Pension Fund to invest $10 million. He and Helmstetter used the money to develop a new line of irons and metalwoods called S2H2, for Short, Straight, Hollow Hosel. (The hosel is the socket, or neck, on the head of the club into which the shaft fits.) S2H2 did well, doubling the company's sales over the next two years.

The Demonstrably Superior and Pleasingly Different (DSPD) Big Bertha

Then came the club that would transform the game of golf and make Callaway the biggest and most important golf-equipment maker in the world: the Big Bertha driver. "For most golfers in the world," Callaway told *Emory*, "the driver was the most feared, least-liked club in the bag." In Japan, Callaway had seen a large-head driver, made of graphite by the leading Japanese sports-equipment manufacturer, Yonex. Callaway liked the idea of the big-head club but didn't like the way it handled or the sound the head made when it came in contact with the ball. He and Helmstetter worked together to create a special sound for the Big Bertha, so that a well-hit ball created a musical, and magical, experience.

Ely Callaway, founder of Callaway Golf, shows a promotional version of the Big Bertha driver. Photo courtesy of Callaway Golf.

Callaway decided to create a driver with a large head made of stainless steel rather than graphite and combine it with the S2H2 technology. "We had to find a way to make it larger by 25 percent, but no heavier than a conventional driver," said Callaway. "That's the secret. It's not just that it's large, but that it is enlarged by a substantial amount for forgiveness without making it any heavier." Helmstetter was skeptical of the idea at first, but Callaway was a persuasive salesman of ideas and products, and eventually convinced his research and development chief. "Ely told me that he had to have a product that was DSPD—demonstrably superior and pleasingly different. Then he gave me the freedom and the money to go and do it."

To create such a large head required that its walls be unusually thin, to minimize weight, and that would make them vulnerable to crushing when the ball was struck hard. Helmstetter got some development help from the Aircraft Engines Division at General Electric, which had developed a process for casting metals that produced thin walls with high strength. Despite the complexities of the process, the prototypes of the new driver were ready in a remarkably short period—just eight months from conception. "In less than a week after we got the first sample parts, shafted them up, and started to hit balls with them, we knew we had a big idea." In tests, they found that golfers were able to hit straighter shots with the new club, even when they hit the ball off-center. They hit the ball farther more often. When it was windy, the ball was less likely to sail high. They could hit the ball more smoothly, even in rough turf. The club felt more stable and responsive in their hands than any other club they had ever tried.

Ely Callaway knew he was onto something, and he believed he could charge a substantial premium for it. The head alone cost Callaway about $20 to manufacture, more than twice as much as the S2H2 head. But he knew that in addition to wanting performance improvements, golfers were also prone to purchasing equipment as a means of expressing Individual Style. They liked owning and showing off the newest clubs and accessories, and they had the money to pay the premium to do so. He decided to price the new club at $250, more than twice the price of a metal head driver from TaylorMade, then the industry leader. "It was a magic price," Bruce Parker, Callaway's chief sales executive, told *Sports Illustrated*.

Callaway also decided to give his big idea an appropriately big name, Big Bertha, a nickname for a huge World War I cannon that could fire a shell over distances up to eighty miles. Helmstetter thought the name would be unappealing and his wife thought it would be offensive to women. Golf pros hated the name. Jack Welch hated the name. According to *Sports Illustrated*, only Callaway and Bruce Parker, the sales head, favored the name. "I didn't know if it was a good name or a bad name," Parker said, "but I knew it was a name people would remember."

The Callaway Big Bertha driver was introduced in 1991 and was an immediate success. In its debut year, Callaway sold some 150,000

Big Berthas, and corporate sales more than doubled—climbing to $54.7 million, up from $22 million in 1990. Demand was so great, in fact, that Callaway was forced to allocate its limited production, and soon golfers were paying a premium—above the already large premium contained in the list price—to any dealer who could get them one of the wonder clubs. From 1991 to 1998, Callaway Golf's net sales increased by at least $100 million each year. In 1992, Callaway Golf went public, achieving a peak market value of $2.5 billion on sales of $849 million with operating income at $214 million.

Callaway marketed the Big Bertha selling direct to existing customers, using word of mouth and a clever mix of influence and event marketing. In the first year, the company used little advertising—just a few print ads in consumer and trade publications, but no television or radio. Callaway understood that the weekend golfer, like many amateur athletes, is strongly influenced by the celebrity player and the professional golfer. Over the years, he convinced an eclectic and wonderful array of golfing enthusiasts to endorse Callaway, including boxer Sugar Ray Leonard, singer Smokey Robinson, and Microsoft founder Bill Gates.

The professional golfer, however, was slower to respond to the new drivers. In 1992, however, Callaway signed Johnny Miller as spokesman. At the time, Miller was a semiretired veteran player who in 1973 had shot the lowest final-round score, sixty-three, in a major golf championship. He had not won a championship in years. By the end of the 1992 golf season, Big Bertha drivers were the number one club used by players on the Senior PGA, LPGA, and Nike (then Hogan) tours. Year-end sales more than doubled once again, to $132 million.

Then, in 1994, Johnny Miller made a comeback, winning the AT&T Pebble Beach National Pro-Am tournament, using Callaway clubs and sporting Callaway logos that showed up nicely on television. In light of Miller's win, other professional players on the tour decided to give Callaway a try. Over the years, Callaway signed up Arnold Palmer, Annika Sorenstam, John Daly, and other leading pros. When Sorenstam shot the first fifty-nine in the history of women's professional golf using Callaway equipment, the company made sure the world knew about it.

In addition to a superior product and a nonconventional marketing program, Callaway—like many other New Luxury players—had to go outside the existing distribution system to reach his audience. At the time, most golf-equipment sales were made through golf course pro shops, which were conservative buyers and slow to stock new or different products. As a result Callaway had been selling its Hickory Stick and S2H2 clubs primarily through off-course retailers. Now the golf course shops wanted the Big Bertha, but Callaway didn't have enough product to satisfy them—and didn't want to jeopardize its relationships with the off-course retailers. The success of the Big Bertha catalyzed a change in the distribution and retailing of golf and other sports equipment. Today, most sales of golf gear are made through off-course retailers such as Golfsmith and Edwin Watts International Golf.

A Thirteen-Times Premium for Emotional Engagement

What would prompt a recreational golfer to pay $4,000 for a Callaway "outfit," as a complete set of clubs is called, when a similar set of clubs can be purchased for less than $300?

At a public golf course in Chicago, we met and talked with Jake, the golf enthusiast and Callaway apostle whom we described earlier in the book. He does not fit the profile of the typical golfer—the well-heeled, executive duffer. He is a thirty-four-year-old construction worker who earns $18 per hour, paid in cash at the end of his shift—less than $50,000 per year. Throughout the eight-month golf season, Jake works the early shift, starting at 6 A.M. so he can be on the golf course by 2 P.M. He plays eighteen holes Monday through Friday and thirty-six holes—two rounds—on Saturday and Sunday. He is a three-index golfer, which means that he is expected to shoot just three holes over par. Jake is single and lives alone in a one-bedroom apartment he rents for $600 a month. He has dated many women but has never found one who will tolerate his "addiction" to golf.

We paired up with Jake at the public course and watched with interest and anticipation as he teed up at the first hole and selected a Callaway Great Big Bertha driver from his bag, which contained only Callaway clubs. His tee shot flew three hundred yards, straight down the fairway. We complimented him on the shot and on his collection of clubs. Jake smiled. "These are the best clubs money can buy," he said. "They cost me a pretty penny, and I had to save money for a whole year to buy them, but they're worth it." He described in detail the technical differences: the titanium face, the expanded sweet spot, the balanced weight, and other features. To afford them, Jake told us that he had to distort his spending—he was a true golf rocketer. "Forty cents of every dollar I make goes for greens fees, equipment, golf clothes, and golf trips," he said. "Golf is my life."

Technical differences and performance improvements were only part of the attraction Jake felt for Callaway. "The real reason I bought them," he says, "is that they make me feel rich. You can run the biggest company in the world and be one of the richest guys in the world, but you can't buy any clubs better than these." Then Jake's comments got a little more personal. "I match up with guys like you all the time," he said. "You are what I call 'an executive suburbanite duffer.' You are tight, stressed, and don't practice very much. When I kick your butt on the course, I feel good, I feel equal. I may make a lot less money than you do, but I think I have a better life."

Jake did, in fact, kick our butt, scoring a seventy-four in our round together—compared to our ninety-eight. When we were finished, as darkness settled in, Jake meticulously wiped and cleaned his clubs and placed them carefully in their assigned positions in his bag. "Thank you, Mr. Callaway, for another fine day," he said. He swung his bag into the back of his pickup truck, climbed behind the wheel, and drove away.

Jake may be atypical in his ability, but his emotional reasons for purchasing premium Callaway clubs are typical. Most recreational golfers will pay dearly for a club that is easier to hit, sends the ball more predictably, and in each round, consistently delivers a shot or two worthy of a pro.

Unlike Jake, the majority of weekend golfers have high incomes and modest innate skills. That is why, according to *Golf* magazine, the average avid golfer spends $4,356 on golf each year. Golfers buy books, videos, and magazines, take lessons, and attend clinics in hopes of improving their game. But the bulk of the spending is on equipment—the average golfer buys ten dozen premium golf balls each year, a new wood and a putter every three years, a new set of irons every five years. Equipment prices vary greatly. At Costco, you can buy a complete set of clubs and a bag under the Jack "Golden Bear" Nicklaus name for $199. But if you appeared on a golf course with them, other golfers would look askance, and your friends would ridicule you from the first tee.

By comparison, a set of Callaway Hawk EyeVFT (Variable Face Thickness Technology) irons retails for $1,599. Add to that three woods, including a driver, priced at $499 each, a putter at $199, and a set of wedges, priced at $159 each. A complete set of Callaway's best clubs, two dozen balls, and a matching bag and towel costs about $3,700. With a pair of Callaway pants, a shirt, a sweater, a jacket, and a hat (all manufactured under license), the bill amounts to $4,000.

That is why sales of golf equipment have grown at a 9 percent real rate over the past decade while the total number of golfers has remained constant.

The Callaway Scorecard

1. *Never underestimate the customer.* "You can't fool the public," Callaway said. "If they are going to buy your product, it has to be better, it has to be right. It has to be truly more satisfying than the existing product."

Callaway demonstrated relentless interest in consumers, obsessively working to create a better game for them. And he never stopped "chatting" with his customers. They are always eager to tell their stories and talk about their hopes, fears, dreams, and wishes—and these can provide inspiration and ideas for product refinements, new features, and new designs.

2. *Shatter the price-volume demand curve.* When the Big Bertha driver was introduced in 1991, it was priced at a significant premium to every other driver on the market at the time. It retailed at prices from $240 to $300. An equivalent TaylorMade club retailed for about $150, and clubs from Titleist, Ping, Cobra, and Wilson sold at prices from $75 to $160. In 1991, Callaway sold more than 150,000 Big Berthas. Callaway had discovered, like his New Luxury

counterparts, that there can be far more volume for premium-priced products than conventional wisdom would suggest.

3. *Create a ladder of genuine benefits.* The ladder of benefits is particularly easy to see with Callaway clubs. The technical differences were obvious and visible: a bigger head, lightweight cast-metal head, S2H2 hosel, and more. The technical differences made a direct, immediate, and also visible difference in performance. Ordinary golfers could hit longer, straighter shots more often. All of this added up to emotional benefits that are almost impossible to describe to a nongolfer. "We sell the physical and emotional experience of hitting a satisfying golf shot, not increasing your distance by eight yards or that your handicap will fall," Callaway said. "Hitting the ball well is the most rewarding part of the game for people, rather than scoring. We're selling the enjoyment of helping the average player pull off more satisfying shots."

4. *Escalate innovation, elevate quality, deliver a flawless experience.* From the beginning, Callaway understood the importance of investing in technology. Callaway knew that his customers—many of whom thought of themselves as "club junkies"—wanted a steady stream of new products, and he provided them. First Big Bertha, then Great Big Bertha, then the Biggest Big Bertha. New technologies including VFT; ERC II with its springlike effect; and the C4 driver, which weighs 25 percent less than comparably sized clubs and has a tungsten-urethane face and a shaft three inches longer, making for even truer and longer tee shots. The company continues to spend more on research and development—about $30 million per year—than most of its competitors. Only Titleist and Taylor-Made spend similar amounts, and they have done so largely in response to the Callaway challenge. At this writing, Callaway holds some five hundred patents and has five hundred more pending.

To aid in the development of its golf innovations, Callaway has also invested heavily in testing and analysis systems and equipment, including hitting robots, air cannons, ultrahigh-speed cameras, distance and dispersion sensors, and the "Sir Isaac" Performance System. Callaway makes its innovations visible and available to customers; every buyer is invited for a free custom fitting at the

Callaway headquarters in Carlsbad, California. The customer spends two hours in a hitting chamber, where his swing is measured and analyzed—club head speed, angle of strike, ball distance. He then receives a "prescription" for a new set of clubs, which are sold only through authorized dealers. The information about these customers—seventeen thousand have visited over the years—is entered into a database which is used to help establish the design parameters for the next generation of clubs.

Callaway himself set the tone for innovation. He spent weekends collecting data on the golf course: seeing what players were playing with which equipment, how they were doing, what they wanted. On Monday morning, he arrived at the office brimming with new ideas. "You had to have your track shoes on," remembers one employee, "because Ely was moving fast."

5. *Extend the price range and positioning of the brand.* Callaway has chosen not to extend the price range of its clubs as broadly as other New Luxury makers. Within a club type, the price range is about 2.5. The low-end irons sell for about $600, while the high-end irons sell at $1,600. But to drive growth and hold consumer interest, the company has been relentless about creating Callaway products in a wide range of equipment and accessories. It offers a complete set of clubs in steel and graphite, including woods, irons, wedges, and putters; it makes a variety of premium balls; and it also sells a range of accessories such as bags, luggage, towels, and umbrellas, as well as apparel.

6. *Customize your value chain to deliver on the benefit ladder.* Out of necessity at first, Callaway helped make golf equipment more accessible to players by offering it in sports equipment retailers off the golf course. With the success of Big Bertha, however, off-course retailers grew in popularity. Because the typical player makes it to the golf course only ten to twelve times per year, the availability of clubs in retail shops has helped to drive purchase and visibility. Selling and merchandising skills that Callaway brought to the mass golf retailer further changed the game.

7. *Use influence marketing; seed your success through brand apostles.* Ely Callaway was particularly effective in getting his products into the hands of influential consumers in highly visible situations. In

1976, during his wine years, his 1974 Callaway White Riesling was chosen as the only wine to be served at a bicentennial luncheon held on July 9 at the Waldorf-Astoria Hotel in New York—the guest of honor was Elizabeth II, queen of the United Kingdom. Callaway attended the affair and was told just afterward that the queen had enjoyed the wine so much she had actually asked for a second glass. "There were ten people from the press standing around listening," Callaway told *Emory*, "so we made every paper in the United States the next day." The wine industry swirled with rumors that Callaway had paid for his wine to be selected for the luncheon, but he denied it. "I didn't have influence with anybody," he said. "The wine got attention and was selected because it was a superior product that was totally different from any other wine in the world." Similarly, Callaway got his clubs into the hands of famous golfers in many walks of life and made sure that the press and his customers knew about it.

As a result, Callaway owners become apostles. Callaway equipment is a "must-have," says one golfer, and owners want to buy the newest model as soon as it is introduced. "At least I like my clubs," said another Callaway apostle, "even if I don't like my swing."

8. *Continually attack the category like an outsider.* "It's very simple," Callaway said. "Develop a product that is clearly more satisfying to the user than anybody else's. To do this, you've got to stick your neck out and gamble. Fortunately, this is an industry where most of the others won't do it." In both golf and wine, Callaway saw industries that had become stagnant, and he entered the industry as an outsider unfettered by the conventional wisdom.

Like all New Luxury innovators, Callaway was infatuated with his product in a way that industry lifers rarely are. "You have to be almost crazy in love with the product that you want to make or the service that you want to sell," he said. "You have to believe in it."

The Callaway Legacy

After its dramatic rise to the top, Callaway Golf peaked in 1997, and the company's growth slowed considerably. During the years 1992 through 1997, sales grew at a 15 percent compound annual growth rate; from 1998 to 2001, sales grew at just 3 percent CAGR. The cooling off came as a result of many factors. As often happens when a New Luxury innovator redraws the demand curve and transforms its category, established competitors took responsive action and new rivals emerged to get in on the action. Rival TaylorMade successfully responded to Callaway's technical lead with innovations of its own. Head, the revolutionary in skis and tennis, is reentering the golf equipment market with a patented piezoelectric technology that stiffens and stabilizes the club head for control and precision. As a result, the production capacity for high-end clubs has come to exceed demand, and the premium makers, including Callaway, have had to resort to discounting. And because of the steady stream of innovations and the regular trading up of many golfers, a large business in used clubs has developed. It is possible to buy last year's Callaway driver at half price. Callaway, in fact, has begun a used-club certification process similar to Lexus's certified used-car program.

Callaway entered the ball market late, in 1999, and invested some $75 million to build a factory with sufficient capacity to enable the company to take a lead position in the market. Although balls are now nearly a $100 million business for Callaway, the company has departed from its influence marketing approach and invested heavily in advertising. As a result of these expenditures, the business has yet to turn a profit, and Titleist, the leading ball maker, maintains its 50 percent market share.

And, of course, Callaway's death in 2001 shook the company. A visit to the sprawling Carlsbad campus is marked by frequent references to the founder and his vision and energy. His spirit remains strong at the headquarters. As we toured the factory, our guide said, "We know he's gone, but his words still drive us—'demonstrably superior and pleasingly different.' He was a very kind man. We all knew him and knew what he believed in." Callaway Golf will doubtless find new ways to innovate, create genuine differences, and deliver on the pledge Ely Callaway made to his customers. He never promised that his clubs would lower their score. All he said was that he would make golf much more fun to play.

His slogan: "Enjoy the game."

Twelve

A Cautionary Tale of an Old Luxury Brand

Well there she sits, buddy, just a'gleaming in the sun, right
There to greet a working man when his day is done
I'm gonna pack my pa, and I'm gonna pack my aunt
I'm gonna take them down to the Cadillac Ranch.

El Dorado fins, whitewalls, and skirts
Rides just like a little bit of heaven here on earth
Well, buddy, when I die throw my body in the back
And drive me to the junkyard in my Cadillac.

Hey, little girlie in the blue jeans so tight
Drivin' all alone through the Colorado night
You're my last love, baby, you're my last chance
Don't let 'em take me to the Cadillac Ranch

Cadillac, Cadillac . . .
Long and dark, shiny and black,
Open up them engines, let 'em roar
Tearin' up the highway like a big old dinosaur

"Cadillac Ranch"
by Bruce Springsteen

The Decline and Fall of an American Old Luxury Icon

In the thirty years after World War II, Cadillac was the epitome of Old Luxury in the American car market—sleek, chromed, and elegant. Most of all, it was emotionally powerful, driven by the most glamorous celebrities—James Cagney, Gary Cooper, Joan Crawford, Bing Crosby, Cary Grant, Elvis Presley, and Jackie Kennedy. After World War II, the operations of German carmakers Mercedes-Benz and BMW lay in ruins, and, in Japan, Toyota struggled to build twenty-seven-horsepower vehicles, known in the industry as "Toyopets." But General Motors, responding to the enormous postwar demand for consumer goods, had the resources and capabilities to create marvels of design—big cars, sporting more chrome than any competitive model. The name Cadillac became synonymous with status, achievement, and recognition, and the brand car became a cultural icon; it appeared in the most successful Hollywood movies, and singers crooned about it in more than a hundred ballads. "Love for your pink Cadillac . . . crushed velvet seats . . . riding in the back, oozing down the street."

Beginning in the mid-1970s, however, with the increase in imports from Japan and Europe, Americans' definitions of quality and luxury began to change, as did our attitudes toward driving performance. General Motors found itself under siege from Toyota and Honda, whose cars offered higher quality at lower prices, and the company began to lose market share in its Chevrolet, Pontiac, Buick, and Oldsmobile divisions. Rather than increase investment in its crown jewel, Cadillac, General Motors starved it of capital and reduced its allocation of engineering resources. As a result, there were few technical improvements in the engine, suspension and handling, computer applications, and paint. General Motors relied instead on cosmetic "flash over function" design updates and superficial styling "improvements."

The consumer was not impressed. With no meaningful technical or functional benefits to sell, the Cadillac dealer network was forced to offer heavy discounts just to move the metal. Although the premium-priced, luxury car market grew during the period of 1975 through 2000—from 5 percent of unit sales to 17 percent, and from

10 percent of profits to 25 percent—Cadillac units declined at a rate of 2 percent per year. The average age of the Cadillac owner climbed from forty-seven to sixty-two. This once-proud symbol of American triumph was nearly destroyed. What had been the ultimate statement of American class became a lament for a bygone era and the butt of jokes by stand-up comedians.

General Motors failed to understand that the American consumer was beginning to trade up to higher levels of quality, taste, and aspiration. The company was focused on other issues: competition from low-cost, high-quality Japanese cars, new fuel-economy regulations, the emergence of sport-utility vehicles (SUVs), increasingly complex and expensive safety and emissions regulations, and the resurgence of Chrysler and Ford as powerful domestic competitors. While General Motors was paddling hard to save its midmarket, midprice offerings, its competitors in Europe were building and selling a new kind of luxury vehicle that redrew the price-volume demand curve. BMW grew from $1 billion to $25 billion globally. Daimler-Benz grew to $40 billion. The Lexus division of Toyota, a latecomer to the market, grew from zero to more than $5 billion. And the premium car market is still on fire, the only segment that achieved growth and profitability in the down market of 2001 to 2002.

Cadillac is a cautionary tale. It shows that there is an important relationship between the high-end and midprice models in the automaker's product range. When the superpremium model fails to offer technical and functional benefits, it can coast for a while on the emotional engagement—but not very long. And no matter how successful—even iconic—a product is, it can swiftly be dethroned by competitors who understand the escalating tastes of consumers and invest in a benefit ladder that aligns with them. In categories of durable goods, the dethroning can take less than a decade. In consumable goods, it can happen in two years or less.

The Best Car in America

Henry Leland founded his company, the Leland Faulconer Manufacturing Company, in 1902, and he introduced his first product—the Cadillac Model A—in 1903. Leland was a machinist with long experience in the production of sewing machines (Toyota has a heritage in automatic looms), and by the age of fifty-nine, when he started his own company, he was an expert in precision engineering and quality manufacturing. Leland's goal was to build the best car in America, and he decided to name his product after the French explorer Antoine de la Mothe, Sieur de Cadillac, who founded Fort Pontchartrain du Détroit, later known as Detroit, in 1701. Monsieur Cadillac spent eight years at the thriving Great Lakes settlement until he was forced out of his post, was eventually recalled to France, and spent time as a prisoner in the Bastille. He never returned to North America. Perhaps the fall of explorer Cadillac foreshadowed the fall of the brand that bears his name.

The Model A was unveiled at the New York Auto Show with a price of $750 for the two-passenger model and $850 for a four-passenger version—as much as a 50 percent premium to competitive models. Even so, Leland's sales manager took orders for 2,286 cars. It featured a single-cylinder copper-jacketed engine.

At the turn of the twentieth century there were more than one hundred small automakers like Leland's in the United States, all of them eager to take advantage of Americans' thirst for mechanical transport. In 1903, entrepreneur William Durant began acquiring some of these producers and cobbling together a conglomeration that would become, in 1908, General Motors. In that year, Durant bought Cadillac from Henry Leland for $5.5 million.

As part of General Motors, Cadillac continued to make engineering advances. Leland had prided himself on advanced engineering and precision manufacture. In 1908, a British Cadillac distributor carried out a remarkable demonstration. He disassembled three Cadillacs, scrambled the parts, and then reassembled them. Everything fit together perfectly, and the three cars drove away—proof of Cadillac's quality and ability to produce consistently interchangeable parts. The company soon developed the world's first production V8 engine, a massive power plant (for its time), which delivered seventy horsepower.

Cadillac also focused on the cosmetic and styling features of the luxury car. By 1924, the Cadillac came with chrome finishing and

Cadillac was the epitome of 1950s Old Luxury.
Copyright Bettman/Corbis.

was available in a wide range of colors. In 1927, Cadillac launched the La Salle convertible coupe, with a side compartment for golf bag and clubs. In 1934, it introduced the first independent front suspension. A sunroof became available in 1938, and the 1941 Series 60 was one of the first models that offered air-conditioning as an option.

Before World War II, Cadillac was just one of several brands that competed at the high end of the U.S. car market, but after the war, Americans were looking for a new way of life that celebrated the U.S.'s triumph and put the deprivation and ugliness of war behind them—and that's when Cadillac became the country's leading luxury car. There were great opportunities available, and much new wealth, and Cadillac aligned its brand with the important emotional themes of the day: status and achievement. It was called the car "where a man is seen at his best." It was designed "for the sheer joy of living." With a Cadillac, "prestige is practical." Cadillac was the car of "taste, quality, supremacy, an enriched life, a symbol of success." By purchasing a Cadillac, you were demonstrating to your friends—and to the whole world—that you had made it.

From 1948 to 1977, Cadillac was the bestselling luxury car in the world and *the* car to own and be seen in. Dwight D. Eisenhower traveled to his 1953 presidential inauguration in an Eldorado convertible, complete with signal-seeking radio, automatic headlight dimmer, leather upholstery, and aluminum wire wheels. In 1955, Cadillac was so dominant it outsold its chief rival, Lincoln, three to one. During those years, Cadillac continued to innovate and offer technical and functional benefits that brought great pleasure to its owners. The 1958 Cadillac Fleetwood 60 Special was "loaded" with engineering advances—including a high-compression, overhead valve engine, power windows, power steering, and power door locks—as well as chrome fins and fenders styled like fighter aircraft. The 1959 Brougham rested on a wheelbase of 149 inches, weighed 5,490 pounds, and delivered fuel "economy" of less than eight miles per gallon.

Then, as reliable, fuel-efficient imports from Japan entered the U.S. market, as well as safer and better-performing cars from Europe, Cadillac began its decline. The flamboyant fighter-jet styling suddenly looked outdated and superficial in comparison to competitors, including Mercedes-Benz and BMW, which offered better driving performance, greater reliability, and more total value. "I drove Cadillacs for twenty years," says fifty-seven-year-old executive Gary. "In the early 1960s, we had a yellow Caddy with bright-yellow interior. All the kids wanted a drive home from Little League in that car. But over time the quality declined. They priced up the cars but provided no innovations. They clung to their reputation, but it was an empty shell. Every three years I was buying the same car. New model year, but no changes. General Motors was milking the brand."

By the late 1970s, Gary's emotional engagement with the Cadillac brand was challenged. "My sons started to make fun of my Cadillacs," he confesses. "They called them fat cars for old men. They joked about the steering and called them boats." In 1982, Gary finally sold his Cadillac and bought the first of a succession of premium European cars. "Today I drive the supercharged V-8 Jaguar," he says. "I've gone from catcalls from my sons, to admiration."

In the early 1980s, when Mercedes-Benz and BMW were becoming serious players in the U.S. premium-car market, Cadillac might have been able to respond to their challenge. But rather than try to understand the benefits these cars offered, Cadillac made half-hearted responses. To try to improve the fuel efficiency of its cars, it developed a diesel engine so poorly engineered that it became a further target for jokes, as well as the subject of consumer lawsuits. In response to Americans' move to smaller cars, Cadillac developed the Cimarron, but it was built on a Chevrolet chassis and looked like a low-price Chevy Cavalier, gussied up with leather and chrome. Cadillac called it "a new kind of Cadillac for a new kind of Cadillac owner." But it offered no technical or functional benefits and couldn't even deliver on the one benefit the true Cadillac apostle still valued—the emotional engagement of a big, flamboyant car—at a relatively small 173 inches and 2,524 pounds. Cimarron sold twenty-six thousand units in 1982 and went out of production in 1986, selling a paltry 6,454 units in that year.

Cadillac lost its leadership because it failed to understand the rules of New Luxury. First—partly as the result of labor strife and strikes at its manufacturing facilities—quality declined. Cadillacs were delivered with wide and uneven gaps between major body panels, ceiling insulation that peeled away, and interior panels with mismatched colors. New Luxury consumers have no tolerance for such defects and performance failures. Second, Cadillac failed to deliver new technical differences and benefits. Rather than invest in engine, suspension, and safety technologies, it relied on model refreshments that offered little more than changes to the shape of exterior body panels.

Most of all, Cadillac failed to understand the change in the emotional drivers of affluent consumers. They no longer wanted to buy Old Luxury cars that were designed mainly to convey status and that had become symbols of conspicuous consumption. They gladly paid a 25 to 50 percent premium for the European models that were better engineered, were more exciting to drive, and made them feel sophisticated and knowledgeable. What's more, a Mercedes-Benz held its value better: After three years it could be sold for up to 70 percent of the original purchase price. A Cadillac lost 35 percent of its value as soon as it left the dealer's lot; three years later, the seller was lucky to realize 40 percent of the original purchase price. Consumers' sense of loyalty to the old image of Cadillac, as well as very generous financial incentives, were all that kept Cadillac's share of the premium car market from declining faster than it did.

A New Definition of Premium: Performance

Mercedes-Benz challenged Cadillac as a different kind of Old Luxury car—safer, more conservatively styled, with higher build quality and engineering advances, but still designed to convey status and success. But it was BMW and Lexus that provided consumers with new ways to think about what a premium car should be.

Bayerische Motoren Werke, or BMW, was founded as an aviation engine company. Toward the end of World War I, its engines were installed in Fokker fighter aircraft, replacing engines made by Daimler (the producer of Mercedes cars). The BMW engines immediately proved to be more reliable, more powerful, and more responsive—pilots found they could fly higher and dive faster. BMW engines became known as the most dependable engines in aviation, and that heritage is still evident in the strategy and culture of BMW.

Between the wars, BMW produced both automobiles and motorcycles, but it returned to production of aircraft engines during World War II. One of its plants, in Munich, was destroyed, but other plants survived. BMW did not begin selling cars in the United States until 1954, and sales were small—under ten thousand units—throughout the 1960s. During its first two decades in the United States, BMW was a cult car, purchased by car aficionados and wealthy driving enthusiasts.

Today BMW, the producer of what the company calls the "ultimate driving machine," has become the most profitable car-company in the world. As a whole, BMW—with sales of 213,127 vehicles in the United States in 2001—achieved a greater profit, $1.87 billion, than any other major carmaker. General Motors, with

U.S. sales of over four million vehicles, earned just $600 million; both Ford and DaimlerChrylser suffered losses. In the down economy of 2001, BMW's U.S. deliveries (cars and SUVs) grew 12.5 percent. In 2002, the company sold 256,622 vehicles (including MINI Cooper sales) in the United States, up 20 percent over 2001, and sold more than one million vehicles worldwide for the first time. By contrast, General Motors unit sales in 2002 were down 1 percent.

BMW has built its success not as an updated version of an Old Luxury car, but as a quintessential New Luxury brand. Dr. Michael Ganal, a member of the BMW board, told us: "BMW produces *premium* cars, not luxury cars. They are engineered by people who love cars. Other car companies concentrate on 'visible' features. We make the best vehicle. We are the advocates for drivers. We invented antilock brakes and traction control."

BMW has extended its position in the premium segment through clever segmentation and maniacal adherence to its core identity as a producer of performance engines. It has made the brand both more accessible to middle-market buyers and more aspirational, with a top-price model (the Z8) at $131,500 and the lowest-priced 3-Series at $27,800.

BMW introduces its new technical and functional innovations in the 7-Series, its superpremium sedan, starting at $68,500. The 2003 7-Series is loaded with technical features that are designed to increase handling, safety, performance, and driving comfort and that deliver functional differences competitive cars cannot match. In addition to a remarkably powerful and efficient 4.4-liter V8 engine that delivers 325 horsepower with 0-to-60-miles-per-hour acceleration in just 5.9 seconds, "enormous" ventilated disk brakes, and a drive-by-wire shifting system, the 7-Series also offers such advanced features as seats that adjust twenty different ways and a Park Distance Control device that signals as the driver approaches the curb. The car can monitor the pressure of its tires, and its headlights adjust their angle during hard braking to provide the driver with optimal visibility. The windshield wipers sense when it's raining, and the washer fluid reservoir is heated so as to better prevent windshield icing. The driver can control the navigation system with voice commands. In case of an emergency, a Mayday system automatically opens a voice line to an assistance center, staffed by people who can help with any need. The Intelligent Safety and Information System monitors the car's safety status with fourteen different sensors. And the iDrive system enables the driver to personalize the settings of many of the car's interior controls.

The innovations that are introduced in the 7-Series soon cascade into the 5-Series, whose models start at $37,600, and the 3-Series, starting at $27,800. These models have enabled BMW to dramatically extend its reach into the middle market. In 2001, 67 percent of BMW sales came from those two models.

In 2001, BMW further extended its reach with the introduction of the MINI Cooper. The MINI is a small classic British car, revitalized with design updates and features that include (on the MINI Cooper S) a six-speed 163-horsepower engine, a six-speaker CD stereo, air-conditioning, and six airbags—offered at $19,425, about 29 percent less than the base 3-Series. It is managed by a separate division at BMW, with its own distribution system and marketing operation. MINI managers often say, "Please don't call us BMW MINI. We're just MINI."

The MINI was launched with a New Luxury campaign designed to position it as an iconoclastic brand and to create apostles—its theme line is "Live me, dress me, protect me, drive me." Consumers can customize their MINIS with colors such as chili red, velvet red, silk green, and pepper white. Options include some of the features pioneered in the 7-Series such as Park Distance Control and sensing wipers. An automotive expert says, "Pound for pound, inch for inch, there's more fun and charm packed into the diminutive 2002 MINI than any car on the market." Or as BMW claims in its new ad, "Small is the new black." The car is a hit, acclaimed for its "fun and charm" and for being "frisky" and "nimble."

Although BMW focuses primarily on the technical and functional benefits of its cars, company managers believe that emotional engagement is just as critical, and they have a thorough understanding of their core consumer. "Most car companies underestimate the psychographic," says Dr. Ganal. "But we are a relatively small, independent company. We have less than 2 percent of U.S. market share. We can't play as big guys—we don't have their large budgets." BMW's chief marketing officer in North America, Jim McDowell, describes the company's target customers as people "who work hard and play hard. They treat fun seriously. They have high personal energy. Quality is very important, and they are prepared to pay more for it. They enjoy driving. Sometimes they don't take the most direct route to work if there is a better road for driving. They feel completely at peace—protected and invigorated in their driving environment. They are far more likely to wash their cars than other people in the same income cohort. One of the company's 'management maxims' is that it is the customer who decides on the quality of our work. The customer decides on BMW's right to exist."

Ted, a reconstructive surgeon who lives in Dallas, is a typical New Luxury consumer—although at the very high end of the income scale—and the kind of buyer BMW attracts. Ted's wife is also a physician, and they have two children. In 1996, Ted bought his first BMW. "First we looked at a Lexus," Ted explained. "But during the test drive, the salesperson drove it 20 miles an hour. Then we went to a BMW dealer and got a salesperson who used to sell cars for Lexus and Mercedes-Benz. She knew that she was selling a hot car with power. My wife went for a test ride, and she came back with her hair standing up. The car was a kick. It seemed as if it were airborne. She was on highway access roads doing 80 miles an hour and coming to a screeching stop. The brakes never failed. It was like being at Six Flags on a roller coaster, only better. I've now had four BMWs, and I'll never ever drive anything else."

BMW has steadily built its presence in the U.S. market—even with substantial price increases over the years, BMW has grown 15 percent every year since 1995—by delivering cars that are thrilling to drive, that offer what owners call a "blend of sport and luxury," and that stay true to the brand's ethos. The company operates by strict design principles, which require the very best components, and it incorporates substantial innovations and improvements into every new model. The cars are among the most expensive in their product segments and therefore sell at premiums, but they are not about Old Luxury or status or conspicuous consumption. Even so, some consumers complain about the high sticker price, which is up substantially since the original launch in the United States, as a result of increased labor costs, intense application of technology, and fluctuations in currency. "We have design that lasts," says Dr. Ganal. "We don't change appearance for the sake of change. You can have a five-year-old BMW that doesn't look old."

Lexus: The Ultimate Reliability Machine

Lexus, the premium car brand of Toyota, presented a different kind of challenge to Cadillac and the other American luxury brands. Lexus patterned itself after Mercedes-Benz, knocking off the German carmaker's flagship sedan, combining Japanese build quality and reliability with an interpretation of European styling.

Toyota began life as a manufacturer of weaving machinery. The Toyoda Automatic Loom Works Ltd. was founded in 1926 and began making automobiles in 1932. Its first model was a hybrid, built on a Chevrolet chassis, with a sixty-five-horsepower engine and a Chrysler body.

Toyota' s factories were converted to military production plants during World War II, but the company returned to car manufacturing in 1947. With Japan's economy devastated, it took years for Toyota to gear up production. In 1955, Toyota was able to produce only seven hundred cars a month. But in the 1960s it dramatically increased production as well as exports to the United States. In 1960, Toyota shipped 6,500 units to the United States. In 1967, exports had grown to 150,000 units. And by 1969, Toyota had become the fifth-largest car producer in the world, after General Motors, Ford, Volkswagen, and Chrysler.

The ethos of the Toyota brand was, and is, quality. The company saw itself as a pioneer in the processes of manufacturing excellence, including just-in-time manufacturing; kanban, a component-tracking system to improve manufacturing work flow; poka-yoke, a system for "mistake-proofing"; total productive maintenance for perfect machinery availability; total system waste reduction; and jidoka, machines with "judgment." The developers built feedback loops into the process, so they could learn from every error that was made on the assembly line. The Toyota Production System, also known as lean manufacturing, enabled Toyota to build cars quickly and cheaply, but with high levels of quality.

Throughout the 1970s, Toyota built its reputation in the United States on quality, fuel efficiency, and reliability—but the styling was bland and there was little driving excitement to be had in a Corolla. In 1978, Toyota launched its first premium model in the United States, the Cressida, with modest success. Then, in 1984, Toyota chairman Eiji Toyoda, cousin to the founder, challenged his engineering staff to create a luxury car to compete with the very best, which at the time was Mercedes-Benz. Toyoda assigned some four thousand engineers, technicians, and designers to the task of creating the new model, code-named F1. To better understand the potential consumer—the affluent, but value-conscious, American—the lead designers spent time in Laguna Beach, California, visiting and studying the American lifestyle. The team dined at fine restaurants, visited elegant homes, and purchased designer clothing. It was an early experiment in "patterning"—finding the key elements in a phenomenon, how they connect with each other, and how the pattern may be applicable to other phenomena.

The Lexus LS400 (Luxury Sedan) was launched in early 1989. It was priced at $35,000, a 40 percent discount to the competing models from BMW and Mercedes-Benz, but the same price as Cadillac. Each buyer received a book about the history of the Lexus and a letter from Toyota's chairman saying, "In our language, we have a saying for the occasion when a daughter is given away in marriage. Here's our cherished child—please take good care of her. This beautiful motor car is, indeed, our cherished child."

The major publications covering automobiles seethed with enthusiasm: "The LS400 is a pioneering vehicle," said *Automobile Magazine*. It was a "remarkable engineering achievement," according to *Road and Track*. *U.S. News & World Report* said, "The LS400 is an exquisite automobile," and J.D. Power and Associates crowned the Lexus "highest on customer satisfaction." The car was applauded for superb ride quality, standard features, top interiors, and reliability higher than all other makes and models. Not everyone was impressed, however. It was dismissed by some German critics as being "less innovative" than their own cars and as being a knockoff that did not pursue "superiority and delight."

Lexus was New Luxury in a different form than the performance-

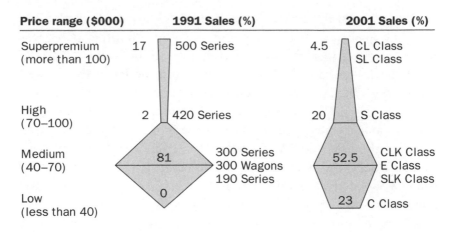

Price range ($000)	1991 Sales (%)		2001 Sales (%)	
Superpremium (more than 100)	17	500 Series	4.5	CL Class SL Class
High (70–100)	2	420 Series	20	S Class
Medium (40–70)	81	300 Series 300 Wagons 190 Series	52.5	CLK Class E Class SLK Class
Low (less than 40)	0		23	C Class

Today Mercedes-Benz makes and sells many more affordable masstige models than just a decade ago.

focused BMW and aimed at a different core consumer than BMW's driving enthusiast—but it was a New Luxury product that delivered on all three rungs of the benefit ladder. Lexus offered technical improvements. The four-liter, four-cam, thirty-two-valve V8 engine used advanced electronics designed to reduce maintenance costs, cut down on vibration, and increase the stability of the car. Aluminum alloys were used to reduce weight. Toyota studied competitive vehicles and developed a list of ninety-six items that would increase the Lexus's longevity, including a paint containing micaceous iron oxide, which resists corrosion. To the driver, these technical improvements translated into a car that was extremely quiet and comfortable, safe, reliable, and easy to maintain.

Lexus also delivered on the emotional level. The company built a dealer network separate from its established Toyota locations, with the showrooms built to a master design scheme, to create a sense of brand consistency and reliability. A dealer was required to display at least four vehicles in the showroom, with media support, and invest $5 million to $10 million in the display and service rooms. The sales staff were trained to promote the safety and service features, including roadside assistance, of the new brand.

Lexus was an immediate success, selling 63,534 units in its first year. By 1991, Lexus unit sales exceeded both Mercedes-Benz and

BMW. Lexus expanded its range in 1993, introducing a performance sedan designed by the design studio of Giorgetto Giugiaro. In 1996, Lexus expanded the line with a four-wheel-drive SUV. In 1999, Lexus introduced its sport coupe with a "hard-top, one-button convertible." Like the Mercedes-Benz SL500, the car featured a hard top that folded into the trunk in less than a minute—but the Lexus was priced 30 percent lower than the Mercedes-Benz.

Lexus was an outsider to the American car industry and broke the rules. It delivered a near-death blow to Cadillac and provided tough competition for the German manufacturers as well. To combat Lexus, Mercedes-Benz and BMW not only revamped their product lines, they also reconfigured their pricing and subsegmentation strategies. In 1980, 70 percent of Mercedes-Benz sales came from its midprice product line, 21 percent from new entry-price points, and 9 percent from the high end. Today the midprice cars represent 45 percent of sales, with 28 percent at the low end, 21 percent at the high end, and 6 percent in a new superpremium segment. BMW followed a similar pattern. Both brands have become simultaneously more accessible and aspirational, with a top price that approaches ten times the lowest. In the down market of 2001, BMW's unit sales grew 13 percent, and average unit price actually rose slightly. Mercedes-Benz, fighting both its integration with Chrysler and multiple product launches, saw both its unit volume and quality ratings decline.

A BMW in Every Driveway?

For the past decade, the premium car category has been the most consistent profit sanctuary for major manufacturers. BMW has become the most profitable major car company in the world. The Lexus division of Toyota delivers an estimated 35 percent of company profitability. Mercedes-Benz funded its purchase of Chrysler with profits from its high-end models.

Virtually every carmaker has tried to capitalize on the New Luxury phenomenon, offering line extensions of superpremium brands, or masstige models between mass and class. Porsche offers the Boxster at $44,000 in comparison to its 911 model, which starts at about $68,000. Mercedes-Benz has the CLK coupe at $42,000 and the SLK roadster starting at $40,000, half the price of the SL class, which starts at $84,000 and sells for as much as $133,000. And BMW sells its Z4 for about $33,000. The cars come equipped with leather seats, cruise control, high-quality sound systems, traction control, emergency communication systems, and more. And each one meets a specific emotional need for the New Luxury buyer.

In the next few years, New Luxury auto manufacturers will extend their brands in new directions and test their ability to maintain the brand ethos while extending its scope and embracing a larger number of consumers. Mercedes-Benz is seeking to push the aspirational limit much higher with its superpremium Maybach models, at prices over $300,000, but it may find that the new model is so far out of reach for middle-market consumers that it is emotionally meaningless to them—just as its 600 model was and as Rolls-Royce and Bentley now are. Porsche has entered the SUV market with its turbo-charged Cayenne model, selling at up to $100,000. It is a very different kind of SUV than the Ford Explorer, capable of delivering 450 horsepower and has a top speed of 165 miles per hour. Concerned that the Cayenne might alter the emotional engagement of the brand and disaffect the Porsche 911 driver, the company claims that Cayenne will "be a one-of-a-kind with the made-in-Germany quality seal. The heart of the matter, as you'll guess, is the genetic code. The Cayenne won't be hip. The Cayenne will be engineered."

As new makers continue to enter the premium market with New Luxury models, there doubtless will be overcapacity. The winners will be the companies that offer genuine technical and functional differences and that continue to enhance them with each model year. Most important, they will deliver the emotional engagement their consumers expect. As soon as the BMW driver detects a bit of mushy handling, or the Lexus driver is treated poorly by a service technician, or the Mercedes-Benz driver notices a sloppy bit of finish work, he becomes a candidate for switching to a different brand. He will not maintain his loyalty for decades as the Cadillac consumer did.

Starting in the late 1990s, Cadillac began taking steps to reverse the decline of its iconic model. General Motors recruited Robert

Lutz, former head of Chrysler, to help return Cadillac to its glory days. "GM had to finally come to terms with the fact that it had allowed the Cadillac to deteriorate," Lutz told the *Economist*. "It had not received the amount of investment and engineering attention that a premium brand would have had if it was stand-alone. Now the company is allocating the money Cadillac needs."

The company has developed a new body style that is still reminiscent of a fighter aircraft but a technologically sophisticated stealth fighter. The engine is a sturdy 4.6-liter V8 branded Northstar tested on the same German road tracks as BMW and Mercedes-Benz. Cadillac is forming new alliances to improve the perception of its cars as performance vehicles—it has become the official supplier of cars to the Bob Bondurant School of High Performance Driving, and the Cadillac CTS models will be customized with racing wheels, rollbars, and dual exhaust.

Although the Cadillac CTS model achieved 16 percent growth in sales in 2002, it may be that Cadillac's enhancements will be seen as simply more of the same old story—changes that do not bring meaningful difference or a new kind of emotional engagement. Cars can be important in all four emotional spaces, but Cadillac will have a difficult time making the case that it is the best car in any one of them. For those who are looking for a Taking Care of Me car, Cadillac won't measure up in terms of safety and comfort in comparison to Lexus. For those who think of a car as a facilitator of Connecting, Cadillac may work for the over-sixty audience, but it is doing much less hooking up than are younger buyers. Cadillac, with its big frame, soft ride, and mushy handling cannot compete with BMW, Porsche, or Mercedes-Benz as a Questing car. And, finally, as an indicator of Individual Style, Cadillac still says, "Out of it."

A return from the dead is unlikely in New Luxury. BMW, Mercedes-Benz, and Lexus have already so transformed the market—making their cars more affordable at the low end and more aspirational at the high end—that Cadillac may not be able to escape death in the middle.

Part Three

Excelsior

Thirteen

The Opportunity

America has not finished trading up.

The phenomenon is almost infinitely extendable because the capacity of businesses to innovate is unlimited and the emotional needs of consumers are never entirely filled. Trading up is not a new phenomenon, of course; America has been trading up since its founding. What were luxuries in the homes of seventeenth-century colonial consumers—including mirrors, chocolates, bedsheets, and salt—are now commodities in almost every home in America.

The trading up of today is very different from the trading up of three centuries ago, however, because it takes place so much faster and involves so many more members of the expanded middle class. It will not take long for the New Luxuries of today—the six-burner cooktops, rain-sensing windshield wipers, premium vodkas, spa experiences, titanium golf drivers, special-formula pet foods, and seamless bras—to become the conventional mass-market products of tomorrow.

So for entrepreneurs and business leaders, the trading-up phenomenon represents a tremendous opportunity—for business growth, increased brand and company vitality, category leadership, and disproportionate share of profits. There remains vast potential to reshape categories, create new winners, dethrone market leaders, simultaneously destroy and create immense value, unleash growth and simulate rebirth in "mature" industries. The list of categories waiting to be transformed—or transformed once again—is long indeed.

But trading up also poses a threat to many businesses. The entry of New Luxury goods generally leads to polarization in its category. Consumers gravitate toward the premium New Luxury goods if that category is important to them. If it isn't, they trade down to low-cost goods. That can often lead to death in the middle for those brands and products that offer no specific reason to buy: a significant price and cost advantage, a genuine technical or functional difference, or an emotional benefit.

Managers of conventional businesses that are threatened with death in the middle often protest, "We can't create a premium product in our category. There's no volume at the high end!" Or, "Our product is a commodity—there are no real differences. We can't create emotionally satisfying goods." But there are emotional issues lurking in every product category, and where there is emotion and a product difference, there can be volume and profits.

As we've explored in this book:

Industry insiders said that consumers had no real interest in *laundry appliances* and would never pay more than $800 for a washer-dryer, until Whirlpool created Duet and consumers fell in love with the front-loading European-style washer-dryer pair selling at $2,000.

Conventional *kitchen appliances* ruled until Viking offered cooktops, starting at $1,000 and selling for as much as $9,000, that gave home cooks bold styling and professional performance.

Consumers thought that a quick lunch had to mean a burger and fries until Panera Bread, Pret A Manger, Cosi, and others helped create a new category of *fast casual restaurants* which proved that people would pay $6 for a sandwich that was quick, tasty, and emotionally engaging.

Beer came either in superpremium three-month-old imports or Budweiser-style kegs before Jim Koch launched Samuel Adams Boston Lager, an *artisanal beer,* for which consumers paid a 100 percent premium and which grew to a $1 billion segment.

There was premium scotch whiskey but no premium *vodka* before Millennium Import LLC introduced Belvedere and Chopin at $30 and up and relegated the former category status brand, Absolut, to a lowly position at the bar.

Women thought that sexy *lingerie* had to be uncomfortable and that comfortable underwear couldn't be sexy, until Victoria's Secret found that American women would pay a threefold premium for a bra and panty set that was both comfortable and sexy seven days a week.

Our idea of Questing in *coffee* was limited to how much milk and sugar was added until Starbucks turned coffee into a drink of endless complexity and created apostles who cannot start the day without a $3 latte.

Golfers thought of their game as "a good walk spoiled" until Ely Callaway created *golf clubs* that offered technical differences that so transform the duffer's game, amateurs are willing to pay a fourfold premium for clubs that make them feel like pros.

Pet food meant horsemeat and kibble until Nutro, Diamond, and other producers realized that many pets are cherished family members and their owners will pay a premium to feed them foods that improve their health and snacks that smell and taste good.

New Luxury goods have transformed these and many other categories, and they will likely do the same in dozens of others that currently lack a brand that offers quality, technical difference, functional superiority, and genuine emotional satisfaction.

The results of our survey show, in fact, that there are many categories that consumers say are emotionally important to them, but in which they currently have few options for trading up. This indicates that in these categories, there is demand for New Luxury goods but not enough supply. Toys, health clubs, bath and body products, and gourmet foods, for example, are categories with relatively high emotional meaning for consumers but that offer relatively few opportunities for consumers to trade up.

The Opportunity in Services

There are many opportunities for growth in durable goods categories, but we believe the greatest potential for New Luxury growth lies in services, including financial and legal services, educational

and health care services, elder care and child care, pet care, travel
and real estate, car care, and home maintenance services.

We are already seeing the emergence of New Luxury in some
professional service categories, such as health care. Personal Physicians HealthCare, for example, cofounded by Dr. Jordan Busch and
Dr. Steven R. Flier, charges a $4,000 annual premium to become a
patient in the practice and delivers on all three benefit levels. The
most important technical difference is that each doctor limits his
practice to three hundred patients, rather than the average three
thousand of a conventional managed-care general practice. There
are further technical differences, including the design of the facility—which looks and feels more like a luxury spa than a doctor's office—and a custom-designed software program that enables doctors
to access patient files from a computer anywhere in the world. The
differences in performance are striking: patients can get same-day
appointments; annual physicals last ninety minutes or longer and
include conversation, advice, and detailed recommendations; doctors make house calls and sometimes accompany their patients to
see specialists; and doctors and staff are always available by telephone or e-mail.

Consumers who choose Personal Physicians HealthCare told us
they do so because the practice fulfills important emotional needs.
Health care is primarily, of course, about Taking Care of Me, and
most of the patients who choose the practice have health concerns—
they are looking for more than an annual checkup and an occasional
prescription for antibiotics. Although Busch and Flier are careful to
say that they do not consider themselves more expert than their colleagues at conventional managed-care practices, they do believe
they can give their patients more time and more focused attention.

New Luxury health-care patients are Connecting—they want to
build a relationship with their doctor. They get to know him personally, and he knows not only their health history but their life
story as well. They are also Questing. There are many patients who
prefer the authoritarian doctor who "knows best," but the patients
at Personal Physicians do not fit that description. They tend to be
people who are generally interested in health and wellness issues,
whether or not they are immediately relevant to their own health.

They like to learn about health, seek new ways to advance their own well-being, and take actions that will avoid illness. At Personal Physicians, they have more time to discuss issues of interest with their doctors—discussions that physicians in a conventional practice would have to limit due to their heavy patient load and tight appointment schedules.

Although premium health-care services, also called "concierge" health-care services, have been criticized as elitist, the doctors at Personal Physicians say their goal is to deliver the kind of health care that all physicians would like to provide but are unable to because they are so hampered by the complexities of managed care. In addition, they say they are now able to provide more pro bono care to disadvantaged patients and communities than when they practiced in conventional health-care groups. Because Personal Physicians HealthCare has been operating for only a year, it is too early to tell whether it will enjoy the kind of financial results that creators of New Luxury goods typically have. But it has had little trouble attracting patients, the practice is nearly full, and, to date, the company is exceeding the financial targets of its business plan.

New Luxury could extend even deeper into the services realm by transforming public and quasi-public services such as transportation and education. There are already some initiatives in the transportation category that might emerge as New Luxury, such as customized railcars, time-share jets, personal aircraft, and alternative forms of street transportation, such as scooters. With the American interest in learning and the current difficulties of public schools, there may be a market for tools and methods of instruction and knowledge attainment that are more effective and more satisfying than current methods of teaching.

Factors That Will Contribute to the Spread of New Luxury

Just as New Luxury has arisen as the result of the confluence of social changes and business capabilities, its spread will be further enabled by a number of factors:

Greater globalization and influence of overseas markets. As the European Union continues to expand and accept new member nations, and as China and other Asian countries become increasingly welcoming to both businesses and travelers, the trading-up phenomenon will become more globally influenced. Consumers will discover new tastes and styles, ideas and interests, and look for their Americanized versions back home. Businesses will have greater access, at lower cost, to ideas and supply chain services in countries throughout the world.

Heightened role of the Web and e-commerce. E-commerce is currently a minor source of revenue for New Luxury creators, but it is growing fast and contributing to sales and brand growth in many ways beyond direct sales.

Although a minor source of revenue for retailers, e-commerce is not an insignificant one. Williams-Sonoma, for example, had $133 million in Internet-based sales in 2001, or 6 percent of net revenues. Pottery Barn's Internet sales grew from $49 million in the second quarter of 2001 to $83 million in the second quarter of 2002, an increase of 70 percent. The American Girl business has a particularly computer-literate customer base. Over 70 percent of its customers have Internet access, well above the 55 percent penetration of the whole U.S. population. Americangirl.com receives over 115 million hits per month, and Web site sales are estimated at $55 million, or about 15 percent of total revenue.

New Luxury creators and retailers understand, however, that the Web is about Connecting and Questing as well as sales. Americangirl.com is rich with content, offering games, polls, e-cards, activity ideas, trivia quizzes, and an advice column for girls. BMW created tremendous buzz with its BMWFilms, action shorts directed by and starring world-class talents and featuring BMW cars. The first round of films was viewed more than fourteen million times. Two million people registered on the Web site, 60 percent of whom opted to receive more information via e-mail. Ninety-four percent of registrants recommended the films to others, feeding into a viral campaign that seemed to encompass the world.

Influence of solo females. Our survey shows that solo working females are particularly active buyers of New Luxury goods. Young singles rocket in a relatively small number of categories, but divorced women told us they rocket in as many as thirty different categories. With the incidence of divorce continuing to rise, and with singles delaying marriage, the pool of solo females is likely to increase—along with their willingness to spend on goods that help mitigate the rigors of Connecting (or not Connecting) and the pain of divorce.

Seniors as heavy spenders. Seniors represent an enormous potential market that New Luxury goods creators have yet to fully tap. Not only is their number growing as Americans live longer (currently there are about forty-six million people over the age of sixty), but they are generally healthier, more active, and more willing to spend on themselves than any previous generation. Our survey results show that seniors are spending on their children and grandchildren, but they are not neglecting themselves to do so; they are particularly big rocketers in packaged travel. There is an opportunity to better serve the senior travel market with clothing, luggage, health care products and services, food supplements, photo and electronic imaging systems, travel planning and support services, and more.

Next-generation consumers: smarter and more sophisticated than ever. It is the "juniors" aged six to eighteen, however, who represent the greatest potential for continuing and expanding the trading-up phenomenon. They are interested in learning, travel extensively, and are highly attuned to brands and products. They have become accustomed to the acceleration of the innovation cycle and are not as exhausted by it as their parents or as bewildered by it as their grandparents. Juniors take it for granted that styles are quickly replaced with new ones and that products should be constantly updated and improved. Neither will they, unlike their elders, have a memory of a time when products did not always deliver quality. They will have little, if any, patience for goods that are poorly made or don't perform as promised. They surf the Web, communicate on many channels, and drive the definition and recognition of what is new.

Most important, juniors have come to expect and appreciate the emotional satisfaction they get from New Luxury goods. As many consumers told us, "It's very hard, if not impossible, to go back" to lower-quality, undifferentiated, emotionally empty goods once you've experienced a New Luxury entry in the category. Americans never like to settle back, give up, and trade down unless they are absolutely forced to by world events or personal vicissitudes. Even when times are rough, they tell us, they continue to hold on to one or two New Luxury items they "just can't live without." Americans, including kids, always want to escalate to still higher levels of quality, taste, and aspiration.

The Demand Society: The Middle Market Takes Control

There is another important aspect of trading up in today's society, beyond its speed and volume. Traditional trading up might be better described as a downward-flowing cascade of innovation. In the past a luxury first appeared on the market in very limited quantities and at very high prices, available only to the rich. It might take years, even decades, for the luxury to become more widely available and for the price to come down to the point where the middle class could afford it.

For example, that most ubiquitous commodity, coffee, began its career as a luxury item. The delights of the coffee bean were probably discovered in Ethiopia before the year 1000, but coffee did not reach Europe until around 1600. It gradually was transformed from a rare and expensive treat into a daily want and, at last, into a necessity of everyday life. In the late 1780s, during the run-up to the French Revolution, the ordinary people of Paris took to the streets to protest the high cost of what they believed were the necessities of life, including sugar and coffee. In our own time, cashmere was for years an expensive luxury, affordable only for the wealthy, with limited supply. With the opening of China, however, supply has increased, and the price of cashmere has dropped considerably. It is now possible to buy a woman's cashmere sweater at Lands' End for just over $100.

The point is that the consumer has traditionally had little control over the pace and timing of the downward cascade of luxury goods. The producer had the control because demand was high and often the supply of raw materials was limited. Besides, the producer often had no great desire to speed up the cascade, because he believed that exclusivity and high margins were the keys to success in luxury goods. But now, because the middle market has become so much more affluent and so much more sophisticated, the luxury producer need not give up those attractive margins in order to gain greater volume.

At the same time, producers of conventional goods are faced with the problem of overcapacity and oversupply. Makers of cars, appliances, clothing, computers, and a dozen other types of goods have become so highly skilled and productive, and so used to selling in huge volumes, that they are making more of their products than consumers want or can buy.

Of course, businesses have been making more goods than American consumers strictly "need" for at least a century. That's what marketing is for— to help create new wants for the consumer. But the "want-creation" industry has hit the wall. Because of all the factors we've discussed, businesses find that advertising, in particular, has lost much of its ability to persuade consumers to buy goods they don't really want. Consumers know too much about product differences and availability, thanks to the proliferation of information available everywhere, especially on the Internet; they have too much choice; and they are too sophisticated about their own emotional needs to settle for mediocre goods.

Suddenly, the middle-market consumer has real control.

It is a control that is very different from the nominal control expressed in the traditional sales bromides—"The customer is always right" and "We don't exist without the customer" and "Our major concern is customer satisfaction." Today's middle-market consumers are active participants in the creation of the goods they want. They don't have to wait for the cascade to reach them; they can demand it because they have the power to buy, the knowledge to select, and the option to choose. They don't really need *anything*, so they are hardly at the mercy of the producer.

We have said that trading up is a historic alignment of consumer needs and business capabilities. It may be more than that—it may represent a power shift from the producer to the consumer, a new dominance of the demand side over the supply side. That will make New Luxury goods all the more important in the years to come since they are harder to create than conventional goods and therefore harder to copy. And they have the great advantage of providing emotional satisfaction, which is the key benefit that today's consumer is seeking.

For Americans in the foreseeable future, the call is "excelsior"—ever higher—and that is what trading up is all about.

Fourteen

A Work Plan

The Impetus

What does it take to succeed in New Luxury?

It is a time of great opportunity for consumer businesses, and New Luxury creators who connect with their core consumers and trade them up are achieving high profits, fast growth, and high market valuations. It is also a treacherous time for consumer businesses. Consumers will ignore goods that don't deliver on the ladder of benefits, and trade down to commodities. The New Luxury winners, as we have seen in the stories in this book, follow a set of practices that enable them to create, build, maintain, and continually improve their businesses. But the practices are general in nature, and sometimes they are more descriptive than prescriptive. In this chapter, we offer a work plan for conceptualizing, developing, and launching a New Luxury business.

Before the work plan, however, there must be an impetus—a driving force and catalyzing energy to create something new. In many of the New Luxury companies we have studied, the impetus comes from an exceptional individual who discovers a business purpose in a personal experience. Some, like Pleasant Rowland, are extremely dissatisfied with the product offerings they find on the market—in her case, it was dolls. Some, like Ely Callaway, are driven by a passion and instinct for a category, in his case, golf. Often, the impetus has a deeply personal and emotional basis. Gordon Segal wanted to live a life of European style and saw Crate and Barrel as a way to do so. Sometimes there is even a dramatic turning point, an Aha! moment, that is later seen to be the beginning of the business—such as Robert Mondavi's violent break with his family.

These entrepreneurs provide interesting and instructive models for others who would like to begin a New Luxury business, not in the particulars of their lives, but in the common patterns of how they achieved their successes. From other stories, however, we know that successful New Luxury goods can be created by large companies and category incumbents that are not driven by an extraordinary leader or entrepreneur on a personal mission. BMW, Whirlpool, Panera Bread, Victoria's Secret—these companies have created New Luxury goods within their established organizations, often going back to their roots for inspiration.

Established companies still need an impetus to get started, however, and it often comes from a competitive threat or the inspired thinking of a manager who is able to think like an entrepreneur. BMW was threatened by the introduction of Lexus and Infiniti into the luxury car market, and it was its response to the threat—a much sharper positioning as a performance brand and a relentless focus on driving excitement—that made it such a potent New Luxury brand and such a successful company. Whirlpool, too, was sufficiently threatened by the success of Maytag's Neptune to bring its own front-loading machine, Duet, to the market. Ronald Shaich built Panera Bread through inspired thinking—he was able to see the potential of the Saint Louis Bread Company concept and had the guts to martial all his company's resources behind it. Leslie Wexner, a serial entrepreneur who had already built a corporate empire, saw the potential for a whole new business in a tiny lingerie shop called Victoria's Secret.

As good as these leaders and entrepreneurs are at creating New Luxury businesses, they are not always able to articulate exactly how they did it. The process, as they describe it, sounds almost haphazard. "I pieced things together," says Wexner. Some of them spend years thinking about their idea and trying out early iterations. Ely Callaway bought Hickory Stick USA in 1982 but didn't launch the revolutionary Big Bertha driver until 1991. Ronald Shaich spent months visiting bakery-cafés; it took him almost a year to sell his concept to the board of directors. Jim Koch of The Boston Beer Company had his idea for the "best beer brewed in America" in his pocket for at least five years before he made the leap. But once they take the plunge, the business can develop with amazing speed. Pleasant Rowland (American Girl), Jim Koch (Boston Beer), Edward Phillips (Belvedere vodka), Ely Callaway (Callaway Golf), and Joe Foster (Whirlpool Duet) went from nothing, or tiny operations, to success with extraordinary speed.

Such success stories may make the process look easier than it is. We can assure you, however, that the billionaires and multimillionaires who have capitalized on New Luxury earned their net worth. This new form of competition generally benefits from first-mover advantage and often requires the outlay of substantial capital for equipment, inventory, trial generation, product improvement, and infrastructure. Winners invest in research and development that delivers technical advantages and in market surveillance that keeps them current, competitively aware, authentic, and fresh. They pay for their new product launches ahead of their success. They often have to go back to the drawing board after initial market reaction to regroup and reignite their enthusiasm.

Although the process is never easy or entirely predictable, it can be understood, defined, planned, and managed. It need not be so meandering as the path followed by some of the leaders profiled in this book, nor does it have to be years in the making. In our work with clients, our approach involves three steps: Vision, Translation, and Execution. In the Vision phase, the idea is developed and defined. In Translation, a product or service prototype is created. Execution is about launching the product and capturing the market, then refining the concept, expanding the business, and establishing an economic formula that pays off.

Vision: Knowing Where and How to Look

To create a vision of a new product or business does not require that the leader undergo an emotional epiphany or a tremendous revelation. At the beginning, the vision may be a simple idea about a market or a group of consumers. Ronald Shaich liked the way people sat around the Saint Louis Bread Company cafés, and he thought there was something important about it. Leslie Wexner, who had lots of experience with apparel, thought that lingerie had a much higher emotional content than plain underwear but that it wasn't being addressed by any product on the market. He saw an economic opportunity for a high-margin product just by looking at the material of the existing offerings and thinking about the likely construction of a better bra. Ely Callaway likewise knew that the recreational golfer needed help, and fast. Such perceptions usually precede the idea for a specific product.

But how do creators get these ideas? They usually come from looking carefully and extensively into a category and gaining understanding, knowledge, and insight about it. First you must decide *where* to look—choosing a category or segment with New Luxury potential. Such categories tend to have one or more of the following characteristics:

Goods are stale and undifferentiated. Any category where the products are similar and no one of them offers a differentiated ladder of benefits represents an opportunity for a New Luxury entrant. This was the case with wine before Mondavi, Callaway, and Jackson; it was true of refrigerators before Sub-Zero; it was true of frozen pizza before DiGiorno. Today, prepared vegetables, corporate hotels, and airlines are categories where the majority of the players look and sound alike.

Goods lack emotional engagement. New Luxury goods are always based on emotional engagement. A category where existing goods do not connect with consumer emotions—or produce negative ones— might be a New Luxury candidate. Consumers knew that there was a lot of emotion involved in doing laundry, but the makers of washer-dryers hadn't made the connection. When market research says the consumer is "bored" or the category "lacks salience," you may be looking at an opportunity.

Compromises to be broken. Established companies often get stuck in the rut of compromise. In quick-service restaurants, the compromise was between speed and quality—it was believed that you couldn't deliver a meal quickly and also customize it and use nonstandardized ingredients. Panera Bread, Pret A Manger, and Chipotle have broken that compromise. Trader Joe's, for all its success, has been unable to break the compromise that remains in the grocery business—stocking private-label specialty items *and* mass-market goods such as eggs, produce, national-brand cereal, milk, and personal-care and home-cleaning products.

Cost could be put in, rather than taken out. We have seen that consumers will pay a substantial premium for goods that deliver on the ladder of benefits and that New Luxury leaders often make a substantial investment in development, raw materials, and production to ensure that their goods deliver technical and functional differences. Over the past decade, the focus for many companies has been on taking cost out of their operations. As a result, their products can lose richness and excitement, as American luxury cars have. Stanley Marcus, who headed Neiman Marcus for many years, said that the same was true of the fur coat business in the late 1930s. "Most of my competitors were always trying to knock off a few dollars on every coat they purchased," he wrote in his autobiography, *Minding the Store*. "I followed the opposite strategy—I offered to pay our manufacturers extra if they could make our garments finer." By putting cost in, Neiman Marcus offered better coats with genuine differences for which it could charge a premium. Similarly, an increased cost of just 5 percent for raw materials in pet food can translate into a 30 percent price premium.

Many categories have experienced "value engineering." Too often that actually means reducing build quality or cutting corners in ingredients or packaging. Such value-engineered products, with their downgraded quality, are potential targets for New Luxury competition.

— *Gaps between mass and class.* When there is a large price gap between the middle-market offering and the superpremium product there is an opportunity for creating a masstige New Luxury product or service. In our work with a number of financial services institutions, for example, we know that consumers are dissatisfied with the undifferentiated products and services offered to the "little guy," as compared to the customized "private banking" services they believe that the rich customers enjoy. Just as Jess Jackson described the wine business, there is a gap in financial services that's so big "you could drive a truck through it."

Craft businesses with middle-market commercial potential. Many New Luxury creators start with a craft business and find a way to standardize the offering enough to produce it on a much larger scale. Starbucks is a scaled-up version of an Italian café that retains some aspects of the original (the barista, custom drinks, and variations in interior design) but has a standardized approach and centralized organization that enables fast build-out, huge volume, and consistent quality.

Technical barriers. In many categories, there is a better product waiting to be introduced but no producer willing to invest the resources and energy, or take the risk, to overcome the difficulties of mastering the process. There were large-head golf clubs on the market long before Callaway introduced the Big Bertha, but no one had figured out how to make them deliver the desired end result— an occasional 275-yard drive for the weekend golfer.

Just as important as knowing *where* to look is learning *how* to look for opportunities within a category.

Patterning. Patterning is a way of gaining insight into and understanding of a category, and it is very different from conducting traditional consumer or market research—such as polling, focus groups, interviews, and the like—or gathering conventional competitive intelligence. Rather than looking at the category as it currently exists, patterning is a process of looking for elements and trends within the category itself, and in other categories, that can provide insight into what the category *could become*.

For established players, this means paying less attention to the nearest competitor and looking more broadly at the entire market by examining every competitive company, including high-end providers, niche brands, companies in other cultures, and start-ups. What are they doing that's working? What is getting in their way of being more profitable and growing faster? It means gathering lots of data—both qualitative and quantitative—about the products on the market, how they are used, how they might be used, who is using them and why.

Leslie Wexner virtually stumbled across the Victoria's Secret shop and, after buying it, just observed it for a while. He realized that the concept had been designed for the male customer, because the founder believed that some specialty lingerie was purchased by men for their women. The element of male fantasy and lack of knowledge of the technical aspects of lingerie (fit and comfort), were keeping the core consumer—women—from buying.

Patterning is also about looking for businesses in other categories that have succeeded by responding to elements and trends similar to those in one's own category. Ronald Shaich believed that he could pattern aspects of Starbucks in creating Panera Bread—especially focusing sharply on a central, emotionally engaging element and building an appealing environment to surround it. Starbucks built its business around coffee; Panera did it around bread. Wexner's search for patterns regularly takes him to fashion markets around the world—from Paris to London to Rio to Hong Kong to South Bend. It is a quest that involves discipline, science, and a kind of "business anthropology."

Idea seeking in different geographies and cultures. The world is full of ideas waiting to be developed, borrowed, copied, adapted, or improved upon. Many New Luxury goods are adaptations of ideas from other cultures, particularly those of European countries. Crate and Barrel, Starbucks, Sam Adams, Kendall-Jackson, Whirlpool Duet—all these brands have roots in western European ideas, primarily because that is where Americans have visited the most in the past three decades. With the increase in travel to Asia, Africa, South America, Russia, and eastern Europe, interest in ideas and styles of those countries will certainly grow. As a creator in search of an idea, you can simply take a trip to an unfamiliar geography or culture. Wander the streets. Go to the markets. Talk to the people. Buy the goods. Eat in local restaurants and stay at local hotels. Watch, ask questions, try things, take goods home and show them to your friends. Find a way to translate the foreign experience into a version that suits American tastes and behaviors.

Social research. New Luxury creators tend to be people who are interested in the world. They want to understand how society is changing and how people are thinking. They read widely and keep an eye on the popular media. What are Martha Stewart and Oprah

Winfrey talking about? What are the magazines covering? What television shows are hot? They watch global trends and local customs and try to make connections between their observations and information and the role of goods and services in our society and in the lives of individuals.

What, for example, does the rise in the average square footage of the American house mean? For Boston University, it meant that its incoming students were extremely dissatisfied with the size and amenities of their dormitory rooms—they were used to having their own, large rooms with a television, phone, and high-speed Internet connection. The university has developed new dormitories, offering single rooms with private baths and is charging, and getting, a premium for them.

Category analysis and the cube. It's important to create a detailed picture of how the category currently appears, using data about trends in mix, growth rate by channel, real price trends, share and profit by segment, consumers, patterns of success by competitors, and a global comparison of the category.

The consumer segmentation cube is a way of expressing the current market by showing the intersection of three elements: the various types of customer, the "usage occasions" (where and when the goods could or might be used), and the attributes of available products. By bringing this information together, you can see the "white spaces"—combinations of customer segments, usage occasions, and product attributes that are empty and represent opportunities for development. The cube can open your eyes to clearly defined but underserved targets, and suggest cues about compelling product benefits and usage occasions.

Victoria's Secret developed such a cube. To do so, the company conducted extensive qualitative research, including one-on-one interviews with category users in their homes, to understand their attitudes, interests, and purchase experiences, as well as their hopes and wishes. With lingerie, there is a great deal of segmentation—by age, marital status, body type, and attitudes toward appearance and sexiness. Because looking good is such a fundamental concern for single women, and so it is closely linked to sexuality, there was an exceptionally wide range of emotions connected to lingerie that could

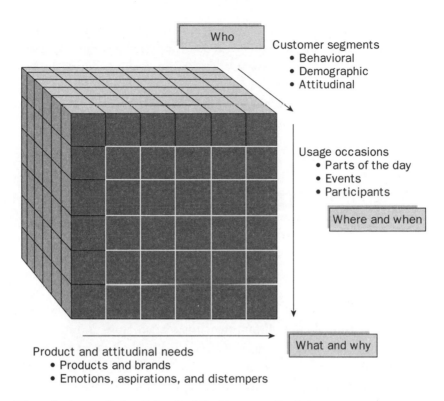

Who

Customer segments
• Behavioral
• Demographic
• Attitudinal

Usage occasions
• Parts of the day
• Events
• Participants

Where and when

What and why

Product and attitudinal needs
• Products and brands
• Emotions, aspirations, and distempers

The cube is a tool that helps find "white spaces" where opportunity might lie.

support a broad variety of product characteristics—from romantic to provocative, from classic to sophisticated, from down-to-earth to naughty.

Market sizing. During this phase, it's important to determine how big the potential market might be. We use a market-sizing device we call the "consumption function" to break out category consumption and define the premium market. In pet food, for example, the consumption function is: Millions of U.S. households × percentage of households with pets × pounds per year per household × price per pound.

As we size the market, we work with consumers to determine what features would justify a premium price. In pet food, for example, we offer them a series of phrases, including "nutritionally complete and balanced," "a perfect blend of taste and nutrition," "scientifically researched and tested," "appetizing aroma," "helps my dog maintain proper weight," "makes me feel I'm doing the best thing for my dog." Consumers prioritize and detail the product's requirements. They also tell us a great deal about their wish lists and exquisitely describe—often with anger—the compromises and disappointments they have experienced with pet foods.

At the end of the Vision phase, you should be able to identify a small number of opportunities that could deliver on the ladder of differences, redraw the demand curve, and transform the category. The opportunities should be tightly defined. You should know whom you want to reach, the behavior you want from them, and how you will connect with them.

Translation: Moving from the Abstract to the Tangible

The Translation phase is about distilling, organizing, and interpreting the information and ideas gathered during the Vision phase and creating a concept for the product and business. The emotional space is defined during Visioning; Translation is about putting together and testing the technical and functional benefits to support the vision.

Concept articulation. This may involve the creation of a white paper—an extensive written description of the concept—but it should always be refined into a clear, easy-to-remember, highly distinct phrase or idea. For Victoria's Secret it was "2/7ths." We learned that young, single women were willing to wear uncomfortable but sexy lingerie for Friday and Saturday night social encounters—two nights out of seven. But even loyal users of glamorous lingerie turned to functional underwear during weekdays—the 5/7ths. Leslie Wexner wanted to create lingerie that was sexy and comfortable for the consumer to wear for those days as well. For Eli Callaway, it was "the perfect shot once a round"—he wanted to develop and market products that would enable golfers to get more enjoyment out of their round of golf. For each golfer, no matter how modest his skill, the club provided a tool for advanced play.

Rapid prototyping. The New Luxury winners develop prototypes quickly and take them into the field for testing with real users and, especially, expert users. Ninety percent of the concept testing we have seen, when done without working prototypes, is a waste of money and time. Consumers are not able to envision the final product; they tend to be too skeptical or overly enthusiastic. In the early stages of development of her American Girl dolls, Pleasant Rowland hired a marketing manager who suggested that she test the concept with a focus group of mothers. The focus group leader orally described the concept to the mothers, and they immediately and unanimously hated it. Then the leader showed the group a prototype doll along with a sample book and accessories, and the mothers changed their minds completely. It was a lesson that Rowland did not forget: "Success isn't in the concept," she said. "It's in the execution."

This does not mean that consumers do not have ideas for better goods and services. They should not be expected to define the product itself, however, but rather how they want to feel when interacting with the category. Karen, a sophisticated twenty-three-year-old, described her vision of a "sexy, comfortable, feminine lingerie line" that would deliver what she called "practical glamour"—and that helped Victoria's Secret create Body By Victoria. Lisa, a thirty-two-year-old mother living in Newton, Massachusetts, complained that "banks don't treat me with respect. My husband and I are educated. But they never ask us, 'Are you happy?'" She then described her vision of a satisfying relationship with a bank that led to the development of an important building block of a new premium financial-services package. Your consumers can tell you about what they want, need, wish for, and only dream about. You will need to help them translate their phrases and nuances of feelings into a big, and workable, idea. It is then up to you to provide the big solution that beams sunshine on their faces.

Input and advice from expert users. Consumers value authenticity and genuineness in New Luxury goods, and they seek the validation of recognized experts and authorities in the category. Viking Range built its reputation by getting expert and professional chefs involved in the testing and refinement of the prototypes. Belvedere vodka enlisted professional bartenders to taste and comment on various distillations and flavors. BMW tests its new technologies on racing versions of its cars and by creating special M-Series models that showcase advanced features.

Value chain definition and scalability planning. The scale-up plan is another key consideration during Translation. It is one thing to deliver prototypes to a small number of expert consumers, but quite another to produce in quantity while retaining the artisanal features and quality—and to do so with speed and consistency. Once the benefit ladder is perfected, the challenge is to determine how to deliver it through "mass-artisanal" production without compromising the quality of the technical features or the integrity of the design.

During the Translation phase, Panera Bread's professional bakers spent hours working in the kitchen and visiting bakeries across the country, experimenting with doughs and sampling different recipes as they worked to perfect new types of artisan breads. Equally important—and perhaps more complex—was the company's ability to organize a delivery system that would enable Panera Bread bakery-cafés across the country to provide these artisan breads, freshly baked and with consistent high quality, to customers every day. That's why the dough for the signature sourdough bread is always made from the original "mother" bread and mixed at central commissaries—there can be absolutely no variation in the flavor, texture, and rising properties of this bread. The other artisan breads, however, are allowed to vary from store to store. This combination of the guaranteed consistency of the sourdough bread and the unpredictable but delightful variation in the artisan breads is an essential aspect of Panera Bread's appeal. Consumers can take comfort in an old favorite, or they can Quest with a sandwich made with one of a dozen different breads.

Execution: From Rollout to Revisiting the Concept

During the Execution phase we take the concept to market. It involves test marketing, a public launch or rollout, and refining and building the concept.

Define and recruit talent. Prior to launch, it's important to evaluate the talent that has helped to create and translate the vision and determine what new talent may be needed to launch and scale up the business. Chuck Williams relied heavily on outside expertise to expand his popular San Francisco shop into the catalog business. But to create the national chain of stores that Williams-Sonoma has become, a very different set of skills was required, and that is why Williams sold the company to Howard Lester, an entrepreneur with a track record for growing small businesses. (Williams remained as merchant visionary.) Building a talented team in the early years provides a powerful foundation for continued technical innovation: teams drive long-term success; teams with a history of working together and creating success drive speed.

Leverage experts. Leveraging the experts, connoisseurs, aficionados, and enthusiasts is the single best way—and is often the least expensive way—to refine early versions of the product, as well as to seed the user group. This group will tell you when your product has hit on the most compelling benefits ladder. In blind and labeled trials, the product should be able to achieve a ninety-to-ten win ratio among target consumers. That is the sign of a product that delivers real advantage. New Luxury winners are authentic and, therefore, credible and authoritative to the category experts.

Experts also provide a critical resource to leverage during the launch. There are many ways to do this: communicating regularly with early users, building customer advisory panels, sampling and conducting trials to provide free goods to high-profile users, and generally catering to the needs of this influential group—your future apostles.

Launch. Experts play a key role in the launch phase. New Luxury marketers know that word of mouth is more effective than advertising—and significantly less expensive. Increased fragmentation among formats, consumers, and behavior has led to diminishing returns on mass media advertising: the cost is up, but reach and depth are down. This is an unattractive prospect for any marketer, but especially for a fledgling New Luxury entrant.

Many New Luxury winners have successfully launched their products by creating an "underground buzz"—whether by design or by good fortune. The 10-50 rule drives most New Luxury launches: 10 percent of consumers deliver 50 percent or more of volume. The early users spread the word and the product can take off. (Pleasant Rowland called it "word-of-mother marketing.") Red Bull, a premium energy drink, spent $4 million to $5 million on a launch that involved sampling among sixteen-to-twenty-nine-year-olds—at health clubs by day, and dance clubs by night. As word of mouth built, volume rose. Then the company began promotional spending—at carefully selected music and sporting events—but only in proportion to sales. The resulting increased volume enabled the company to work with a stronger distributor and begin radio advertising, and finally, to go "mainstream" with television and trade advertising.

Launch checklist. Before you launch, it is wise to evaluate the product or service by asking a series of questions about it:

Is it aspirational? Have test users become emotionally engaged with it? What is its primary emotional space? What is its secondary emotional space? Is it differentiated, pleasing to use, and a beautiful solution to a vexing problem? Can you imagine your consumer saying, "Thank you for creating this"?

Is it unique? Are there other products or services on the market that are similar? Are its technical features truly different? Does it deliver genuine performance differences?

Will it be the first in the market? Are you sure? If not, what genuine differences does it offer from those products that are already available?

Who is the core consumer? Can you describe the heavy users in detail? Have you met and talked with any of them? Have you visited their homes and workplaces and used the product with them? Do they crave it? Does it fit tightly into their lives?

Is it authentic? Do the technical differences contribute to performance benefits, or are they merely "cool features" or, worse, meaningless "bells and whistles"?

Is it authoritative and expert? How have respected experts in the category responded to the product? Have they tried it? Have they helped develop it?

Is it extendable through segmentation? Who else beside the core consumer might be interested? What other uses or situations might it be extended to?

Is it supported by a synchronized and informing business system? Do you have more than a strong concept and an exciting prototype? Do you have an organization in place that can manage the scale-up of production, expand distribution, and continue to deliver innovation?

Does it deliver on the ladder of benefits? Is it technically strong but weak on emotional engagement? Does it trade on emotion but not deliver on performance?

Do you have the next generation of innovation in process now? The fashion cycle is collapsing, and many New Luxury goods must be considered as fashion—even as the current product is being launched, the next iteration should be in the prototype phase.

Have you lined up influencers to seed usage? Who is going to speak up for the product? Who will tell their friends about it? Where and when will they be seen?

And one final question: *How do you feel about the product?* Do you love it? Do you enjoy using it yourself? Do you believe the world needs it? Do you want people to embrace it? Are you also dissatisfied with it and do you want to make it even better? Can you imagine spending the next ten years of your life working with it, promoting it, refining it, building it into a respected New Luxury brand?

If you answered yes to all the above, we want to buy whatever it is you're selling.

Fifteen

A Call to Action

It takes committed leaders to seize the trading-up opportunity.

As a result of the work we've done with our clients and the research we've conducted into the power of New Luxury brands, we're convinced that traditional management techniques are outdated and, at best, lead to slow incremental change and, at worst, to stagnation.

The product development paradigm for most traditional consumer companies is no longer working. The time frames are too short, there is too much turnover in their executing teams, and there's not enough emotional connection. The people that are guiding the new product-development effort have an eighteen-month time horizon—get in, get out, make their mark, and get to the next promotion.

Brand managers are forced to plan using flawed consumer-and-market research. They try to find opportunity and achieve growth by asking consumers what they want instead of developing a better vision for the category and involving the consumers in refining that vision. Ask consumers what they want, and they will stare blankly at you. Engage them in the category and ask for improvements, and they will work with you. Most of the innovations in the thirty categories we have studied would have been killed by traditional customer research. There is an important role in connecting and understanding and involving the customer, but it's a very different role than has historically been played in large packaged-goods companies.

Brand managers spend too much time analyzing their nearest competitors and developing new promotions to respond to the promotions their competitors are running. The really important competitors are off their radar screen. Brand managers are often unable to see their category in context and to understand major shifts in their consumer base. We're trying to widen the field of view, so that companies can have a broader perspective on their customers, their categories, and how they can build emotional connection.

This book is for the next generation of leaders, for people who want to get ahead by leaps—not creeps.

Is a Premium Price Strategy Risky in the Current Global Economy?

Reports about the death of the American consumer are greatly exaggerated. The economic forces that permit trading up are not subject to moderate business-cycle forces. More than twenty-five million households in the United States have incomes over $75,000; these are the households that are driving the New Luxury movement. These are households with men and women who are educated, well-traveled, adventurous, and who seek responses to their emotional needs. Although they may have suffered economically in the recent downturn, their overall net worth is slightly up, their incomes are growing in real terms, and they have been insulated from changes in the unemployment rate.

Now is the best time to invest for growth in the coming upswing in the economic cycle, because it takes twelve to thirty-six months to develop a powerful, technically true, emotionally engaging New Luxury product. Consumers in the target market may be anxious, but they have money in their pockets, and they want to press forward. They will buy at any time and in virtually any economic cycle.

During the downturn from 2001 through 2002, the dividing line between New Luxury and Old Luxury became clear. Many Old Luxury brands showed substantial declines while most New Luxury brands demonstrated their resilience and were able to grow. Starbucks, BMW, Williams-Sonoma, Panera Bread, Coach, and The Cheesecake Factory all grew during the downturn. Why? Because they tapped into the emotional needs of their customers.

The forces that fuel trading up have been gathering force for decades and will continue to gain power for decades to come. Women will continue to play an important role. People will continue to be pressured by the demands of work and family. On the supply side, global sourcing costs will continue to fall. Technology will continue to drive down product cost and features. The cascade of innovation from the high-end market to the middle market will grow increasingly shorter. The polarization of retail will continue to permit consumers to trade down and trade up.

From 2002 to 2003, we saw consumers cling to their New Luxury goods. They protected themselves emotionally with their New Luxury favorites, seeing them as a way to achieve safety, security, and identity.

A Challenge to Our Readers

We hope readers will respond to the case studies and relate to the individuals highlighted in this book. But we want more than that. We want you, the reader in business, to start a New Luxury response in your current company. We want you, the reader who is primarily a consumer, to see the pattern in your purchases and feel supported in your need for better and best goods. We want the service economy to come alive with interest in this opportunity. We hope the medical, financial services, and grocery sectors will see the obvious voids in the market and react.

This is partly about inspiration—having confidence because you know that New Luxury can succeed in virtually any category. All it takes is imagination, creativity, and the skills to create a vision, to translate the vision, and then have flawless execution. It also requires staying power because you're only as good as your latest launch. If your current product line stands still, you're going to get knocked off. It requires a comprehensive and long-term effort to get to the top of the mountain.

What Can Companies Caught in the Middle Do?

Ask yourself the difficult questions now.

Which side of the road do you want to play on? Who are your customers, and what are their hopes and dreams? Have you patterned the world, looking for solutions better than yours? Have you dumbed down your product in an attempt to maintain profitability? Have you stripped the competitors' solution and rigorously gauged relative performance? Have you asked your product-development teams to dream? Have you pressed your organization for incremental profit growth and squeezed, squeezed, squeezed?

One of the biggest dangers for companies in the middle is the rules of thumb they develop about what can and cannot be—in terms of profitability, sales per square foot, and consumer experience. They define for themselves a very narrow range of possibilities, and that pushes them to reinforce the currently eroding position. They can't break away and imagine a different world. But that's what you have to do—imagine a completely different world where sales per square foot are higher than you've ever seen before, a higher profitability in percentage of sales and a higher consumer draw, higher repeat rate, higher loyalty.

Bring in new talent and tell them to create a business that's going to make your current business obsolete. Become the outsider who attacks your own business. Give your team a chance to take whatever resources they want and to reject any resources they don't want. Make them entrepreneurs and offer them tantalizing rewards to make it happen.

Most important for executives of companies caught in the middle: you need to dream about a different, better way.

Why Is There Urgency to Act Now?

It is always easier to delay and wait for a phenomenon to hit before responding. It seems as if it will be less costly to lie low, hope the New Luxury phenomenon passes by, and doesn't affect you.

That is fantasy. Outsiders have great access to capital. They can build and prepare prototypes more cheaply than most big companies can. They can test the market, gain first mover advantage, and own New Luxury. Reacting to a well-developed, clever, emotionally gripping competitor is very difficult. The pain of losing shares, losing momentum, losing confidence, losing users is a real and present danger.

The mass middle market is large and has enormous resources. Middle-market consumers can make trading up happen in any category. There are many proud and currently successful companies with wonderful histories who are choosing to ignore the New Luxury phenomenon, but they do so at their peril. We ask you, our reader, to take up the battle cry with purpose, with honor, and with all your heart.

Part Four

___

The Back Story

___

Luxury: A Philosophical and Historical Context

For centuries, people of the world have been trading up—seeking to enrich their lives and engage their senses and emotions through wonderful goods. And, for centuries, luxury has been a subject of intense debate and discussion.

To the ancient Greeks, luxury was a political issue. Luxury items were condemned "because they fostered effeminacy and thus undermined virtue and corrupted both the individual and his homeland," according to Dr. Christopher Berry, a leading expert on the subject. Warriors who indulged in luxury would be emasculated and less inclined to fight. The Stoics argued for living "the natural life" rather than the life of luxury and desire, and the Greek authorities sought ways to control and police the use of luxury goods.

The ancient Romans, as they extended their tentacles throughout the world, found all kinds of new pleasures and delights abroad and brought them home to enjoy—gold, olive oil, and honey from Spain, fresh figs and fragrant citron wood from Africa, herb-infused wines and woolen cloaks from northern Gaul, dogs and washing tubs from Britain. Luxury became closely associated with women and the physical pleasures, especially eating and drinking. The Romans were concerned enough about the effects of too much enjoyment on their society that they passed sumptuary laws, meant to regulate consumption of certain goods. One forbade a woman from possessing more than a half ounce of gold. But Romans continued to indulge—in chariots, armor, swords, private baths, villas, exotic food and wine, and other luxuries.

In the seventeenth and eighteenth centuries—as trade among countries widened and class tensions increased—many of the great philosophers, economists, and social analysts took up the debate about the meaning of luxury. John Locke (English philosopher, 1632–1704) wrote that desire is an "uneasiness of the mind for want of some absent good." This presages the rise of the "want-creation" industry which taps into, and sometimes exploits, the longing for goods (tangible or intangible) the consumer does not have but may not need. David Hume (Scottish philosopher-economist, 1711–1776) argued that "luxury is pernicious only when it ceases to be socially beneficial." This is a key aspect of the luxury debate. Critics argue that New Luxury is just the most recent manifestation of consumerism and unnecessary consumption. But New Luxury creators often see a social good in their products, and consumers often think of them as social tools rather than as indulgences. Hume also made the intriguing comment that in ages of luxury, "industry, knowledge, and humanity are linked together by an indissoluble chain." This is similar to our belief that our current age of New Luxury is the result of a rare alignment of business capabilities (industry), educated consumers (knowledge), and emotional needs (humanity).

Adam Smith (Scottish philosopher-educator-economist, 1723–1790), author of *Wealth of Nations* and a "father of capitalism," can be read as a booster of luxury. He argued that opulence and freedom are "two of the greatest gifts a man can possess" and that "real happiness" is about "ease of body and peace of mind." He believed that the individual desire for "improvement" led to a collective economic good, creating employment for many and wealth for the state. In other words, trading up brought both personal and societal benefit.

Karl Marx (German historian-economist-revolutionary, 1818–1883) wrote partly in reaction to Smith's idea that workers could never earn much more than needed for the survival of the race and as a continuation of the ideas of David Ricardo (English economist,

1772–1823), who wrote about the inevitable impoverishment of the masses, the inevitable enrichment of those who own production, and the fundamental conflict between wages and production. Marx believed that every society has within it "immanent forces" that give rise to contradictory forces—or disequilibria—that can be resolved only by replacing the old system with a new one; he argued that capitalism would eventually die and be replaced by a classless society. It would be hard to make the case that Marx was an advocate of trading up or that New Luxury signals the end of capitalism. It does, however, suggest a modification of the system that gives more consumers—if not all of them—more power and influence over the producers than they have had before. The trading-up phenomenon is practiced by the majority of American households. Marx could not have foreseen a world where twenty-five million households in a single country could earn $75,000 or more a year.

In the late nineteenth century, we began to see that production might not only serve a society, but could also become its master. Max Weber (German sociologist-economist, 1864–1920), in *The Protestant Ethic and the Spirit of Capitalism*, described this uneasy relationship between production and consumption in American society and argued that the "Calvinist Diaspora is the seedbed of capitalist economy." He referred, of course, to John Calvin (French theologian, 1509–1564), who believed in "election by grace," which means that God decrees everlasting life for some people and everlasting death for others. There is no way for a person to change God's decree by what he accomplishes, or fails to accomplish, during his time on earth. Moreover, it is impossible to tell from people's behavior who is chosen and who is not. Even so Calvinists came to value labor but feel guilty about consumption.

Many Americans still wrestle with the guilt associated with consumption. We believe that work and production are good for society. We feel ambivalent about whether consumption, especially the consumption of luxury goods beyond our survival needs, is a sign of status and power or a signal of indulgence and weakness.

Thorstein Veblen (American economist–social scientist, 1857–1929), in *The Theory of the Leisure Class* (1899), saw that the debate had become even more complicated and that goods were no longer simply a matter of production and consumption but had become a language of social dialogue. Veblen writes that "pecuniary strength" is the "basis on which good repute in any highly organized industrialized community rests" and that the "means of showing pecuniary strength are leisure and a conspicuous consumption of goods." No class will deny itself this "spiritual need," he says; in fact, "very much of squalor and discomfort will be endured before the last trinket or the last pretence of pecuniary decency is put away." Veblen coined the phrase "conspicuous consumption," which has proved very durable and is often applied to the trading-up phenomenon. New Luxury consumers do not wish only to show their "pecuniary strength"; they demand that their goods have technical and functional benefits, aspects that Veblen's consumers cared little or nothing about.

The 1950s and 1960s in the United States saw much discussion about the relationship of business, society, and the individual. Sloan Wilson in *The Man in the Gray Flannel Suit* (1955), William H. Whyte Jr. in *The Organization Man* (1956), Vance Packard in *The Hidden Persuaders* (1957), and David Reisman in *The Lonely Crowd* (1961) explored the effects (largely negative) of large corporations, advertising, and a mobile society on the individual and the culture. In *The Affluent Society* (1958), John Kenneth Galbraith (American economist-educator-writer, born 1908), argues that the debate about consumption and production, want and need, is fundamentally different in affluent societies than it was in earlier cultures. Historically, he says, most societies have been poor. And, as Ricardo argued, most people were unable to live a life of anything more than bare subsistence. In affluent societies, however, even the average person can be materially well-off.

Galbraith says that American society is based on the idea that production of goods and services is of paramount importance, primarily because it provides employment—our great goal is "the expanding economy." However, we quickly became so proficient at production that we created an oversupply of goods. Accordingly, we became expert at "creating wants"—primarily through marketing and advertising—so that consumers would continue to buy goods even after they had long since satisfied their basic needs. Then we became so good at creating wants to sell the goods we're so good at producing that, in order to expand the economy, we have had to make credit more available so that a wider population can afford things.

In the last few years, aspects of the trading-up phenomenon have been explored by a number of writers and analysts. Writer David Brooks, in *Bobos in Paradise* (2000), says that our current condition is the result of a coming together of Bohemian (Bo #1) ideals that became fashionable in the 1960s and the conventional, bourgeois (Bo #2) American drive to succeed materially—we want to make "being good compatible with making good." He describes many of the emotional drivers, including travel as a search for spirituality, that we talk about in this book. He defines a phenomenon that he calls "income-status disequilibrium," in which a person's status does not match his wealth: for example, a professor with a Ph.D. who earns $80,000 a year, and an executive with a high school education who earns $1 million a year. This disequilibrium can influence many purchasing decisions. The professor expresses his superior intellect in his choice of goods that he can afford, such as wines and travel, but opts out of the dialogue conducted in automobiles. The executive declares his "pecuniary strength" through big-ticket items, including cars, boats, and homes.

The trend toward middle-market consumption of premium goods has also been sharply criticized as a negative phenomenon in our society. Juliet B. Schor, author of *The Overspent American* and many other works, believes that "the new consumerism has led to a kind of 'overspending' within the middle class. By this I mean that large numbers of Americans spend more than they say they would like to, and more than they have."

As believers in the essentially positive nature of New Luxury, we are not, however, advocates of consumer debt, pathological spending, or the use of goods to create class divisiveness. In fact, we believe that New Luxury purchasing—as distinct from conventional American middle-market spending—is a partial solution to the ills that Schor and others describe. People, no matter what their class or status, use New Luxury goods to help alleviate the stresses of modern life and to realize their aspirations. In our interviews, we learned that most people do not fool themselves that such goods solve their root problems or take the place of essential needs such as wellness and human connection; most people are well aware of the limitations of goods.

Furthermore, as businesspeople, we believe that production is not only a positive, but also the very foundation of our country and that the market economy is a reality that is likely to expand rather than shrink. As Fernand Braudel (French historian, 1902–1985) writes in *The Wheels of Commerce*, "Man can still live in some places on the globe outside the market economy 'like a snail in his shell.' But he is a condemned man on temporary reprieve." The system may require further modification to avoid oversupply and overcapacity, and New Luxury is one modification that both the consumer and the producer can approve, but we doubt that a fundamentally new economic system will replace capitalism within the span of influence of this book.

In addition to the social and economic issues that surround luxury, there has long been a discussion of the psychology of acquisition and consumption, from the writings of Aristotle (Greek philosopher, 384–322 B.C.) to the work of Abraham Maslow (American psychologist-philosopher, 1908–1970), and many others. Most recently, analysts such as Daniel Goleman, author of *Emotional Intelligence*, have begun to link human physiology, particularly the structure of the brain, to emotional drives and consumer behavior.

The popular media have recently become aware of the trading-up phenomenon, and they tend to ascribe it to certain key influences. Often mentioned is the issue of "emulation"—consumers buy premium goods because they want to "keep up" and attempt to gain status through their possessions. It is argued that the desire for emulation is heightened by the extraordinary exposure that American consumers have to "premium lifestyles" thanks to the media, coupled with high-powered encouragement to "live large" from such cultural icons as Oprah Winfrey, Martha Stewart, and dozens of other models of self-actualization and self-improvement in business, education, politics, and the arts. As a result, consumers compare themselves not only to the Joneses next door, but to celebrities and public people throughout the world. This is exhausting, frustrating, and ultimately—for the vast majority of consumers—an impossible endeavor.

We do not define New Luxury as a phenomenon based primarily on emulation. Today's consumers certainly compare themselves and their possessions to a much wider cohort than ever before. The consumer is as likely to compare her shoes to whatever Sarah Jessica Parker is wearing on *Sex and the City* as to what her friends wear to a party, and her home-cooked meals to those she has eaten at the Wolfgang Puck restaurant at O'Hare International Airport or to what Martha Stewart prepares on *From Martha's Kitchen*. For centuries, the middle class has been accused of emulating the styles and manners of the privileged classes, but there is plenty of evidence that it is more a matter of what one observer calls "appropriation"—and that it is hardly a one-way street. When, for example, you see the owner of a large pleasure yacht observing with envy a lobsterman firing up his four-stroke premium Honda outboard on his twelve-foot punt, you realize that classes and cultural groups borrow and appropriate from each other—up, down, and sideways—all the time. The New Luxury consumer gathers ideas from others and watches for signals but is not a slavish emulator of any one class or individual. Such consumption is much more a selective and discerning emulation than it is a thoughtless rush to be "just like" this or that media star.

We believe that New Luxury purchasers are inherently educated consumers. They do not buy foolishly, and they don't buy junk; they are aware of the companies that create the goods they purchase, and they seek to align themselves with companies that share their values. Often, New Luxury consumers are antiwaste, suspicious of big business, respectful of the environment, and wary of credit card debt.

So while we agree with the social critics that there are negative aspects of overconsumption, as well as overproduction, we believe they are less prevalent in the New Luxury consumer and in New Luxury companies.

For centuries, people have wanted to trade up. Now more people can do so, and more often. And the goods they trade up to are of higher quality and deliver greater emotional engagement. Whatever negatives are involved with New Luxury, we see it as a largely positive phenomenon.

About Our Sources

In researching and writing *Trading Up*, we have drawn on a wide variety of sources. Although there is a brief review of our primary sources and methodologies in chapter 1, this section is intended for readers who want a deeper understanding of our process.

Much of the information in this book was gathered from public sources. We reviewed SEC filings, annual reports, and company news releases to obtain data on revenue growth, profitability, store productivity, and other measures of performance. These data were also used to develop our own estimates of the economics of specific products and units such as pints of ice cream or pounds of dog food. They also fed into our analyses of large trends, such as the relative performance of specialty stores and department stores or the capital freed up by discounters.

We often supplemented the published information with our own "patterning," which included field research such as store visits, as well as analyses of printed and online materials. It was through patterning that we made observations on assortment, price ranges, and merchandising—as well as an evaluation of the linkage between technical, functional, and emotional benefits of specific products and services. When possible, we integrated and compared our findings with information from analysts' reports, the popular and trade press, consulting work, and quotes from our own primary consumer research. All of the information gathered was evaluated in the light of the knowledge gained in the course of our literature review of more than eight hundred books, articles, and other materials. These included published works of history, philosophy, sociology, criticism, and fiction, from Plato to David Brooks. The articles covered an extraordinary number of topics and trends, from cosmetic surgery in New York to apparel manufacture in China.

The author team was greatly aided and owes tremendous thanks to the exceptional professionals in the Chicago-based Knowledge Group—Vera Ward, Pat Heidkamp, Bill Hagedorn, Jill Jaracz, and Wanda Perkins—of The Boston Consulting Group. The breadth of subjects covered in this book attests to their skills, tenacity, resourcefulness, and dedication.

Chapter 2. The Spenders and Their Needs

A good deal of the information for this chapter was drawn from U.S. Census Bureau data, most of which are available online at www.census.gov. The sources from which we drew most heavily were the historical income and housing tables—particularly for data "cuts" by household and quintile. Data on educational attainment and the changing family structure were obtained through the Census Bureau's Current Population Surveys, published annually in March, and supplemented with information from the National Center for Health Statistics (a branch of the Centers for Disease Control). The Bureau of Labor Statistics was an additional source for information on working women.

Not all census data were available in a pretabulated form, so we obtained some information through custom online searches and ordered special-request queries from the Census Bureau; in other instances, we were able to find useful information in special Census Bureau reports that included time series data spanning several decades.

There are multiple sources for our other inquiries on spenders. Our analysis of net worth was based on Federal Reserve flow of funds data as well as a particularly interesting report, written by Dean M. Maki and Michael G. Palumbo, titled "Disentangling the

Wealth Effect: A Cohort Analysis of Household Saving in the 1990s" (a paper in the Finance and Economics Discussion Series published by the Federal Reserve System, April 2001). Travel data are currently tracked by the U.S. Travel and Tourism Administration, though historical (pre-1992) data capture was the domain of the U.S. Bureau of Economic Analysis. The cost of passenger travel derives from published fares unearthed by extensive literature searches, with help from the researchers at Northwestern University's Transportation Library.

The four emotional spaces are based on the results of our primary research—a quantitative survey of 2,300 people in households with incomes of $50,000 and above. The survey vehicle and methodology are discussed in more detail under the chapter 4 heading.

Finally, we drew on an August 2002 interview with Dr. Michael Ganal and Jim McDowell, BMW's worldwide sales manager and vice president of North American marketing, respectively.

Chapter 3. The Creators and Their Goods

To gain insight into the creators of New Luxury goods, we conducted interviews with the leaders of some of the most important and intriguing New Luxury companies. In August 2002 we spoke with Ellen Brothers, president of Pleasant Company and an executive vice president at Mattel, to learn more about the benefits ladder of the American Girl brand. In January 2003 we talked with Leslie Wexner, CEO of Limited Brands, and tried to get into the mind of a master of patterning.

Various other sources were consulted in researching this chapter. The Securities Industry Association publishes an annual factbook that contains data on capital raised through initial public offerings; additional data were gathered from the Forbes Interactive IPO data bank. The decline in international freight rates is tracked by U.K.-based Containerisation International's Freight Rate Database. Like the data from other sources, current dollars were adjusted to constant (real) dollars using NASA's Gross Domestic Product deflator.

Chapter 4. Where Goods and Emotions Intersect

To create a statistical fact base about spending on premium goods, we conducted a quantitative survey of American households, in partnership with HarrisInteractive, a leading marketing research firm.

Utilizing Harris's extensive panel, we polled 2,333 adults over the age of eighteen with annual household incomes over $50,000. Using a twenty-five-minute Internet survey, we asked questions regarding luxury purchases and attitudes about luxury shopping and spending in general, as well as specific questions about the luxury categories most important to those adults. All data were weighted using Harris's proprietary propensity-weighting technique to be representative of the general population of adults with household incomes over $50,000.

The data were analyzed using a variety of statistical techniques. The groupings of emotional drivers were derived through factor analysis, a multivariate statistical method that aligns attribute statements onto common factors or vectors on the basis of their intercorrelation.

The quantitative survey raised many new questions about consumer motivations—particularly concerning why certain types of people traded up in certain brands or categories. To gain further insight, we interviewed thirty respondents from our survey. We spent an hour on the telephone getting to know these people, learning about their lives, their work, their friends, their attitudes toward spending and saving, their hopes and fears and motivations. These interviews supplemented other consumer interviews and focus groups conducted for this book, as well as for consulting work (involving, over many years, hundreds of people), to help us refine the profiles of the emotional spaces that were derived from the survey. This research took place in research facilities, as well as in people's homes, on the golf course, on airplanes, and at the mall.

In addition to the interview program, we relied on a number of outside sources in researching this chapter, primarily trade groups and industry associations. These include the International Spa Association's *2002 Spa Industry Study*, the National Restaurant Association, the American Society for Aesthetic Plastic Surgery Web site and statistical reports, the *Travel Industry World 2001 Yearbook*, and the Cruise Lines International Association. Finally, we drew on research conducted by the National Marriage Project based at Rutgers, the State University of New Jersey.

Chapter 5. The World Is a Sexy Place

BCG's relationship with Limited Brands and Victoria's Secret goes back several years. During this time, in our capacity as thought partners, we have had many discussions with Leslie Wexner, the company's visionary founder and CEO. The Victoria's Secret story as it is recounted in these pages reflects these conversations, as well as our own experiences working with the brand during the course of many projects spanning five years.

Chapter 6. Eating As an Emotional Experience

Researching this chapter was especially fun, as it enabled us to spend a good deal of time talking about food with some of the most engaging New Luxury leaders. Ronald Shaich of Panera Bread shared his observations on "decommodification" with us in December 2002, as we discussed the evolution of his company over the past decade. We also had the pleasure of an impromptu meeting with David Overton, the CEO of The Cheesecake Factory, and Mats Lederhausen, president of McDonald's Development Group.

More generally, we drew on information from NPD Foodworld reports to learn about the performance of various segments within the food industry. These data supplemented our internal knowledge of the away-from-home food industry that has resulted from multiple client projects over the course of several years.

Chapter 7. Only the Best for Members of the Family

To supplement information from our interview with Ellen Brothers (referenced in chapter 3), we consulted an interview with American Girl creator Pleasant Rowland, which was published in *Forbes Great*

Minds of Business (John Wiley & Sons, 1998). We also visited American Girl Place in Chicago with a an eight-year-old consumer and American Girl enthusiast, and we spoke with her mother about their relationship with these extraordinary dolls.

Our research into the pet market relied on a variety of sources, including the American Pet Products Manufacturers Association 2001/2002 National Pet Owners Survey, the Pet Food Institute, the American Pet Association, and the American Animal Hospital Association. The May 2002 issue of *American Demographics* featured a particularly interesting article by Rebecca Gardyn, titled "Animal Magnetism," which contained other useful data. The pet food market is tricky to track because there is no single, definitive industry source. So we gathered data from a handful of sources and triangulated them in order to size the various market segments over time. These sources included the Business Communications Company's Pet Food Report, Euromonitor, and the Maxwell Report. Our analysis of pet food economics also drew on information from a 2001 analysts' report by Deutsche Bank Alex. Brown.

Chapter 8. Inside the New American Home

The housing market is well tracked by a small number of key sources. These are the U.S. Census Bureau, the U.S. Department of Labor's Bureau of Labor Statistics, the National Association of Realtors Housing Affordability Index, and the U.S. Department of Housing and Urban Development. Additionally, there were two reports of particular note related to trends in the evolution of U.S. housing: The National Association of Home Builders' 2001 report, "Housing Facts, Figures and Trends," and Harvard University's Joint Center for Housing Studies' "The State of the Nation's Housing: 2001." For background information on Fred Carl, Jr., founder of Viking Range, we relied on an article, "He's Cooking Now," by Maridith Walker Geuder, that appeared in the fall 1998 issue of *Mississippi State Alumnus* magazine.

In addition to the sources cited above, we conducted a variety of interviews. We spoke with Joe Foster, marketing director–Whirlpool Brand Fabric Care, and Gordon Segal, the visionary founder of Crate and Barrel. We also had the opportunity to sit in focus groups with a passionate group of Duet owners who made us think twice about the boundaries of the relationship between person and machine.

_____

Chapter 9. Awakening the American Palate to Wine

Three sources account for the majority of our information on the wine industry: the Wine Institute; the U.S. Department of Agriculture's Economic Research Service for Wine, Beer and Spirits; and the Impact Databank Review and Forecast's annual report, titled "The U.S. Wine Market." For more flavor on the history of the wine industry, we consulted various books, including Paul Lukacs's *American Vintage: The Rise of American Wine* (Houghton Mifflin, 2000) and Robert Mondavi's autobiography, *Harvests of Joy* (Harvest Books, 1999).

Information on Kendall-Jackson accolades was obtained from Varietal Fair's series "California Wine Winners 1994–2003: The Best of the 1993–2002 Judgings," 1994 through 2003 editions. Our research was topped off with a memorable interview with Jess Jackson, conducted atop a mountain that overlooks his ranch estate and the Alexander Valley.

_____

Chapter 10. The Old World in New Luxury Bottles

Volume and some price data on vodka were obtained from the International Wine and Spirits Record and *Impact* trade magazine. The majority of price data is based on supermarket channel prices as tracked by Information Resources, a market research firm that tracks the checkout scanners of over thirty thousand points of sale. In addition, we talked at length with Edward Phillips at Millennium Import LLC, the man responsible for bringing Chopin and Belvedere vodkas to the trendier members of the middle market. To learn more about beer, we spoke with former BCG manager Jim Koch, who is the founder of The Boston Beer Company.

Chapter 11. Demonstrably Superior and Pleasingly Different

Though we are golf enthusiasts, we consulted several outside sources in researching the Callaway story. We gained information from "The Golf Club Manufacturers U.S. Sales at Wholesale," a report by the Seidler Companies, and "State of the Industry" annual report from the Sporting Goods Manufacturers Association. This chapter also relied on articles from a variety of popular publications and associations, including *Golf Digest*, *Golf* magazine, and PGA.com. We also took a field trip to Callaway Golf in Carlsbad, California, to visit the campus and talk with president and CEO Ron Drapeau and Larry Dorman, senior vice president–global press and public relations. We also spoke with Mark King, president of TaylorMade–adidas Golf.

Chapter 12. A Cautionary Tale of an Old Luxury Brand

There is no shortage of information available on the car market in general, and Cadillac in particular. *Ward's Automotive Yearbook* was the primary source for unit volume and list price data for all car brands and models from 1970 to the present. We found additional Cadillac-specific information, including some history of the brand, in the *Standard Catalog of Cadillac, 1903–2000*, by James T. Lenzke. While *Ward's* provided historical (pre-1970) figures for American models, we needed to consult other sources for earlier data on imports to the United States. We were able to fill in the gaps with information from James Flammang and Mike Covello's *Standard Catalog of Imported Cars, 1946–2002* (Kraus Publications, 2002). Brian Long's book, *Lexus* (Velace, 2001), also provided interesting context for the public information available from Toyota. To supplement these sources, we visited edmunds.com for price and feature information. And, as mentioned in the chapter 2 summary, we interviewed Dr. Michael Ganal and Jim McDowell, BMW's worldwide sales manager and vice president of North American marketing, respectively.

Acknowledgments
___

Creating *Trading Up* involved the work of many contributors.

Trading Up would not exist without the early and continuing efforts of a number of champions, advocates, and partners. Bill Matassoni, who is a legendary figure in the world of consultancy marketing and now the steward of The Boston Consulting Group (BCG) brand, recognized the potential of our ideas early and helped shape them. He helped put together a formidable team of partners, including our agent, Todd Shuster of Zachary Shuster Harmsworth; Adrian Zackheim, the founding editor of Portfolio and a renowned figure in the world of business books; and our collaborating writer, John Butman. John was a fantastic writing partner—strong willed, with strong opinions, collaborative, sympathetic, kindhearted, and fun.

Most of the members of our core team were based in the Chicago office of BCG, and were responsible for gathering data, conducting content research, and helping to develop and refine our ideas. Special thanks go to Tamara Duker, our longest-serving and most dedicated team member, for her extraordinary work ethic, insight, analytical skill, wit, and diligence. Jill Corcoran, Jonathan Cowan, and Suzy Oudsema were key team members who made valuable contributions as researchers and thought partners. Tina Choi, Aaron Dannenbring, Lily Yao, Danielle Harbison, and Mary Egan conducted research into specific categories and helped us understand the implications of their findings. Jeannine Everett, based in the Boston office, led the effort in developing our consumer survey and understanding the emotional spaces surrounding trading up. Special thanks to Christine Beauchamp, one of the first team members from BCG at The Limited, for insight, spark, and creativity. We also want to acknowledge five BCG partners for their help and support: Patrick Ducasse, Barbara Hulit, George Stalk, Miki Tsusaka, and Adrian Walti.

We received valuable support and guidance from our senior management at BCG—Carl Stern, our former CEO; John Clarkeson, our chairman; and Hans-Paul Buerkner, who succeeded Carl as CEO in the spring of 2003. Thanks to them for understanding that a body of work that combines data with anecdotes, sociology with business practice, and rationality with emotion, is a wonderful expression of the BCG ethos and expertise.

An important and enlightening part of our research was the interviews we conducted with the leaders of our featured New Luxury companies. We greatly appreciate the time we spent at BMW with Dr. Michael Ganal, worldwide sales manager, and Jim McDowell, vice president North American marketing; at Mattel with Bob Eckert, CEO, and executive vice president, Ellen Brothers, president, Pleasant Company; at Limited Brands with Leslie Wexner, founder and CEO, Ed Razek, chief marketing officer, and Dan Finkelman, senior vice president; with Grace Nichols, CEO, Victoria's Secret; Ronald Shaich, chairman and CEO, Panera Bread; David Overton, CEO, The Cheesecake Factory; Mats Lederhausen, president, McDonald's Development Group; Joe Foster, marketing director— Whirlpool Brand Fabric Care; Gordon Segal, founder and CEO, Crate and Barrel; Jess Jackson, founder, Kendall-Jackson; Jim Koch, founder, The Boston Beer Company; at Callaway Golf with Ron Drapeau, president and CEO, and Larry Dorman, senior vice president–global press and public relations; with Mark King, president, TaylorMade; and with Dr. Jordan Busch, cofounder, Personal Physicians HealthCare, and an instructor in medicine at Harvard Medical School.

We thank the dozens of consumers we interviewed, both formally and informally, as part of our research. Many of them appear in the book, and although we gave them fictitious names, we did not invent details or alter their stories or the critical details of thir lives. We also thank the 2,300 consumers who participated in the Harris-Interactive poll and the dozens of those who agreed to further interviews with our team. We also conducted a series of focus groups with Whirlpool customers, and we very much appreciate their enthusiastic participation. In the course of our work over the years, we have visited and interviewed hundreds of consumers, and we thank them for their comments, ideas, attitudes, and insights.

We and our core *Trading Up* team have had the benefit of an expert and hard-working support team. In Chicago, Kristin Claire, Debra Price, and Marge Branecki were our key administrative team members. Vera Ward, Pat Heidkamp, Bill Hagedorn, Jill Jaracz, and Wanda Perkins provided extensive and knowledgeable research support. Our thanks for varied contributions to our BCG colleagues Eric Gregoire, Peter Truell, and Susan Bergel in New York; KC Munuz, Jeri Herman, Christine Vollrath, and Irene Blach in Boston. Thanks to Sally Seymour, based in Chicago, for writing advice and counsel.

We also received valuable support from a number of outside contributors. At Sommerfield Communications in New York, Frank Sommerfield, Penny Peters, and Elizabeth Case expertly helped us bring our ideas to the press and the outside world. At *Harvard Business Review*, we developed a fruitful working relationship with Ben Gerson, Suki Sporer, and Cathy Olofson who helped us shape our ideas and material for the HBR audience. Ashley Siegel and Jonathan Dowds assisted John Butman in conducting the literature review and managing the voluminous materials and many tasks of writing; Toni Baccanti developed the customized database that holds and optimizes those materials. Elyse Friedman provided expert copy editing.

Throughout the course of our work on the book, we have turned to our partners at BCG for their ideas, insights, and counsel. We are fortunate to have a worldwide network of people with extraordinary expertise and experience in a wide range of practices, disciplines, and industries.

Thanks go to: René Abate; Nina Abdelmessih; Charbel Ackermann; John Akin; Harri Andersson; François Aubry; Brad Banducci; Felix Barber; Julie Barker; Mary Barlow; Tommaso Barracco; Ivan Bascle; Pedro Bastos Rezende; Herbert Bauer; Jorge Becerra; Jean-Marc Bellaïche; Marc Benayoun; Joël Benzimra; Kilian Berz; Rohit Bhagat; Laurent Billés-Garabedian; Lamberto Biscarini; Eric Bismuth; Rolf Bixner; Mark Blaxill; Renata Bochi; Ralph Boehlke; John Bogert; Marcus Bokkerink; Elaine Boltz; Philippe Bongrand; Michael Book; Lucy Brady; Andrew Brennan; J. Kevin Bright; Christophe Brognaux; Sophie Bromberg; Charles-André Brouwers; Vivian Browning; John Budd; Marc Budim; William H. L. Burnside; Sylvia Butzke; Charmian Caines; Alain Calmé; François Candelon; German Carmona; Paul Carr; Phil Catchings; Jean-Michel Caye; Christian Cerda; Jacques Chapuis; Thierry Chassaing; Vincent Chin; Soyoung Choi; Tina Choi; Hervé Chopard; Jeffrey Chua; Raffaele Cicala; Stéphane Cohen-Ganouna; Jennifer Comparoni; Christophe Condat; Alessandro Coppo; Thomas Corra; Carlos Costa; Ken Crumley; Stefan Dab; François Dalens; Nan DasGupta; Joe Davis; Niamh Dawson; Emmanuel De Courcel; Jesús De Juan; Bruno De Saint-Florent; Filiep Deforche; Michael Deimler; Ulrika Dellby; Sebastian DiGrande; Yves Djorno; John Dunlap; Sylvain Duranton; Christophe Duthoit; Muzaffer Egeli; Petter Eilertsen; Henry Elkington; Laura Entwistle; Pedro Esquivias; Philip Evans; Jeannine Everett; Paul Fenaroli; Alastair Flanagan; Colm Foley; John Frantz; Michel Frédeau; Mark Freedman; Grant Freeland; Daniel Friedman; Ian Frost; Xavier Galtier; John Garabedian; Gerardo Garbulsky; Jeff Gell; Marc Gilbert; David Gilmour; Reginald Gilyard; Marin Gjaja; Karen Gordon; Paul Gordon; Emile Gostelie; James Goth; Gregory Gottlieb; Antoine Gourevitch; Oliver Graham; Cliff Grevler; Claus Peter Groos; Howard Grosfield; Robert Grübner; Steven Gunby; Manish Gupta; Julie Han; Tracy Hankin; Gerry Hansell; Nicolas Harlé; Brian Harris; Jens Harsæ; Pat Heidkamp; Andre Helfenstein; Katrina Helmkamp; James Hemerling; Jérôme Hervé; Dieter Heuskel; Ralph Heuwing; Matt Holland; Dave Houggy; Hubert Hsu; Emmanuel Huet; Rich Hutchinson; Jean Manuel Izaret; Alan Jackson; David Jacobs; Dan Jansen; Yvan Jansen; Jill Jerez; Jim Jewell; David Jin; Dan Johnson; Mark Joiner; Barry Jones; Lidia Juszko; Osamu Karita;

Errol Katz; Gerhard Kebbel; Donna-Marie Kelly; Ben Keneally; Simon Kennedy; Jaap Kerstjens; Nicholas Keuper; David Kim; Suyeong Kim; Kermit King; Mark Kistulinec; Martin Koehler; Kim Wee Koh; Satoshi Komiya; Dietmar Kottmann; Jeffrey Kotzen; Elena Krasnoperova; Stephen Kremser; Matthew A. Krentz; Kaj Kulp; Doug Kush; Marion Kusterer; Robert Lachenauer; Jonas Lagerstedt; Edwin Lai; Federico Lalatta Costerbosa; Alvin Lam; Mathieu Lamiaux; Peter Lawyer; Jean Lebreton; Marjorie Lee; Rich Lesser; Kevin Lewis; Tian Shu (Carol) Liao; Tomas Lindén; John Lindquist; Alexander Lintner; Derek Locke; Roland Loehner; Ross Love; Mikael Lövgren; Jim Lowry; Mark Lubkeman; Tom Lutz; Robert Maciejko; D G Macpherson; Katherine Manfred; Joe Manget; Sharon Marcil; Todd Marsh; Bjørn Matre; Steven D. Matthesen; Bengt Maunsbach; Heino Meerkatt; Antonella Mei-Pochtler; José Manuel Méndez; David Michael; Arnaud Miconnet; Anna Minto-Sparks; Arnon Mishkin; Takashi Mitachi; Jean Mixer; Heinz Möllenkamp; Neil Monnery; Nuno Monteiro; Sandy Moose; Yves Morieux; Atsushi Morisawa; Jeff Mory; Kiyan Nouchirvani; Holger Odenstein; Paul Orlander; Shinji Oshige; Kent Owens; Sang Yong Park; Boyd Pederson; Stephanie Peponis; Wanda Perkins; Guillermo Peschard; Pramoad Phornprapha; Nicola Pianon; David Picard; Stéphane Potier; Anthony Pralle; Paige Price; Daphne Psacharopoulos; Collins Qian; Stuart Quickenden; Stefan Rasch; Vaishali Rastogi; Martin Reeves; Michael Regnier; Joey Reiman; Axel Reinaud; Byung Nam Rhee; Laurent Richaud; David Rickard; Martina Rißmann; Félix Rivera; Philippe Roch; Catherine Roche; Tad Roselund; François Rouzaud; Richard Rubenstein; Immo Rupf; Carl Rutstein; Hideaki Saito; Rohan Sajdeh; Camille Saussois; Katharine B. Sayre; Olivier Scaramucci; Jacob Schambye; Jan Scheffler; Eddy Schmitt; Wouter-Jan Schouten; Erik Schumacher; Just Schürmann; Friedrich Schwandt; Naoki Shigetake; Harold Sirkin; David Skeels; George Stalk; Peter Stanger; Simon Stephenson; Karen Sterling; Abraham Stern; Carl Stern; Rainer Strack; Hiroaki Sugita; Greg Sutherland; David Tapper; Lars Terney; Steven Thogmartin; Frédéric Tiberghien; Peter Tonagh; Carlos Trevijano; Ricard Tubau; Jari Tuomala; Kazunari Uchida; Tetsuya Uekusa; Rob van Haastrecht; Laurent van Lerberghe; Bruno van Lierde;

Geoffroy van Raemdonck; Mark Verheyden; Nicolaus von Harden-berg; Carina von Knoop; Kevin Waddell; John Wallace; Bernd Wal-termann; David Webb; Thomas Wenrich; Tania Elizabeth Whyte; Jens Willenbockel; Alan Wise; John Wong; Wendy Woods; Thomas Wurster; Yuichi Yatsuhashi; Xudong Yin; Jun Yokohama; Byung Suk Yoon; Mehmet Yukselen; Marie-Thérèse Zambon; Yu (Vivian) Zheng.

In addition, we would like to acknowledge the contributions of other local colleagues in Chicago, including Georgia Alexakis; Nik Bafana; Patrick Campbell; Kristen Didio; Steven Gearhart; Karthik Hariharan; Doug Hohner; Dennis Howe; Sims Hulings; Jill Jaracz; Paul Jene; Kevin Kornoelje; Kelly Ladiges; Jill Linderoth; Katie Moody; Julie Nelson; Hajo Oltmanns; David Panzer; Gaurav Sharma; and Terrilynn Short.

Index